A GOVERNMENT OF STRANGERS

EXECUTIVE POLITICS IN WASHINGTON

HUGH HECLO

How do political appointees try to gain control of the Washington bureaucracy? How do high-ranking career bureaucrats try to ensure administrative continuity? The answers are sought in this analysis of the relations between appointees and bureaucrats that uses the participants' own words to describe the imperatives they face and the strategies they adopt.

Shifting attention away from the well-publicized actions of the President, Hugh Heclo reveals the little-known everyday problems of executive leadership faced by hundreds of appointees throughout the executive branch. But he also makes clear why bureaucrats must deal cautiously with political appointees and with a civil service system that offers few protections for broad-based careers of professional public service.

The author contends that even as political leadership has become increasingly bureaucratized, the bureaucracy has become more politicized. Political executives—usually ill-prepared to deal effectively with the bureaucracy—often fail to recognize that the real power of the bureaucracy is not its capacity for disobedience or sabotage but its power to withhold services. Statecraft for political executives consists of getting the changes they want without losing the bureaucratic services they need.

Heclo argues further that political executives, government careerists, and the public as well are poorly served by present arrangements for top-level government personnel. In his view, the deficiencies in executive politics will grow worse in the future. Thus he proposes changes that would institute more competent management of presidential appointments, reorganize the administration of the civil service personnel system, and create a new Federal Service of public managers.

Hugh Heclo is a senior fellow in the Brookings Governmental Studies program. In 1975 he won the Woodrow Wilson Foundation Book Award for his *Modern Social Politics in Britain and Sweden* (Yale University Press, 1974).

Hugh Heclo

A GOVERNMENT OF STRANGERS
Executive Politics in Washington

The Brookings Institution
Washington, D.C.

THE BROOKINGS INSTITUTION is an independent organization devoted to nonpartisan research, education, and publication in economics, government, foreign policy, and the social sciences generally. Its principal purposes are to aid in the development of sound public policies and to promote public understanding of issues of national importance.

The Institution was founded on December 8, 1927, to merge the activities of the Institute for Government Research, founded in 1916, the Institute of Economics, founded in 1922, and the Robert Brookings Graduate School of Economics and Government, founded in 1924.

The Board of Trustees is responsible for the general administration of the Institution, while the immediate direction of the policies, program, and staff is vested in the President, assisted by an advisory committee of the officers and staff. The by-laws of the Institution state: "It is the function of the Trustees to make possible the conduct of scientific research, and publication, under the most favorable conditions, and to safeguard the independence of the research staff in the pursuit of their studies and in the publication of the results of such studies. It is not a part of their function to determine, control, or influence the conduct of particular investigations or the conclusions reached."

The President bears final responsibility for the decision to publish a manuscript as a Brookings book. In reaching his judgment on the competence, accuracy, and objectivity of each study, the President is advised by the director of the appropriate research program and weighs the views of a panel of expert outside readers who report to him in confidence on the quality of the work. Publication of a work signifies that it is deemed a competent treatment worthy of public consideration but does not imply endorsement of conclusions or recommendations.

The Institution maintains its position of neutrality on issues of public policy in order to safeguard the intellectual freedom of the staff. Hence interpretations or conclusions in Brookings publications should be understood to be solely those of the authors and should not be attributed to the Institution, to its trustees, officers, or other staff members, or to the organizations that support its research.

For my mother, Adeline Heclo

Foreword

WORK ON THIS BOOK began as Richard Nixon was preparing to resign from office and ended as Jimmy Carter was making plans to assume the presidency. These changes symbolize the subject dealt with here. Political leadership in Washington is fragile and transient, perhaps more so now than ever. This is a fact of life for presidents and all the people they bring with them to help run the government. Hugh Heclo has tried to describe the relationship between the fleeting and enduring forces in government and to suggest ways in which the inevitable tensions could be handled more constructively.

The relations between political appointees and high-level bureaucrats—or what the author terms "executive politics"—have been largely ignored by the public. The conventional approach to analyzing dissatisfaction with government performance is to define Washington as the problem. It is less popular but more important to try to understand the problems that people in Washington have. Such understanding is basic to improving government performance; little can be achieved simply by insisting that people in government must do better.

Mr. Heclo, a senior fellow in the Brookings Governmental Studies program, describes the underlying significance of relations between political executives and bureaucrats, as well as trends and practices that have made it increasingly difficult to reconcile the dual need for change and continuity in government. He analyzes the different personnel systems and strategic settings for both political executives and civil servants and evaluates the probable effects of different strategies for dealing with the bureaucracy. Finally, he considers the deficiencies that seem inherent in the current structure of executive politics and proposes reforms that could help ensure more constructive working relations between political appointees and bureaucrats in Washington.

The many hours of interview notes for this study were patiently transcribed by Gloria M. Jimenez and Radmila Nikolić, both of whom also typed the manuscript in its several stages. The manuscript was edited by Tadd Fisher and indexed by the author. Clare and Frank Ford prepared the figures.

The views expressed in this book are those of the author and should not be ascribed to the trustees, officers, or other staff members of the Brookings Institution.

GILBERT Y. STEINER
Acting President

January 1977
Washington, D.C.

Author's Preface

As NEW political executives are installed in office to "take control of the
bureaucracy," they usually acquire a collection of wall photographs signi-
fying their association with the great and near-great of a particular administration. Often it takes time (sometimes forever!) for a newcomer to
realize that these visual associations and other accoutrements of office
are substantially irrelevant to his effective power in the bureaucracy. The
pictures convey no more than a grant of "Best Wishes" from distant persons who will probably never see or understand the organization and officials with which the political executive has to deal.

At the outset I had hoped to write a book that would help such public
executives and that would elicit a broader understanding of the need
for political competence in Washington. In the end I had to conclude
that many of the problems related to the interaction between political
leadership and bureaucratic power are structural, not personal. Merely
urging people in government to try harder and use more statecraft is unlikely to help. Improvements are possible, but winning them is a very
difficult and lengthy process.

The evidence used in reaching such conclusions is rather unusual and
deserves comment. The research for this book was conducted during
1973–76. It is the result of what might be called an unassembled seminar,
with approximately 200 interviewees as the teachers and me as the stu-
dent. Extensive discussions were conducted with a range of present and
former government executives, the oldest with Washington experience
going back to the Hoover administration, the youngest a newly arrived

aide in the Carter transition group. In all, the data base amounts to about 3,000 man-years of experience in government.

I do not claim to have constructed a random statistical sample. In general my aim was to weigh rather than to count opinions and to counterbalance self-serving statements with responses from other participants whose views could be expected to be self-serving in a contrary direction. Thus I sought out Republican and Democratic appointees, bureaucrats from old and new agencies, people with intimate and distant ties to Congress and interest groups. Always I tried to find people who had closely observed one another in action and who were thought to be particularly effective or (for a balance of experience) ineffective in dealing at the political-bureaucratic interface. Such as it was, my sample was drawn by using the real scales by which people are weighed in Washington—that is, their reputations.

I have chosen to tell the story in the participants' own words, having assured them that they would not be identified (even when they wanted to be). My use of so many anonymous quotations may possibly disturb some readers, but I have not tried to reconstruct a particular historical event from unattributed sources. The few historical facts recorded in what follows may or may not be distorted by selective perceptions. That is largely irrelevant. The reliability of the book ultimately depends on how perceptively I have heard what was being said. The analysis is mine, not the interviewees'.

This book could give rise to two serious misunderstandings, however. On both counts there is little that can be done except to put in an initial disclaimer.

To some readers, the discussion of strategies and ways of using people may seem manipulative, not to say Machiavellian and sinister. But all of us, even though we may not care to admit it, are always using people to get what we want, whether for narrow self-interests or for the general public interest. At least that seems a more realistic way of looking at the way people behave than to imagine they are acting to fulfill some abstract role expectation or a sense of uncalculating altruism. It is my hope that those who are disturbed by this approach will read more closely and see that the actual experiences discussed do not support any type of slick expediency or ruthless use of subordinates. On the contrary, it often turns out that straightforwardness and sensitivity and willingness to shoulder responsibility are the best policies. To those who say that these are home truths, I would respond that many people who are put in charge of the public's business do not act as if they know these things, or they learn the lessons too late.

Second, some may gain the mistaken impression that all people in government care about are personal motives, jockeying for position, and directionless power. The fact is that vast numbers of public officials are concerned about the substance of government policies and the conduct of the public's business; they take their oaths of office seriously. That is why they struggle so hard to get their way. Here I can only acknowledge that in focusing on the pragmatic rules that help them achieve their ends, I have been unable to do justice to the underlying motives of countless outstanding public servants.

Like some of the executives described in this book, I have extended my debts and lines of obligations in many different directions. Thanks are particularly due to the men and women who took hours of their time to talk with me, often at the end of an exhausting day at the office or as an interruption to their well-deserved retirement. I hope they will feel that the results justify their expense. Many colleagues at Brookings were also a constant source of ideas and good advice. Finally, among all the other participants in Washington, one creditor in the Bureau of Reclamation holds the least redeemable debt of all. A book dedication seems small return.

H. H.

Contents

1. People in Government   1

What Is at Stake   3
The Search for Political Leadership   8
The Idea of Civil Service: A Third Force?   19

2. Setting: The Executive Mélange   34

Who's Who?   36
Trends   55
Results   64
Summary   81

3. Political Executives: A Government of Strangers   84

The Political Executive System   84
The Selection Process   88
Characteristics of Political Executives   100
A Summary and Look Forward   109

4. Bureaucrats: People in the Machine   113

The Higher Career System   114
Job Protection   133
Bureaucratic Dispositions   142

5. Working Relations: The Preliminaries   154

Self-Help: The Starting Point   156
Self-Help Is Not Enough   170
Whom Do You Trust?   181

6. Working Relations: The Main Event   191

    Using Strategic Resources 194
    Using People 213
    Mutual Support and Its Limits 220
    Conclusions 232

7. Doing Better: Policies for Governing Policymakers   235

    The Case for Reform 236
    The Shape of Reform 243
    A Third Force: The Federal Service 249
    Costs and Prospects 261

Index   265

Text Tables

2-1. Approximate Number of Noncareer and Career Positions, U.S.
     Government, by Rank, 1975–76   38
2-2. Postwar Growth of U.S. Congressional Staffs   59
2-3. Previous Government Experience of Incumbent Assistant Secretaries
     for Administration, Selected Years, 1954–74   79
2-4. Government Experience of Bureau of the Budget/Office of
     Management and Budget Executive Personnel,
     1953, 1960, and 1974   81
3-1. Full-Time Political Appointments in the Executive Branch,
     June 1976   85
3-2. Political Executives' Years of Experience in the Federal
     Government, 1970   101
3-3. Tenure of Political Executives, 1960–72   104
4-1. How Career Executive Positions Have Been Filled
     before and after 1967 Reforms   118

Figures

2-1. Political and Career Executive Positions in the Department of
     Commerce and in the Department of Housing and Urban
     Development, June 10, 1974   42
2-2. Management Organization of the Department of the Interior,
     1924 and 1976   58
2-3. Index of the Growth of Mid-Level Executive Positions
     and Federal Civilian Employment, 1961–74   63
4-1. Procedures for Hiring a Career Executive   122

CHAPTER ONE

People in Government

The true test of a good government is its aptitude and tendency to produce a good administration.
—Alexander Hamilton, *The Federalist*, no. 68

EVERY new administration gives fresh impetus to an age-old struggle between change and continuity, between political leadership and bureaucratic power. Bureaucrats have a legitimate interest in maintaining the integrity of government programs and organizations. Political executives are supposed to have a broader responsibility: to guide rather than merely reflect the sum of special interests at work in the executive branch.

The search for effective political leadership in a bureaucracy of responsible career officials has become extraordinarily difficult in Washington. In every new crop of political appointees, some will have had government experience and a few will have worked together, but when it comes to group commitment to political leadership in the executive branch they constitute a government of strangers. And yet the fact remains that whether the President relies mainly on his White House aides or on his cabinet officials, someone is supposed to be mastering the bureaucracy "out there." For the President, his appointees, and high-ranking bureaucrats, the struggle to control the bureaucracy is usually a leap into the dark.

Despite a host of management and organization studies, Washington exposés and critiques of bureaucracy, very little information is available about the working world and everyday conduct of the top people in government.[1] Even less is known about the operational lessons that could be

1. Several useful discussions are in Francis E. Rourke, *Bureaucracy, Politics and Public Policy* (Little, Brown, 1969); Marver H. Bernstein, *The Job of the Federal Executive* (Brookings Institution, 1958); and Robert C. Wood, "When Government

1

drawn from their experiences. Congress is widely thought to have lost power to the executive branch, but congressional rather than executive behavior remains a major preoccupation in political research. Observers acknowledge that no president can cope with more than a tiny fraction of the decisionmaking in government, yet we know far more about a president's daily social errands than about the way vital public business is conducted by hundreds of political appointees and several thousand top bureaucrats who take executive actions in the name of the United States government—which is to say, in the name of us all.

In this book I explore the important but relatively unknown process by which high-ranking political executives and bureaucrats interact with each other in Washington, concentrating on the people themselves rather than on particular institutions, questions of legal authority, or organizational divisions of power. How do those interested in political control and those interested in administrative continuity take the measure of each other? Why do some people in government do better than others in getting what they want? To what extent can any political leader hope to guide what government does—programs—by controlling the people who do it—personnel?

Before trying to answer these questions (in chapters 5 and 6), other questions must be considered. Who are these political executives and bureaucrats? How do they come to positions, not necessarily of power, but of potential for power? What are the important calculations and constraints in their working worlds?

A focus on the participants themselves means dealing with the relatively soft data of individual thoughts, of experiences, and not least, of emotions. But that is not always a disadvantage. Often it is easy to forget that those we label politicians or bureaucrats are also people in government doing many of the things we might do in similar circumstances. The participants speak for themselves throughout this study, revealing that life at the top of the government bureaucracy is far different from the strict procedures, written orders, and rigid hierarchies generally associated with the term "bureaucracy."[2] It is, in fact, a highly personalized realm,

---

Works," *The Public Interest*, no. 18 (Winter 1970), pp. 39–51. Some of the best recent work is on agencies concerned with foreign affairs. See, for example, I. M. Destler, *Presidents, Bureaucrats, and Foreign Policy* (2d ed., Princeton University Press, 1975); and Donald P. Warwick, *A Theory of Public Bureaucracy* (Harvard University Press, 1975).

2. The quotations appearing throughout the text are taken from interviews conducted with 200 present and former government officials. Because all respondents were

even when dealing with the rules and regulations of government personnel administration—surely one of the most procedurally bureaucratized
subjects in Washington. Those who expect to stand on formal memos or
live by the book cannot hope to play an important part in executive politics.

No systematic body of knowledge or special training exists to instruct
political and bureaucratic executives on how to handle their mutual relationships. They may have technical or professional qualifications, but
their interactions are not derived from professional expertise. Instead, operations are based on craft knowledge—understanding acquired by learning on the job. Hence this book is not so much about office-holding as
about office-using by people in a variety of circumstances at the top of the
executive branch; that is, the *statecraft* of political administration. Far
from being a peripheral concern or a mere residue of nonpresidential details, the relationship of political executives and bureaucrats is a persisting
and growing problem that goes to the heart of a modern democratic
government.

What Is at Stake

If popular impressions are any guide, few job titles are more suspect
than "politician" and "bureaucrat." Periodic polls have shown that while
most parents might want their offspring to become president, they dislike
the notion of their becoming politicians. No pollster has dared to ask
Americans what they would think of their children growing up to become
Washington bureaucrats.

Yet in many ways the American form of government depends not only
on a supply of able politicians and bureaucrats, but even more on a successful interaction between these two unpopular groups. At stake are
issues of both negative control and positive performance.

Control

One of the central premises of democracy is that those in positions of
power should be accountable to and ultimately controlled by the people.

---

assured anonymity, the quotations must appear without attribution, but in most cases
I have tried to identify the general rank or position of the person being quoted. I comment more fully on this point in my preface.

Hence considerable attention is devoted to selecting, electing, and remov-ing the political leaders who wield such power. The traditional assump-tion has been that if the people can control their elected representatives, they will perforce control their government.

The continued development of large-scale administrative structures has made such democratic assumptions much more tenuous. To accom-plish complex social, economic, military, and other tasks, modern govern-ment has evolved immense administering organizations that can readily exercise a will of their own. Ultimately, important actions by today's po-litical leaders—a president exercising his power and influence, congress-men passing a law or overseeing its execution, political parties organizing their followers, candidates making election promises—are all likely to be directed toward getting large groups of government officials to do or to stop doing something. However one might debate the merits of presi-dential or congressional or party government, bureaucratic government seems a fact of contemporary life. If democracy is to work, political repre-sentatives must not only be formally installed in government posts but must in some sense gain control of the large-scale bureaucracies that con-stitute the modern state.

But to say that government bureaucracies need to be under political control may mean anything from a somewhat vague overall moral re-straint within official psyches to the most detailed political direction of the bureaucrats' acts. How much political control should there be?

No final answer to this question is possible because a number of differ-ent and somewhat contradictory objectives are desirable. Americans want administrative machinery that will respond to political leadership, but they do not want it to be so dominated by a particular party that it fails to resist illegal or improper demands—or so loyal that it is unable to re-spond to a new set of leaders. There should be enough control to hold superiors responsible for what is being done, but not enough to destroy individual responsibility and judgment in subordinates. When effective executive action is stymied by fragmented authority Americans complain that power should be commensurate with responsibility, but they also worry that fully commensurate power—an unchecked capacity to take action—can be arbitrary and can corrupt absolutely. Although a clear division of responsibilities is essential for public accountability, too clear a division can create structures of self-defense that are impervious to out-side criticism. The smooth operation of government seems to require co-operation between career officials and political executives; in recalling past disclosures of abuses and cover-ups by both politicians and bureaucrats, ordinary citizens may rightly worry when the two sides are getting along only too well with each other.

Obedience and independence, stability and adaptability, power and restraints on power, cooperation and resistance—the problem of political control of the bureaucracy is obviously one of relative dilemmas. Hence this book is also about changeable balances that need to be struck rather than about absolute solutions. The only way to judge any appropriate next step for reform is to look at the balances as they actually operate at present.

Performance

It would be a mistake to stress the importance of political-bureaucratic interaction only in terms of negative constraints. Whether they want more or less federal government, most Americans probably want better government—one that promises what is needed and delivers what it promises. If democratic institutions are to work, government must not only be checked from doing what is not wanted but must also be competent as an administering organization to do what is wanted. Particular pieces of bureaucracy may be cut, rearranged, and reconstituted, but there seems to be no way to separate government performance from the valuable services offered by officialdom. Bureaucracies can be indispensable in translating abstract intentions into workable programs of action, in performing the substantive work associated with executing a policy intention, in providing information based on institutional memory and continuity, in offering practical advice on what can be done, and in giving some accounting of what is being done.

Imagine, for example, a political leader committed to replacing government regulation with market competition and incentives. Of course the bureaucracy immediately becomes a key participant inasmuch as it must be, at a minimum, sufficiently responsive to stop generating and enforcing its customary regulations. But there are more positive ways in which some measure of bureaucratic activity can aid any such effort to "debureaucratize" government policy. To create a market where none has existed before implies some forethought about how far it will extend, what transitional arrangements should be made for lifting existing regulations, how this will affect programs in related areas, what are fair and enforceable rules of the competition; enter planners, market analysts, economists, and so on. Once in operation a fully competitive market may not be permanent or self-sustaining; enter antitrust lawyers, inspectors, score-keepers on the market's functioning, and enforcement machinery for rules of the game.

As the market continues to operate, many may feel that it is in some sense unfair to let the costs of private market operations lie wherever they fall; thus the other officials may be joined by purveyors of compensations and subsidies, guardians against environmental or other spillovers, and still more analysts. And since the preceding public officials (or private contractors hired for such work) are using the taxpayers' money, there must be overhead units to ensure that the public's money is properly ac-counted for, procurement procedures followed, and so on. All these adjuncts to the free market will probably have to subdivide their tasks and order their activities on a relatively permanent basis—in other words, they will become public bureaucracies.

The example of replacing bureaucratic regulation with market mech-anisms clearly simplifies what in practice would be a complicated set of actions, but it is perhaps sufficient to make the basic point: to achieve practical results, democratic political power must for the most part trans-mit its strength through government officialdom. Although public atten-tion may focus on recurring campaigns to cut bureaucracy or on dramatic exposures of individual misdeeds, the relationship between political and administrative officials persists as one of the linchpins of effective govern-ment performance. Between the politicians' intentions and the govern-ment's final action passes the shadow of the bureaucrat.

Leadership and Power

American political institutions have many different ways of tackling the twin tasks of controlling and making positive use of Washington's bureaucracies. Congress provides legislative decisions on what the law to be executed should be; it also appears to be becoming more interested in post hoc evaluation of what administering authorities have actually done. The courts and administrative law proceedings have become im-portant in directing the executive branch to correct what are judged to be errors of omission and commission. The public media continue to probe for administrative misdeeds that seem newsworthy, and interest groups have their own special claims to press on particular government agencies.

But none of these devices, either alone or in combination, can substitute for the direct everyday guidance that becomes available when political representatives are placed in positions of authority in government organizations and held accountable for bureaucratic performance. The justification for spending proportionately more of the taxpayers' money on top government salaries is not that political executives are necessarily smarter or more meritorious than anyone else but that they are supposed to have the greatest responsibility for establishing a sense of direction and taking the public heat for what government does.[3]

The tasks of direction-setting and heat-taking broadly define what I mean by *political leadership* in the bureaucracy. If democratic political power is the raw material created by the representation of voters and other publics, political leadership has to do with the craft of using and risking such power through action. Political leadership is transient, in that it depends on a particular individual and his or her changing supplies of outside power. Political leadership in the bureaucracy is also problematic inasmuch as it is heavily contingent on how political executives themselves choose to act. Some will know or learn how to string together connections to light up the right circuits and run the government engines. Others will not.

By comparison, *bureaucratic power* is nonproblematic and enduring. It is automatically attached to those people who continuously operate the machinery of government. Unlike the blackouts or brownouts that may affect political leadership, bureaucrats are able to generate their own power through an ability to give or withhold compliance, advice, and information. Their circuits are firmly based in loyalties to particular programs, functional specialties, and institutions rather than to any particular leader of the day. The essence of bureaucratic power lies in both the service and resistance that officialdom can offer to political leaders.

Government performance (in the sense of both negative constraints and the positive use of bureaucracy) can be thought of as the product of political leadership times bureaucratic power. A product rather than merely a sum is at stake because, depending on how politicians and bureaucrats are linked, either one can diminish or magnify the impact of the other on total performance. At the same time, the formula suggests the importance of a separation as well as links between the two groups. If there is no distinction between the roles of transient political leaders and enduring bureaucratic operators, one of two results seems likely: the

3. For example, current salaries range roughly from $47,500 a year for a deputy assistant secretary, to $66,000 for a cabinet secretary, to $200,000 for the President.

ascendance of bureaucratic leadership over national political life or the entrenchment of personal political power in the machinery of government.

The Search for Political Leadership

If political leadership vis-à-vis the bureaucracy is so important, where is it to be found? Customarily the answer has been to look to the presidency. Many reasons, however, suggest a need to look beyond the White House to the public executives operating throughout Washington's bureaucracies. To do so does not discount the importance of presidents, but it does begin to draw attention to the large number of other participants who have also become vital to the politics and policies of the executive branch.

Beyond Presidential Leadership

Late on a Thursday afternoon in August 1974, fifty or so onlookers outside the northwest gates of the White House managed to gain a final glimpse of President Richard Nixon as he returned the twenty yards from his hideaway suite in the Executive Office Building to the Oval Office. Most of the spectators dispersed, presumably to have supper and watch the resignation announcement on television.

For a unique interlude the President had virtually ceased to exist as a political force in Washington. Yet if they could have looked elsewhere in the executive branch, the worried, amused, or curious spectators would have seen how much government activity went on beyond the pall that had settled over the White House. This work of political and bureaucratic policymakers involved not only routine operations but matters of considerable importance in Americans' lives.

It was a week when financial experts in the Treasury Department and Federal Reserve Board polished contingency plans in case the growing financial strain in New York led to a chain of defaults and panic among banking institutions. The Defense Department announced sixty-one new contracts funneling three-quarters of a billion taxpayers' dollars to private industry (as well as an airlift of 2,500 cots and 3,000 blankets to victims of the fighting on Cyprus). In the Department of Housing and Urban Development, officials returned from congressional offices to report mixed success in their lobbying efforts: not all of the desired cuts in public housing subsidies could be made, but Congress would enact a bill to recast the basic structure of federal support for housing and community development. One floor above the President's hideaway office a top bureaucrat continued to receive congressional inquiries about the administration's position on particular pieces of legislation; he explained to a visitor that even with a politically crippled President in the White House, congressmen still found it useful to touch base with the Executive Office of the President in order to learn about potential objections to legislative proposals. Some administrators in the Transportation Department were completing paperwork for $433 million in mass transportation grants, other officials authorized to approve capital grants for highways were fending off pressure from a Republican governor up for reelection, and still others were readying proposals for a new experiment that would alter how Americans told time in the winter months.

And much more was going on beyond the White House gates. A few leaders in the young Environmental Protection Agency were making the first major effort to enforce compliance with air pollution regulations in metropolitan areas; officials in the even younger Federal Energy Administration were searching for a means of counteracting oil companies' efforts to increase gas sales in an era of supposed conservation. The Labor Department was issuing new regulations for the employment and training of migrant farm workers, while at the Department of Health, Education, and Welfare debate continued on old regulations that allowed federally subsidized medical students to work in the most remunerative locations rather than in geographic areas of greatest medical need. Government lawyers in the Justice Department were succeeding with indictments against government-licensed grain inspectors charged with taking bribes; they were failing in lobbying efforts to make congressional markup of the forthcoming Privacy Act more administratively feasible. Leading government spokesmen publicly reaffirmed that unemployment would remain below 6 percent during the year, while a few Labor Department officials privately tried to prepare the unemployment insurance machinery for a surge that would soon top 8 percent of the labor force.

Two hours after taking the oath on Friday the new President met with his advisers to review the puzzling economic situation: consumer prices up 12 percent and real output down 4 percent in the first half of 1974. A new "canvassing of the options," as it was termed, produced a list that was largely indistinguishable from that worked out in the bureaucracy for the former President. The crisis in the White House, which many commentators misdiagnosed as a general paralysis throughout the entire government, was over.

If a little slower than most, the week of President Nixon's resignation was not particularly unusual in the rest of the executive branch. Each federal agency, whether it is in a so-called inner department (State, Treasury, and Defense) or outer one (Labor; Health, Education, and Welfare; Transportation; etc.), can expect most of its work to arouse little presidential attention most of the time. What was unusual as the Watergate crisis reached its denouement was that every agency was devoid of presidential involvement in any of its work all of the time.

Even under the most favorable circumstances (typically at the beginning of a new administration), a modern chief executive and his personal aides face severe constraints in trying to breathe new life into the executive branch. Many opportunities for political leadership have to be forgone by the White House and are picked up by other political executives or not at all. The reasons go deeper than a mere shortage of time and manpower in the west wing of the White House. In part they lie in the following limitations that any new administration brings to the job:

Unoperationalized goals. Political campaigns highlight a number of general goals applicable to the major foreign and domestic issues of the day, but they do not produce specific action programs that can be enacted and handed to the bureaucracy to be put into operation. During a presidential election and possible transition, some officials in the bureaucracy can usually be found trying, without much success, to distill tangible policy options from the cloud of party pledges and campaign speeches. For the most part, however, the important detailed work on practical measures must await the arrival of not only a new president but of hundreds of new officeholders in the executive agencies. Without strong political leadership "out there," the fresh impetus of a new administration easily sags under the strain of reconciling general promises with the inherited problems and everyday flow of government business.

Mixed mandates. The presidential election conveys a very small amount of information: the name of the next person to take the presidential oath of office. The policy measures of the presidential candidate may be poorly delineated in his own mind and even more fuzzy in the party platform, but they are positively shapeless as reflected in the final electoral choice. Whether the electoral margin is narrow or wide, there is no way to distinguish to what, among all the things that are said in an election campaign, the mandate applies. No greater or lesser mandate applies to promises to reduce unemployment than to those to curb inflation, to improve health policy than to cut government spending and interference. Mandates become further mixed because, regardless of election promises, unexpected circumstances may require considerable rethinking of policy intentions. Such rethinking is also part of the President's mandate and, unless omniscient, he and his personal aides are likely to require help from other political executives and their organizations. Their analyses can help the President think and rethink priorities. Equally important, their advocacy will provide vital signals about who cares how strongly about what. Weak executives outside the White House produce weak analyses and useless or misleading signals.

Disorganized teams. Even if the presidential election could produce a clear mandate and an unwavering set of policies, a new president arriving in Washington would find that other elections—to Congress and to state and local governments—have produced people who think that they too are being paid to have priorities. While congressmen and subnational officials may be members of the President's party, they are not part of his administration, and what they see are mainly their own mandates to do or not do something. The President and his personal aides can help with the biggest problems, but the bulk of persuasive efforts on the Hill and in the state capitals must rest with the political executives in the agencies.

Yet as chapters 2 and 3 will show, the President's executive team itself is likely to be poorly organized. If the American national parties and electoral process did automatically produce sets of mutually familiar and committed political executives led by the President, there would be little need to look beyond the presidency in the search for political leadership. But that does not happen. In Washington, administrative teams of political leaders, insofar as they exist, are created after rather than before a government is formed. That effort at team-building—in the agencies as well as in the White House—is one of the principal tasks of political leadership in the bureaucracy.

Strategic calculations. Another major reason to look beyond the presidency for direction-setting and heat-taking is that the chief executive has little choice but to act selectively. Strategic calculations as well as personal predilections will impel different presidents to take the lead in some areas rather than others. As he concentrates on what are to him the *crucial* issues, the President and his staff must leave to other execu-

tives those issues that are merely *important* to national policy. As he prudently seeks to calculate and marshal his own power stakes, the President
of necessity leaves his nonpriority areas vulnerable to others. Taking operational control of a foreign policy crisis means a more hurried sign-off on
an education option paper, framing a new social program that will bear
his name means less attention to an emerging controversy with labor, and
so on indefinitely. Hence presidential leadership is like a spotlight that
can sweep across the range of executive activities but can concentrate on
only a few at a time. Political leadership in the bureaucracy needs to extend much further out to the mass of government decisionmaking that
lies in the shadows beyond the glare of publicity surrounding the White
House.

The case for looking beyond the White House gates becomes even
stronger if one considers some of the established forces in Washington
that greet any new administration and that often focus leadership opportunities in the operating departments and agencies.[4]

Legal constraints. The Constitution vests all executive power in the
President, but Congress also enacts laws requiring executive officers in
the various agencies to take given actions. A great deal of authority in
executive agencies flows directly from Congress to the agency head or in
some cases to lower officials, not through the President. The legal implications are of little concern here.[5] What is relevant is that frequently these
legal requirements are vague, or inconsistent with other authorizations to
the same agency, or in conflict with what other agency heads have been
told to do, or all three. Each of these circumstances creates a potential
need for political leadership to translate the vagueness into concrete proposals, to choose among the inconsistencies, and to try and resolve the conflicts with other agencies. Only the biggest problems can ultimately reach
the President. The others have to be dealt with elsewhere.

Divided organizational loyalties. The administrative machinery in
Washington represents a number of fragmented power centers rather
than a set of subordinate units under the President. As many observers

4. For a fuller discussion and specific examples of many of the same points, see
Bradley H. Patterson, Jr., *The President's Cabinet: Issues and Questions* (Washington,
D.C.: American Society for Public Administration, 1976).

5. President Nixon's final legal battles did highlight the basic issues, many of
which were summarized in "Symposium: The United States Versus Nixon," *USLA
Law Review*, vol. 22 (October 1974), pp. 116–40.

have noted, the cracks of fragmentation are not random but run along a number of well-established functional specialties and program interests that link particular government bureaus, congressional committees, and interest groups. People in the White House are aware of these subgovernments but have no obvious control over them. They seem to persist regardless of government reorganizations or, perhaps more to the point, they are able to prevent the reorganizations that displease them.[6] In coping with these Washington subgovernments, the real lines of defense and accommodation are out in the departments, with their mundane operations of personnel actions, program approval, budget requests, regulation writing, and all the rest. These are the unglamorous tools with which political leaders in the agencies either help create a broader approach to the conduct of the public's business or acquiesce to the prevailing interest in business as usual.

Operating realities. Every new administration encounters constraints of a public administration nature at the White House level. These, for want of a better term, might be labeled operating realities. Since the end of the Eisenhower administration, enough experience has accumulated to suggest that whenever an activist president tries to run a large number of government operations directly from the White House he also runs into considerable trouble.[7] There were precedents in the Kennedy and Johnson administrations, but it was toward the end of Nixon's first term that the effort to create a central operating staff in the White House went further than ever before. Yet even at the height of the administration's power in 1972, Nixon aides had rediscovered the disadvantages of direct White House operations.[8] Rather than helping the President, these arrangements increasingly sucked problems into the White House, complicated major choices with irrelevant details, confused signals going out in the President's name, and made the White House itself into a slow-moving bureaucracy. The next step was an attempt to create an "adminis-

6. Harold Seidman, *Politics, Position and Power* (London: Oxford University Press, 1975), chaps. 3 and 4.

7. The general record is set out in Thomas E. Cronin, *The State of the Presidency* (Little, Brown, 1975). An interesting fact the author did not point out is that according to his tables even former White House aides are as critical of failures at the White House level as they are critical of the departments and about as many recommend more constructive relations with the departments as suggest strengthening the White House. See tables 6-1 and 7-2, pp. 163 and 203.

8. Richard P. Nathan, *The Plot that Failed: Nixon and the Administrative Presidency* (Wiley, 1975), p. 61.

trative presidency" by placing personal presidential loyalists in the departments and agencies. Whether one prefers that idea (which puts the
President's power and credit on the line everywhere in the executive
branch) or stronger, more independent cabinet officials, the point is the
same: there are severe limits on what can be run directly from the White
House. With or without the President's imprimatur, the search for political leadership in the departments and agencies has to go on, not least of
all so that the White House can be left to function effectively.

   More could be added, but these seven circumstances constitute an im-
posing list of limitations on the President—as manager-in-chief and as the
sole focus for understanding political leadership in the executive branch.
To a large extent they seem inherent. American electoral processes will
probably go on producing unoperationalized goals, mixed mandates, and
disorganized teams, at least until that unlikely day when a centralized
national party organization wins control of the government with a cadre
of executives ideologically committed to a given blueprint for the future.
Presidents will probably go on making strategic calculations and leaving
important areas of political direction-setting and heat-taking to others.
A constitutional structure of divided institutions sharing powers will no
doubt go on producing crisscrossed legal requirements and divided organizational loyalties. The same operating realities will probably intrude
into the splendid plans of every White House staff. In short, if political
leadership in the bureaucracy depends mainly on what the President can
supply, there is unlikely to be enough to go around.

A Growing Problem

   As pressures constantly push much (although obviously not all) of the
need for executive leadership beyond the President's office, the search
for such leadership is becoming even more difficult. In the next chapter,
I examine some of the difficulties associated with executive personnel
themselves, specifically the politicization of the bureaucracy and the bureaucratization of the political layers. But even if everything about the
executive personnel system had remained unaltered, changing features in
the substance of government activity have intensified the problem of creating productive relations between political executives and the bureaucracy. The features traditionally identified have to do with a growing reliance on the technical expertise of the bureaucracy and its powerful client

groups.[9] There are, however, at least four other trends that are equally ominous for future executive leaders. None of them are particularly dramatic, but taken together they promise to make it increasingly difficult to answer the basic question of political leadership: who is setting directions and being held accountable for what is happening in Washington's bureaucracies?

Proliferation. Few people would doubt that the activities of the national government have grown immensely. For the post–World War II generation, "big government" in Washington has been an enduring part of life. Each of the two world wars had a notable "ratchet effect" (a sharp increase and then a decline to a higher than original level) on the trend of government spending and employment. But whereas after World War I Republican administrations did much to dismantle the instruments of national government power accumulated during the war, the ratchet effect was much larger after 1945. Post–World War I federal employment was up 20 percent over the average of prewar years, but after 1945 it remained 120 percent larger than in the immediate pre–World War II years; federal spending tells a similar story.[10]

More government activity has meant more agencies to do the work associated with more policies and programs. The birth rate of government agencies has easily exceeded the death rate, leading to a rapidly growing total population of government bureaucracies. Even by conservative estimates (i.e., that the birth rate will stay the same and not continue growing as it has in the past), there are strong grounds for thinking that the future Washington environment will be crowded with government agencies that are not only much more numerous but also proportionately longer-lived and hence possibly more entrenched in their ways.[11] None of this makes political leadership atop these government agencies impossible. It does suggest a growing need for careful attention to the compe-

9. Rourke, *Bureaucracy, Politics and Public Policy*, chaps. 2 and 3.

10. Total civilian employment in the executive branch averaged 450,000 during 1913–15 and 550,000 during 1922–25. In the pre–World War II years it averaged 890,000 but 2 million during 1947–49. The respective figures for total federal spending were $983 million and $2,633 million for World War I and $7,718 million and $33,904 million for World War II. See Solomon Fabricant, *The Trend in Government Activity in the United States since 1900* (New York: National Bureau of Economic Research, 1952), tables B 6 and D 7, pp. 182 and 240.

11. Herbert Kaufman, *Are Government Organizations Immortal?* (Brookings Institution, 1976), pp. 70–76.

tence and organization of political executives if they are to have some coherent influence in the bureaucracy.

Interdependence. Questions of public policy once thought to be manageably within separate corners of government are increasingly seen to impinge on each other. Case studies suggest, for example, that after having eroded for the past fifty years the foreign policy–domestic policy distinction has virtually disappeared, or soon will.[12] Similar interdependency has emerged among social and economic policies that interact with each other in unexpected and perplexing ways.[13]

Meeting the need for increased coordination will depend heavily on executive leaders and staffs that can work together effectively across agency lines, a capability that has not been especially strong among the disorganized teams of political appointees. The recommendation to create a new central coordinating mechanism under the President comes easily and may often be desirable. But trying to design any new presidential machinery around weaknesses in agency leadership is also likely to create hollow, pro forma mechanisms irrelevant to those actually executing the everyday work. White House coordinators will be at a considerable disadvantage if they are able to deal only with department executives who cannot go beyond their predetermined agency briefs and agendas.

Momentum. Two generations of big government have created a policy momentum that is immense compared with the opportunity for political executives to provide fresh directions. Political power in a democracy may be personal and transient, but margins for significant decisionmaking seem increasingly to be a long-term proposition. Budget analyses invariably show, for example, that uncommitted resource margins are in the nature of a wedge, extremely narrow in the immediate years and widening only in later periods that lie well beyond the tenure of most political executives. A new president or assistant secretary arriving in Washington can find that total resources are already so committed that the scope for new initiatives in the next year or two is zero or even nega-

12. Peter L. Szanton, "The Future World Environment: Near-Term Problems for U.S. Foreign Policy," in U.S. Commission on the Organization of the Government for the Conduct of Foreign Policy, *Appendices* (Government Printing Office, June 1975), vol. 1, p. 8. See also the case studies in Griffenhagen-Kroger, Inc., "Cases on a Decade of U.S. Foreign Economic Policy: 1965–74," ibid., vol. 3.

13. See Hugh Heclo, "Frontiers of Social Policy in Europe and America," *Policy Sciences*, vol. 6 (December 1975), pp. 403–21.

tive.[14] In every new administration the significant margins for action appear not in this year's global budget figures but only here and there today, farther up the road tomorrow. Far from rendering political decisionmaking in the bureaucracy irrelevant, such constraints reinforce the importance of controlling the margins for action that do exist and of scrutinizing the immense base from which they grow. Reexamining such well-established forces of inertia is likely to require considerable feats of executive leadership.

Permeability. Compared with other nations, the United States has long been noted for having executive institutions that are highly accessible to outside pressure, particularly by organized interest groups. The executive branch's growing involvement with complicated national policies—environmental protection, civil rights, health care, energy planning, educational assistance, and so on—has, if anything, increased this permeability.

The most obvious examples are lobbying organizations interested in specific government activities and the vastly expanded network of private contractors and consultants who perform a significant portion of the government's work. In the past two decades the total number of federal civilian employees has changed little and their payroll costs, once the largest item in the federal administrative budget, have been far surpassed by the costs of government contracting.[15]

Many other forces are also impinging more and more on the work of public executives. Congress, for example, has become more inclined to participate in detailed administrative decisions. Since 1932 almost 300 provisions have been enacted to allow Congress or its committees to review, defer, approve, or veto executive actions before they take effect. Of these provisions, four-fifths have been enacted since 1960 and over one-half just since 1970.[16] Several agencies in recent years have even been

14. Roughly these kinds of constraints greeted the new Nixon administration in analyses of possible spending cuts and the amount of resources free for presidential action. See U.S. Office of Management and Budget, Director's Review Material, Fiscal Year 1970, "Budget Issues: General," box 7202-4; and for Fiscal Year 1971, "Overview" and "Elimination" files, both in series 60.25.

15. For a general discussion of the extent of government contracting, see Daniel Guttman and Barry Willner, *The Shadow Government* (Pantheon Books, 1976); and Comptroller General of the United States, *Annual Report* (GPO, 1973), chap. 6.

16. Clark F. Norton, "Congressional Review, Deferral and Disapproval of Executive Actions: A Summary and an Inventory of Statutory Authority," Congressional Research Service, Library of Congress (Library of Congress, April 30, 1976; processed), table 1, p. 8.

required to submit their budget proposals to Congress at the same time they send them for inclusion in the President's budget, defying the system of central control in executive branch budgeting that has prevailed since World War I.

The courts have also become increasingly involved as administrative participants. Responding to a flood of lawsuits, contemporary judicial decisions not only enforce but often direct executive actions in policies dealing with the environment, prisons, education, housing, welfare payments, civil rights, health, and many other fields. At the end of the 1950s, for example, the secretary of health, education, and welfare had several hundred lawsuits pending against him; at the end of 1975 he faced approximately 10,000 lawsuits, a large portion of which challenged some use of executive discretion.[17] The recently enacted Freedom of Information Act (which does not apply to Congress) has opened up large amounts of written material within the executive branch. This opportunity is gradually being used more extensively, particularly by those with a vested interest in particular programs,[18] and more exposure seems likely in the future, given current proposals for "sunshine" laws that would widen access to the internal processes of executive policymaking. On top of all this, government employees have drawn lessons from the private sector and have become more adept at organizing and exerting demands on their own behalf; in the process, the huge public work force seems likely to see itself as more distinct from "management" and to become one more social faction making claims on the government and its beleaguered leaders.

No doubt many of the trends making for more openness and wider participation are desirable and worth encouraging. But there is also no mistaking the difficulties raised for political leadership in the executive branch. As more participants in and out of government become critical to the development of complex modern policies, hard-pressed political executives can find themselves nominally in charge of not only a particular government agency but of a societal process in which it is difficult to

17. The changing role of the courts has been discussed in Donald L. Horowitz, *The Courts and Social Policy* (Brookings Institution, 1977); and in Abram Chayes, "The Role of the Judge in Public Law Litigation," *Harvard Law Review*, vol. 89 (May 1976), pp. 1281–1316.

18. The Freedom of Information Act of 1966 (5 U.S.C. 552) as amended in 1974 (88 Stat. 1561). The act's operation is described in Richard E. Cohen, "New Information Law Gets Heavy Use from Public, Business," *National Journal Reports*, vol. 7 (July 5, 1975), pp. 985–92.

have any clear idea of who is responsible for what is happening. The buck can readily seem to stop everywhere and nowhere. This situation is not so much a threat to political executives (since it also creates new opportunities for leadership) as it is a challenge to them to attain higher standards of craftsmanship and competence. More sensitivity will be needed to deal with the growing number of actors, more flexibility to navigate across unfamiliar boundaries, more perseverance to cope with the accumulating momentum of policy, and more self-assurance to represent the larger public that is not privy to opportunities for penetrating and influencing executive decisionmaking.

To summarize, the search for political leadership in the executive branch has to extend beyond the presidency. Moreover, the need for such far-flung executive guidance throughout the bureaucracy is being intensified by trends in the substance of government activity. To speak of somehow counterbalancing bureaucratic power and political leadership is easy; it is far more difficult to see how some sort of balance might be worked out in the years ahead.

The Idea of Civil Service: A Third Force?

Political leadership seems problematic and bureaucratic power unavoidable. The Political side (with a capital "P") of people in government evokes an image of changeable personal, party, or philosophical loyalties. Bureaucratic figures may have no less political acumen (i.e., small "p" in the sense of how to get things done), but they also suggest a more institutional commitment to established programs, procedures, and organizations.

There is another force at work in executive politics that is less familiar and somewhat more difficult to visualize. Political leaders in the executive branch deal not simply with bureaucrats but with career officials who are part of a civil service system. The civil service is a personnel structure (or more accurately a collection of structures) manifested in a dozen or more statutory laws, in hundreds of executive orders by the President, and in literally thousands of rules and regulations supervised by the U.S. Civil Service Commission. But the core of the civil service is an idea rather than a body of personnel regulations. This idea is somewhat distinct from notions of either political leadership or bureaucratic power.

In a sense bureaucracies are a "natural" phenomenon in modern society; they have occurred and grown without anyone having to decide or
plan consciously that they should do so. The civil service, however, has
been a kind of social invention. Deliberate planning and struggle for the
establishment of a civil service system can be traced back a hundred
years or more.[19] Unlike the fact of bureaucracy, the design of the civil
service was normative, a statement of what should be.

Throughout its history, the civil service idea has rested on three basic
principles: (1) that the selection of subordinate government officials
should be based on merit—the ability to perform the work rather than
any form of personal or political favoritism; (2) that since jobs are to be
filled by weighing the merits of applicants, those hired should have
tenure regardless of political changes at the top of organizations; and
(3) that the price of job security should be a willing responsiveness to
the legitimate political leaders of the day.

Because preconceptions abound, it is worth pointing out that nothing
in the basic civil service idea requires that such an official be passive
rather than actively responsible for expressing his views, or politically
insensitive, or on the right side of some mythical line separating administration and policy. In fact, at the higher levels of nonroutinized work, the
merit principle's stress on competent performance may imply just the
opposite. Neither does the basic idea suggest that the civil service is created primarily for the sake of providing job security to public employees.
Rather, security of tenure was a by-product of assuring the competence of
government personnel by an open, competitive examination of merits in
hiring.[20]

19. The best historical treatments of the U.S. civil service are Paul P. Van Riper,
History of the United States Civil Service (Row, Peterson, 1958); and *History of the
Civil Service Merit Systems of the United States and Selected Foreign Countries*, compiled by the Congressional Research Service for the Subcommittee on Manpower and
Civil Service of the House Committee on Post Office and Civil Service, Committee
Print 94-29, 94 Cong. 2 sess. (GPO, 1976). George A. Graham attempted to distill
what is in essence a civil service concept of public administration in "Ethical Guidelines for Public Administration: Observations on Rules of the Game," *Public Administration Review*, vol. 34 (January-February 1974), pp. 90–92.

20. The Civil Service Act of 1883 provided for no restrictions on the removal of
civil service employees. At Civil Service Commission urging, President McKinley in
1897 issued the first rules restricting removal. These, together with clarifications issued
by President Roosevelt in 1902, are still the applicable basic provisions. See U.S. Civil
Service Commission, *14th Report*, 1896–97 (GPO, 1897), p. 24; and *19th Report*,
1901–02 (GPO, 1902), p. 18.

Potentially at least, the civil service concept adds a third dimension to the interaction between top political executives and officials in the bureaucracy. It may mitigate and soften though it does not entirely eliminate the apparent conflict between purely political and bureaucratic self-interests. Unlike archetypal "bureaucratic man" interested in protecting existing operations and organizations, the civil servant is supposed to be responsive to the legal authority of political heads. Unlike pure "political man," the civil servant has a responsibility that is institutional and enduring, whoever the political figures in charge might be. To institute a civil service system is to accept the idea that competent personnel manning the government machinery should be available for use by—but not at the absolute disposal of—any political group arriving in office through legitimate means. If there is an analogy, it is to be found in the differentiation of a career military service from both the self-contained private armies of the past (one of the earliest forms of bureaucracy) and from the inchoate militia that (much like sets of democratic politicians) were periodically called on to exercise the power of the state. Thus to some extent the civil service idea can be an important fulcrum for trying to balance the demands of political leadership and bureaucratic power. How far it actually does so can only be determined by looking at the actual practices of people in government. The following two sections suggest why the historical and structural context reduces the odds for the civil service performing such a role in Washington.

A Precarious Idea

Relevant rules and regulations are well ensconced in personnel offices throughout Washington, but the basic idea of a civil service has always had a precarious existence. One reason stems from the original design of American national government. Having settled on a single rather than a plural executive and a sharing of powers among the three branches, the Founders could easily relegate the rest of government administration to a matter of "executive details."[21] The advent of modern bureaucracies, however, added the civil servant as an unexpected and insecurely placed participant to the original grand design of American government. Higher civil service officials are apt to find themselves in the middle—a part of the

21. Alexander Hamilton, James Madison, and John Jay, *The Federalist, or, The New Constitution*, Max Beloff, ed. (Oxford: Basil Blackwell, 1948), no. 72, p. 369.

unitary executive branch under the President's guidance but also dependent on a Congress sharing important life and death powers over their work. As civil servants, the price of their secure tenure is supposed to be responsiveness to political leadership, but both presidents and congressmen can legitimately claim that role. Thus on the one hand, smart bureaucrats with their own program loyalties can play presidents and congressional committees against each other.[22] On the other hand, even without such intrigue, civil servants can easily make a misstep that destroys the trust and understanding they need from all sides. To protect and advance the aims of their organizations, officials have to deal with large numbers of power centers outside the executive branch. But bureaucratic entrepreneurs who build this needed support can also become visibly identified with special interests and less responsive as civil servants.

In its search for an accepted role the U.S. civil service has been the victim of not only constitutional design but also of its own history. The U.S. civil service system, unlike that in other Western democracies, developed well after democratic political parties and mass political participation but somewhat ahead of industrialization and the accompanying expansion of central government bureaucracies (through business regulations, health and safety requirements, technical standard-setting, and so on). In the last quarter of the nineteenth century, when the first stirrings of modern bureaucratic power associated with industrialization were being felt, civil service reformers were already concentrating on an older American problem: how to reverse the intrusion of political party spoils into the work of government administration.[23] History thus bequeathed a concern that focused somewhat more on negative protections and somewhat less on the positive duties and direction of the U.S. civil service. Many reformers also recognized that without responsibility to political leaders, the protected civil servants could themselves become a threat to democracy. But in general there was little need to pay attention to the problems that would face future political executives who would have to deal with the

22. For a discussion based on this perspective, see Richard E. Neustadt, "Politicians and Bureaucrats," in American Assembly, Congress and America's Future (2d ed., Prentice-Hall, 1973), pp. 118–40.

23. The reform movement emerged and gathered momentum in the 1860s and 1870s, finally culminating with the Civil Service Act of January 16, 1883 (22 Stat. 403). By contrast, there were almost no statutes of national importance regarding U.S. commerce before the Interstate Commerce Act of 1887.

growing power of the bureaucracy.[24] The arrangements created by the Civil Service Act of 1883, which remains applicable today, represented an ingenious and necessarily ambiguous attempt to straddle these cross pressures of protecting and directing the civil service.

On the one hand, the act not only accepted but reemphasized the President's constitutional position as the ultimate repository of executive power: rules and regulations for civil service personnel actions in the executive branch derive their authority from and are proclaimed by the President.[25] The Civil Service Commission was created "to aid the President as he may request in preparing suitable rules for carrying this Act into effect," and the same perspective was deliberately expressed by making commissioners serve at the pleasure of the President.

On the other hand, the concern for protection from politics was expressed in the creation of a Civil Service Commission that would be more insulated from political influences than any of the government departments (it was in fact the first attempt to stretch the three-branch constitutional structure by creating a separate regulatory commission). This effort to distance the commission from the regular political apparatus was signified by providing three commissioners, only two of whom would be members of the same party, and by making the commission a separate agency permanently outside the existing hierarchy of government departments. Since 1883 the customary but obscure terminology has been that the commission is a "semi-independent" agency. If it is responsible political leadership that worries people, emphasis can be put on "semi"; if political partisanship seems the threat, one can always accentuate the "independent" side of things.

This ambivalence has received unexpected emphasis in recent years. It is not just that civil servants have quietly become a major component of the ostensible political leadership in the executive branch. Experiences with the Nixon administration have raised doubts once more among many of the public administration experts who had previously sought

24. The somewhat divergent aims were described by a leading reformer, William D. Foulke, in his memoirs, *Fighting the Spoilsmen* (Putnam, 1919).

25. The heart of the provision (22 Stat. 403 [1883]) reads as follows:
The President is authorized to prescribe such regulations for the admission of persons into the civil service of the United States as may best promote the efficiency thereof, and ascertain the fitness of each candidate in respect to age, health, character, knowledge, and ability for the branch of service into which he seeks to enter; and for this purpose he may employ suitable persons to conduct such inquiries, and may prescribe their duties, and establish the regulations for the conduct of persons who may receive appointments in the civil service.

with moderate success to downplay the negative, protectionist tradition in favor of more flexible and positive approaches to managing the career public service. The mea culpa of a distinguished Civil Service Commission adviser and personnel expert shows how much feelings have changed:

> We, professionally, are very largely responsible for the attitude that gave the Nixon staffers a rationale in their own minds as to what they were doing. That was this business of control. Our profession has constantly preached that a guy can't have responsibility without the requisite authority, that he can't direct a staff of people unless he has selected them. . . . Our doctrine has been that you have to have this personal, individual administrative control of selection of people in order to direct their activity. . . . [The Civil Service Commission] did pull in their horns a little bit. They did modify their role of protecting the merit system.[26]

Such complaints reflect not only the misdeeds of one administration but also a feeling that the basic concept of civil service has been lost from view with the passage of time. This historical precariousness of the civil service idea has only been accentuated by uncertainty about the organizational structure for guiding personnel policies in Washington.

Four Decades of Truncated Reform

Toward the end of every decade since the 1930s efforts have been made to restructure the organizational arrangements inherited from the nineteenth century. Two questions have remained as basic to the reform efforts during this period as they were to the 1883 act. First, what sort of central authority, if any, should guide the civil service system as a whole? Second, how should responsibility for protecting the civil service from political partisanship be organized? Both questions are important to institutionalizing the civil service idea; if anything, both have become more pressing than they were in the days when presidential power was in repose and the federal bureaucracy left the average citizen alone.

Looked at as a whole, none of the reform efforts have succeeded in creating the major change intended, that is, strengthening central institutions for guiding and protecting a governmentwide civil service system. But this has not been for want of proposals. In 1937 President Franklin Roosevelt and his administrative advisers advanced a plan to replace the Civil Service Commission with a single-headed Central Personnel Agency directly under the President and a wholly separate Civil Service Board. The presidential agency would perform the positive work of setting

26. "Discussion of the Federal Personnel Crisis," *The Bureaucrat*, vol. 4 (January 1976), p. 377.

standards and policies for nonpolitical personnel throughout the executive branch, while the independent board would perform the traditional role of protecting the civil service from partisan and personal favoritism. Despite a combination of forces defending the commission and numerous complaints about presidential dictatorship, the plan failed by only eight votes in the House of Representatives.[27]

The 1937 defeat was the closest reformers have ever come to major structural change since 1883. What has occurred instead has been a series of attempts to modify—first this way and then that—central staff for overseeing the career personnel system. In a scaled-down reorganization plan of 1939,[28] FDR used his new discretion to appoint a respected civil servant as Liaison Officer for Personnel Management, who thus became one of the six new personal assistants to the President in the newly created Executive Office of the President. By the end of the 1940s the liaison office was being run by a political aide and was heavily involved in trying to manage the system of political appointments as well as advise the President on civil service policies. In 1949 the first Hoover Commission on government reorganization proposed that the chairman of the three-member Civil Service Commission should become its chief administering officer and also serve as staff adviser to the President on all policies affecting career employees.

This plan was adopted at the outset of the Eisenhower administration,[29] but the "two-hat" arrangement for the Civil Service chairman did not work satisfactorily. By 1956 the top presidential advisers on civil service personnel were themselves dissatisfied with existing arrangements. As both White House aide and Civil Service Commission head, the chairman was strained between divers part-time roles as an advocate for what the commission staff wanted, as a personal adviser trying to look at matters strictly from the President's point of view, and as a nonpartisan commissioner appearing before a Democratic Congress suspicious of Republican raids on the civil service.

Thus in the last half of the 1950s the cycle of reform sentiment swung forward again. Early in 1957 Dwight Eisenhower's advisers on career per-

27. President's Committee on Administrative Management, *Report with Special Studies* (GPO, 1937), pp. 95–101; and Richard Polenberg, *Reorganizing Roosevelt's Government* (Harvard University Press, 1966), pp. 47, 80–84, 93–94, 129.

28. Executive Order 8248, September 8, 1939.

29. *First Report of the Commission on Organization of the Executive Branch of the Government*, H. Doc. 55, 81 Cong. 1 sess. (GPO, 1949), pp. 23–25. The plan was implemented in Executive Order 10452, May 1, 1953.

sonnel policies recommended to the Republican President a plan that
was basically the same as the one sought unsuccessfully by Franklin
Roosevelt twenty years earlier. Reacting against efforts to politicize the
civil service in the early Eisenhower years (see discussion of the Willis
Plan in chapter 2), a few members of Congress and civic group leaders
introduced similar proposals to recast the top structure with a presidential agency for civil service policies and a separate unit to police the civil
service rules.[30] But again Congress and public employee groups showed
little receptivity, and the President was reluctant to push the issue. In
fact, far from wishing to strengthen the President's hand in personnel
policies for the executive branch, the Democratic Congress easily and
without hearings passed legislation moving the Civil Service Commission
somewhat further from direct presidential control.[31] Rather than risk
presidential prestige by proposing major structural changes, the Eisenhower administration after 1957 reverted to the earlier pattern and replaced the Civil Service chairman's job in the White House with a special
presidential assistant for civil service policies. In 1961 the Kennedy administration abruptly abolished the special assistant's office for civil service policies, in large part because of the last Eisenhower assistant's
political activities in the 1960 campaign.

With several important variations, the 1960s repeated what was by
then a familiar story of pushing civil service policymaking in and out of
the White House advisory system. Increasingly in the Johnson administration, the White House relied directly on the Civil Service chairman
for advice on personnel policies. Yet what developed after the 1964 election until the end of the Johnson administration was not, as many observers assumed, simply a return to the "two-hat" model of the first
Eisenhower term. In effect there now evolved a tripartite role for the
Civil Service chairman—one as administrative head of the commission,
a second as presidential adviser on civil service policies, and a third as
operational director of the White House office responsible for staff work
and advice on political appointments. The first two roles were known

30. See *Administration of the Civil Service System*, Report to the Senate Committee on Post Office and Civil Service, Committee Print 2, 85 Cong. 1 sess. (GPO,
1957), and *Federal Personnel Administration*, S. Rept. 1545, 86 Cong. 2 sess. (GPO,
June 10, 1960).

31. Public Law 854 of 1957 established six-year overlapping terms for the commissioners; it thus subtly modified the reasoning of 1883; i.e., that since personnel
policy was part of the President's general responsibility for executive branch management, Civil Service commissioners should serve only at his pleasure.

to Eisenhower's chairman; the second and third had occupied Harry Truman's liaison aide on personnel, but never before had all three been put together at once. While by all accounts the arrangement worked fairly effectively in the Johnson years, the potential for abuse seemed clear. As one former White House aide put it:

> [The Civil Service chairman] is a man of high integrity. The civil service work was done over in the commission office from 8 A.M. to 2 P.M. and political appointments handled in the White House office from 2 P.M. to 8 P.M. . . . Still, you had one man in the middle instead of people on both sides. There was no one to see if the civil service side of things or the political side of things were encroaching on each other.

The advantage gained, of course, was access to the President and support for a number of things wanted by the personnel experts in the Civil Service Commission.

The close working relations between commission and White House in the Democratic administrations fueled suspicions in an already distrustful Nixon White House. More than ever after 1968, the Civil Service Commission found itself cut off from personal access to the President but subject to political pressures from the White House in its work. At the same time, management experts advising the President returned to a familiar theme. Surveying the operation of government personnel policies at the end of 1969, they concluded that as part of his management responsibilities the President needed a direct capability in the Executive Office. Against the objections of the Civil Service Commission and several members of Congress, the Bureau of the Budget—now the Office of Management and Budget (OMB)—was "charged with advising the President on the development of new programs to recruit, train, motivate, deploy and evaluate the men and women who make up the top ranks of the civil service, in the broadest sense of that term."[32] One month later, OMB acquired a new Division of Executive Development and Labor Relations to carry out this responsibility.

Hence if the basic overall structure for guiding the civil service system has remained unchanged since 1883, it is also true that the relationship between civil service leadership and the presidency has never been firmly established. That relationship has regularly oscillated between more and less White House proximity, between more and less clarity in distinguishing personal political advisers to the President from civil service policymakers.

32. Executive Order 11541, July 1, 1970.

Throughout these decades the Civil Service Commission itself has undergone important changes in its approach. By the end of the 1960s the trend was well established—away from the traditional emphasis on negative protections and detailed control of personnel operations and toward what the commission has viewed as a positive approach to allow greater executive flexibility in the agencies for managing career personnel. Gradually in the past forty years, the bulk of routine operations have been decentralized to personnel offices in the agencies, with the commission concentrating instead on setting standards, overseeing the procedural rules it promulgates, and auditing personnel operations. Its desire for a positive approach to civil service employment has been reflected in new programs for training, college recruitment, civil service awards, and manpower planning. And as the "management" side in government labor relations, its policymaking role has been heightened by the growing power of public employee unions. If presidential advisers persisted in recommending the creation of a central capability under the President for leadership in civil service policy, it was not because officials at the Civil Service Commission failed to claim that they were already performing that role.

But experiences in the Nixon years also showed that the commission's emphasis on flexibility and managerial discretion was to some extent purchased at the price of its policing role. In part there was the gradual accumulation over many years of "flexible" arrangements that violated the spirit and occasionally the letter of civil service rules. In part, too, the commission's vigor in protecting the civil service idea was muted by a desire to establish good relations with an especially suspicious Nixon White House. During 1976 a self-evaluation by the Civil Service Commission showed that in the years 1969–73 (1) staffing and examining processes had been subject to manipulation in a way inconsistent with merit principles; (2) commission officials and employees had actively participated in these and other improper acts of favoritism and preferential treatment; (3) the commission had lacked the will to respond to allegations of political intrusion into the civil service system; and (4) once started, its enforcement efforts were ineffective and superficial.[33] Far from

33. A *Self-Inquiry into Merit Staffing*, Report of the Merit Staffing Review Team, U.S. Civil Service Commission, for the House Committee on Post Office and Civil Service, Committee Print 94-14, 94 Cong. 2 sess. (1976), pp. 14, 65, 82. The evidence for an even more damning indictment of the commission's work is contained in *Final Report on Violations and Abuses of Merit Principles in Federal Employment Together with Minority Views*, Subcommittee on Manpower and Civil Service of the House

being in a position to discipline others, the Civil Service Commission by 1976 had to admit that it had been part of the problem.

None of this is to say that the majority of commission activities have been handled improperly, and procedures have been tightened up since 1973 (see chapter 4). Yet seen in perspective, the commission's recent failings have shown that the question hedged in previous decades is still alive. Can the commission be an agent of presidential leadership in guiding civil service policies and a watchdog for impartially protecting merit system principles? Many reformers have thought not, but none of their efforts to recast the top personnel structures for dealing with the bureaucracy have been realized. The civil service remains a precarious idea in an ambiguous organizational structure.

The same problems have emerged in accentuated form with regard to higher civil servants, the ones who are likely to deal personally with political executives. This, too, is a story of truncated reform inasmuch as organizational arrangements for top careerists have aroused considerable dissatisfaction but little concerted change. The Classification Act of 1949 created a more uniform schedule of job classifications for the many employees bunched at the top civil service grade, then GS 15. The act was primarily intended as a pay and classification reform, however, and in no way attempted to create a higher civil service with distinctive responsibilities.[34] In 1955 the second Hoover Commission on government organization gave an unprecedented amount of attention to problems of the higher civil service and proposed the creation of a senior corps of up to 3,000 civil servants who would carry their high rank with them as they moved throughout government, breaking the tradition of making civil service rank the attribute of a particular classified job.[35] Supported by the Eisenhower White House, the idea encountered strong opposition from top careerists in various agencies and their friends in Congress. Presidential attempts to initiate a scaled-down version of the same plan were defeated when Congress attached an appropriation rider denying any funds to administer such a program.[36]

Committee on Post Office and Civil Service, Committee Print 94-28, 94 Cong. 2 sess. (GPO, 1976), pp. 1–138.

34. Ismar Baruch, "The Supergrade Story, 1949–1952" (Ismar Baruch Collection, U.S. Civil Service Commission Library, Washington, D.C., n.d.).

35. See Commission on the Organization of the Executive Branch of the Government, *Task Force Report on Personnel and Civil Service* (GPO, 1955).

36. The events are recounted in George A. Graham, *America's Capacity to Govern: Some Preliminary Thoughts for Prospective Administrators* (University of Alabama Press, 1960).

The first significant reform occurred only in 1966, when the Civil Service Commission was able to use its rapport at the White House to gain support for some modest changes at the top career levels. In 1966 the new Executive Assignment System created a somewhat neater typology of appointment authorities and a computerized inventory with biographical information on 25,000 high-ranking federal employees that could be used by all agency heads in filling vacancies.[37] At the same time, a new Bureau of Executive Manpower was created in the Civil Service Commission to encourage the development of and planning for top career personnel, a mission it began sharing in 1970 with the OMB's new Division of Executive Development.

To date the results of these changes have been meager. Hiring officials often complain that the computerized inventory merely produces lists of names but offers no in-depth evaluation of the people or their qualifications. More important are doubts that an admonition from the commission or the OMB is capable of penetrating the territorial boundaries that separate the bureaucrats' agency-centered careers, much less promote movement toward a governmentwide personnel system for higher civil servants. Far from demonstrating a serious concern for top civil service manpower, the new arrangements have remained undermanned, underfunded, and politically undersupported. With the exception of a few efforts confined to certain agencies, the overall executive development program can be rated a failure in its attempt to generate groups of more broadly experienced and more organizationally mobile career executives.[38] In 1973, for example, a new Federal Executive Development Pro-

37. In brief, the system established three types of appointments at the supergrade level: career executive assignments for positions in the career service filled through the competitive staffing process; noncareer executive assignments to replace the old schedule C for supergrade positions involving advocacy or confidential or policy responsibilities; and limited executive assignments, which are career-type assignments for a short duration or to meet emergency needs. In addition there remain appointment authorities under schedules A, B, and C. Noncareer executive assignments and the various schedules are defined and discussed in chapter 2. For a more complete description, see the annual report of the U.S. Civil Service Commission, Bureau of Executive Manpower, *Executive Manpower in the Federal Service*, for January 1972 and following years.

38. William A. Medina offers one assessment in "Factors Which Condition the Responses of Departments and Agencies to Centrally Mandated Management Improvement Approaches" (Ph.D. dissertation, American University, Washington, D.C., 1976), chaps. 4–6. The formal guidelines for executive development are set out in *The Federal Personnel Manual*, chap. 412, app. A. The Internal Revenue Service is generally regarded as having one of the best-established programs of this kind. For a description, see U.S. Department of the Treasury, Internal Revenue Service, *The Executive Selection and Development Program*, Doc. 5659 (rev., GPO, 1974).

gram was started with high hopes for centrally identifying, training, and assigning a few promising career executives on a governmentwide basis. By 1976 the hopes were gone and the program had retreated to a position of allowing agencies to select their own candidates for executive development; each of these careerists is to be trained to advance slowly within his own agency and to meet its specific needs. One of the officials in charge of executive development in the civil service described it in the following manner in the summer of 1976:

> We haven't accomplished much. A number of those selected in the first two years felt they were taken out of the stream for promotions in their old bureaus. And the bureaus resisted because they knew the whole idea of this program was to arrange things so that a good guy didn't necessarily return to spend his entire life in one bureau. I guess I shouldn't have been so surprised at how unwilling and parochial the agencies would be. . . . So now we've trimmed our sails to cope with the reality that the departments are conglomerates and the real management is at the bureau level. I've got to work with the bureau chiefs, not fight them. Now it's just a program for encouraging them to develop better personnel systems for their own use.

Even less was accomplished when the Nixon administration and the Civil Service Commission proposed creating one common pool of government career executives who could be moved at the discretion of agency heads. By 1972 the intentions of the Nixon White House toward the civil service were already arousing suspicion, and no one was surprised when the House of Representatives rejected the plan.[39]

Meanwhile, Congress has continued to play an important but disorganized part in managing the civil service system. By adding to governmentwide quotas on supergrades, exempting particular bureaus from overall personnel ceilings, creating uncoordinated provisions for ranking and classifying civil service positions—in these and other ways it has become customary in Congress to bypass House and Senate civil service committees and to develop civil service policies through the ad hoc actions of committees that deal with particular agencies and programs. For example, 400 new supergrade positions created in 1949 were established as a single governmentwide quota allocated by the Civil Service Commission acting for the President. In 1951 Congress passed the first of its "special authorizations," and since then new supergrade positions have come to depend

39. See *The Federal Executive Service*, Hearings before the Subcommittee on Manpower and Civil Service of the House Committee on Post Office and Civil Service, 92 Cong. 2 sess. (GPO, 1972). Incredibly, a revised version of the same plan was proposed one month before the Nixon resignation. See "Government Executive Development" (White House press release, Office of the White House Press Secretary, San Clemente, Calif., July 17, 1974).

on special congressional provisions rather than on a centrally allocated quota.[40]

Likewise, no one appears to have control over personnel totals, for when a bureau's activity appeals to a particular committee, presidential personnel ceilings can make little difference.[41] As a manager of other civil service policies, Congress has been rated by its own analysts in much the way that reformers several years ago described its incoherent control over budget totals and their allocation.

> Subject matter committees of the Congress do not coordinate their actions on the classification or ranking of positions with the Post Office and Civil Service Committees of the Senate and House. This is the basic cause of inconsistencies and inequities among the classification, ranking, and pay systems throughout the Federal Service.[42]

Thus most attempts to plan and coordinate the civil service system as a whole have been accepted only grudgingly, if at all, in Congress; by contrast, detailed administrative interventions on those personnel issues of particular interest to individual congressmen find ready acceptance on Capitol Hill.

THESE FACTORS taken together suggest that while in theory the civil service idea in Washington may be a counterpoint for balancing strictly political and bureaucratic demands, in practice it rests on slippery foundations. Constitutionally, it leads a precarious existence between separated executive and legislative institutions that share important powers over each other's work. Historically, a tradition of party spoils has encouraged more attention to preventing patronage abuses than to building the civil service

40. From 1963 to 1974 the commission's governmentwide quota increased by only 350 positions, but special congressional authorizations increased by 780, and the so-called nonquota positions (first instituted in 1963) grew by 1,660. See U.S. Civil Service Commission, Bureau of Executive Manpower, *Executive Manpower in the Federal Service* (GPO, September 1975), table 2, p. 2.

41. Frequently, this is apparent in the language of appropriation committee reports. In one recent example the directive to an Interior Department bureau was as follows:

> The Committee expects these new 683 positions to be filled without regard to Departmental restrictions imposed under position ceilings fixed by the Office of Management and Budget. These added positions shall not, under any circumstances, be filled at the expense of personnel allocations to other agencies.... Although reluctant to write personnel provisions into the bill itself, the Committee is prepared to take this step if positive directives accompanying this appropriation are not followed.

Department of the Interior and Related Agencies Appropriation Bill, 1977, Senate Appropriations Committee Report 94-991, 94 Cong. 2 sess. (GPO, 1976), pp. 13–14.

42. *Report on Job Evaluation and Ranking in the Federal Government*, H. Rept. 91-28, 91 Cong. 1 sess. (GPO, 1969), p. 11. An earlier summary of the role of Congress in dealing with civil service policies is in Joseph P. Harris, *Congressional Control of Administration* (Brookings Institution, 1964), pp. 163–203.

as an instrument of improved government performance. Structurally, there has been persistent ambivalence about how close or how far from the White House the direction of civil service policies should be. Administratively, attempts to reform the top career levels suggest the ease with which any idea of a governmentwide civil service becomes subordinated to particular bureau and congressional interests. Recent events have only reemphasized the strength of the prevailing crosscurrents: since 1969 it has been possible to have both a lapse in the traditional negative protections of the civil service and a record of continued frustration in reforms trying to create more positive management of the career system.

In general, then, as the search for political leadership has become more demanding, answers to the two basic questions about the bureaucracy's civilian personnel system have remained relatively unchanged since the decision of 1883. What sort of central authority should there be? Never have reformers managed to create a single presidential staff arm for a governmentwide civil service policy. Instead, a bureau-level focus in using civil servants has been coupled with central regulation over procedural techniques for taking personnel actions. This process regulator has remained the Civil Service Commission, which is located ambiguously as more central than the departments but more peripheral than the Executive Office of the President. How should protection be organized? The answer has continued to be reliance on the "semi-independent" status of the same commission—part presidential agency and part policeman against political intrusions. And always in the background has loomed a Congress that is vocal in support for better management but jealous of any rearrangements that might disturb its own diverse lines into each fragment of the bureaucracy.

It is within this historical structure that American national government seeks to cope with the problem of relating political and bureaucratic executives. But the structure itself does not reveal very much about what these relationships of executive politics are like or how they work. For that it is necessary to watch and listen to people in government who have had the actual experiences.

CHAPTER TWO

Setting: The Executive Mélange

[I am] particularly anxious that the executive should be properly constituted. The vice here would not, as in some other parts of the system, be curable. It is the most difficult of all rightly to balance the executive.
—Gouverneur Morris, *Constitutional Debates*, July 24, 1787

SEVERAL GENERATIONS ago, the formula emerging to balance political leadership and bureaucratic power seemed clear enough. After surveying in detail the history of departmental management, two leading administrative experts concluded that a "fulfillment of tendency" was at hand. Gradually, departmental management was coalescing under a stable, professional cadre of civil service executives. These career executives were becoming an instrument of leadership indispensable to the small, clearly demarcated teams of political policymakers that were also developing at the top of government departments.[1] Moreover, central capabilities that embraced all the departments were being improved so as to put the President "in effective control of administrative policy and operation. . . . The departments have lost their independent and uncoordinated position and have been coordinated into a single national administrative machine."[2]

Today it is clear that no such tendencies have been fulfilled. The proper role of the President and his men in the federal executive branch arouses continuing controversy. If anything, the position of higher civil servants and the lines between political and career appointments have become even more complex and uncertain. The same refrain can be heard on all sides. "In my mind," said an intimate White House aide of

1. Arthur W. Macmahon and John D. Millett, *Federal Administrators* (Columbia University Press, 1939). See especially pp. 116 ff.
2. Leonard D. White, *Trends in Public Administration* (McGraw-Hill, 1933), p. 174.

34

a former President, "the whole political-bureaucracy thing is all mixed up. I don't have a strong sense of where the line's drawn." Out in an operating department an assistant secretary declared his job to be

> one of the most impossible in government, given the diversity of activities under me. Two offices are headed by political appointees. Two others are headed by civil servants. Two others are headed by deputy assistant secretaries, but I'm not sure to what extent they're career people. I know they come and go a lot as assistant secretaries change.

Looking at the same situation from the other side, a high civil servant in another department reflected on his prospects:

> I don't know what I'm up against. As a career man, you can never be sure where the boundary is between civil service and politically appointed jobs, and once you think you know it, at this level you can easily find the situation has changed, leaving you with no focus for career ambitions.

Clearly something has happened that was not expected by the experts who were writing as the modern era of big government began.

What has happened to the setting for executive politics is not a neat or simple story. In this chapter I attempt to unravel some of the complexity by looking at the cast of characters. The first section describes formal designations of people and the informal procedures surrounding these designations. While the formal categories of people and jobs may seem a jumble, ambiguity is vastly increased by the unofficial arrangements that fill the working lives of people in government. The second section puts an otherwise static picture in perspective by examining the trends generating the mélange of political and career executives. These trends tell a story of fragmentation and layering high in the executive community. I conclude the chapter by assessing some of the results for the executive personnel system. Occupying positions of ostensible leadership, more top-level political appointees are segmented within more government layers and they confront even more compartmentalized bureaucratic executives and specialists. Thus as political leadership has become more bureaucratized, the incentives have also grown for politicizing the bureaucracy.

It is not surprising if all of this presents a confused picture to outside observers. Trying to figure out who is who is not a passing stage for the uninitiated but a preoccupying and enduring question in Washington politics. The ambiguity that surrounds any answer is one of the most important factors conditioning the relationship between political leadership and bureaucratic power.

Who's Who?

A conventional image of pyramid-like structures in the executive branch, with a neat division of politicians above and bureaucrats below, is badly misleading. Rather than picturing a single, clearly defined boundary line, one should think instead of an erratic smudge that is jagged (occurring at different levels within and among different agencies), variable (moving up and down at different times in the same agency), and blurred (being subject to compromise by informal understandings even at one place and one time).

Formalities

At its extremes, the formal personnel picture seems fairly clear. Presiding over the approximately 2.8 million civilian employees of the federal executive branch is the President, the men and women he appoints as heads of the executive agencies, and their principal subordinates. During recent years these top (executive schedule) posts have numbered about 700.[3] For most of the postwar period a handful of these high executive jobs have been explicitly designated for civil servants, but more recently they have often reverted to de facto political appointments. A few of the dozen or so cabinet secretaries and agency directors may be known to some of the general public. The rest of the 700 top executives—deputy secretaries, undersecretaries, deputy undersecretaries, assistant secretaries, administrators, deputy administrators, commissioners, and so on—are known and build reputations only within the narrow confines of Washington politics.

At the other extreme are about 2 million federal employees—roughly grades 1 through 12 in the civil service general schedule (GS)—performing the largely routine tasks attached to their positions. Scattered throughout this lower level is a relatively small number (about 500 in 1976) of noncareer employees coming in with their politically appointed bosses to perform personal chores (secretaries, chauffeurs, etc.).

3. This figure includes line and staff positions in the departments and agencies, regulatory commissions, the White House Office, and the Executive Office of the President; almost 90 percent of them are presidential appointments, usually with Senate confirmation. It does not include all the higher political appointments in the executive branch. There are also approximately 100 ambassadors; 725 judges, U.S. attorneys, and U.S. marshals; and over 2,000 presidential and 10,000 departmental part-time positions on advisory boards and commissions.

Between these two extremes of the executive establishment lies a patchwork of intermingled political and career appointments that becomes more tentative and variegated in the higher levels. Grades 12 through 15 include another 500–600 (in 1976) exempt positions for political appointment. While a few of these jobs are formally labeled "policy-determining," nine out of ten have such vague catch-all designations as "administrative" or "special" assistant to higher political executives. In theory all these so-called schedule C positions are civil service jobs subject to rules prohibiting political activity and laying down qualifications and standards of conduct; formally speaking, these political appointments are merely exempt from a competitive examination of qualifications. In practice top political executives are usually quite free to appoint whomever they want to these positions, and prohibitions against their partisan political activity are rarely enforced. Yet schedule Cs are also assigned an official grade and salary indistinguishable from that of regular career officials.

Climbing still higher one reaches the so-called supergrade level (GS 16–18) and the beginning of what the Civil Service Commission terms the "executive population" of the federal government.[4] Roughly speaking, the supergrades comprise about 7,000 positions and it is these, along with the 700 top political executive posts mentioned earlier, that are the main focus in this book. As table 2-1 suggests, it is at the supergrade level that the intermixture of career and noncareer positions increases rapidly. Since this is also the range where the interactions of executive politics begin, it is worthwhile having a closer look at the formal job classifications.

THE MID-LEVEL MUDDLE

The largest single portion of the supergrade executives, approximately 5,500 in 1976, fall under the general schedule of the Civil Service Commission. But by no means are these positions all career "civil service" jobs in the sense of being filled by an open, competitive examination of qualifications. Approximately 500 are jobs exempt under so-called schedules A and B and are filled predominantly by lawyers. This arrangement is formally justified on the grounds that it is impractical to hold a competitive examination for such work; in effect, the practice is due to a long-standing

4. While the Bureau of Executive Manpower's categorization of the executive population is based only on salary level, i.e., those paid at rates equivalent to GS 16 and above, the majority of people concerned are said to have management duties.

Table 2-1. *Approximate Number of Noncareer and Career Positions, U.S. Government, by Rank, 1975–76*

Schedule	Political, or excepted, noncareer positions[a]	Competitive civil service career positions[b]
Executive schedule		
I	12	. . .
II	71	. . .
III	115	. . .
IV	353	4
V	194	19
General schedule supergrades		
18	246	221
17	386	771
16	646	3,213
Public law 313 supergrades		
16–18	430	808
Other general schedule grades		
15	310	28,940
14	150	50,930
13	140	108,100
12 and below	720	2,100,000

Source: Compiled from unpublished figures made available by the U.S. Civil Service Commission and by the White House, and from *Executive Manpower in the Federal Service*, the annual report of the commission's Bureau of Executive Manpower first published in 1972.

a. Includes all presidential appointments; schedules A, B, and C; and NEA and miscellaneous noncareer appointments excepted from competitive civil service examinations.

b. Includes only career positions falling under Civil Service Commission purview.

rule laid down by Congress prohibiting the expenditure of funds to examine lawyers.

Another 500 to 600 supergrade posts are exempted as noncareer executive assignments (NEAs) with the justification that they involve the advocacy of administration positions, political policymaking responsibilities, or personal assistance to a political executive. They are political appointments in the sense that they are excepted from the competitive staffing procedures of the career system, and appointees do not have the tenure of career civil servants. The concentrations of these noncareer jobs are especially heavy at the highest bureaucratic levels. A young careerist ambitious for what might superficially seem to be the top rung of the competitive civil service ladder—the GS 18 level—would have found in 1976 that over two-fifths of such top supergrade posts in the cabinet departments were exempted NEA positions. They might be open to him as an individual, but they were closed to him as a career civil servant. In departments such as Interior, Justice, and Housing, NEAs held over half of the GS 18 jobs.[5]

A cabinet member or assistant secretary, however, might also feel frustrated, or at least confused, when told that these NEA slots are available for his or her political appointments to put the administration's stamp on government programs. It is the officials in the Civil Service Commission who determine that a job meets the NEA criteria, where it should be located in the salary scale between grades 16 and 18, and whether a potential appointee meets the qualifications for the specific job. As with schedule Cs, the agency is supposed to police these "political" appointments against certain prohibited political activities (an NEA can watch but not participate in a political convention, contribute as an individual but not help raise funds for partisan political purposes, join a party but not help manage a campaign, and so on). If a political executive wishes to move his NEA appointee to any other position, even at the same level within the same agency, Civil Service Commission approval will be required. Although a top political executive can fire his NEA appointee, if the latter is a military veteran with one year of continuous employment, a long list of procedures will have to be followed. These procedures for "adverse action" will require thirty days' advance warning specifying charges, opportunities for written answers, and then a written notice of the adverse decision and right of appeal to the Civil Service Commission.[6]

In addition to the 5,500 general schedule jobs, 1,200 executives are in so-called Public Law 313 positions. These were first established in 1947 to compensate scientific and research professionals in the defense agencies and are now comparable to GS 16–18. About two-thirds are career civil service positions and one-third are noncareer positions outside the purview of the Civil Service Commission.

Hence for almost 7,000 people near the top of the government, the formal demarcation between bureaucrat and political appointee is far

5. Data supplied by the U.S. Civil Service Commission, Bureau of Executive Manpower. Almost half of the temporary NEA officials report they have managerial line authority over operating programs. Bureau staff speculate that this may be an exaggeration because "many [NEAs] have so little government experience that they are uncertain as to what an operating organization program is."

6. For a description of the formal system for executive personnel, see two pamphlets of the U.S. Civil Service Commission: *Employment Rights and Responsibilities of Noncareer Executive Appointees* (GPO, 1974); and *Your Executive Team: A Guide for the Noncareer Executive Appointee* (GPO, 1974).

from obvious.[7] Depending on who is doing the counting, noncareer "political" positions can be taken to mean only NEAs or all positions exempt from the competitive career service. Thus anything from 9 percent to 25 percent of the executive supergrade positions can be considered as political appointments. That experienced government leaders disagree so widely on the actual proportions is itself indicative of the murky boundaries between political appointees and civil servants.[8] Whatever the intricacies of body counts in the personnel system, the major point is that somewhere in this smudgy zone between top presidential appointees and the several thousand officials below them, the vital interface of political administration occurs, for better or worse in terms of government performance.

Variety is the primary constant. For example, a bird's-eye view of the formal designation of positions in the Housing and Commerce departments (figure 2-1) suggests the ragged terrain across which political and career positions are mixed within the same agency and at different levels in different organizations. It is not particular details but the overall image of variability that makes these departments typical of the federal executive branch.

If organization charts could be made into moving pictures, they would show that the formal political or career label attached to a particular position can change at different times. In approving a reorganization plan or an appropriation or other piece of legislation affecting government personnel, Congress may change its mind about the respective merits of having particularly important jobs in or out of the general classified service or possibly in a separate personnel system. Together, the President and the Civil Service Commission can also exercise considerable discretion in reclassifying positions from career service to exempt noncareer jobs or something in between. In the 1960s, for example, an aspiring civil servant might have successfully set his sights on a senior position as regional director in one of the domestic departments. After a series of complicated changes, the same jobs in 1970 were being filled, not as if they were the

7. Another 3,100 executive positions (not shown in table 2-1) are in totally separate personnel systems, such as the State Department's foreign service corps, the Central Intelligence Agency, the Atomic Energy Commission, and the Tennessee Valley Authority.

8. See, for example, the conflicting testimony of the chairman of the Civil Service Commission and the comptroller general on this point in *The Federal Executive Service*, Hearings before the Subcommittee on Manpower and Civil Service of the House Committee on Post Office and Civil Service, 92 Cong. 2 sess. (GPO, 1972), pp. 15, 216.

top of a career ladder, but by persons given a limited contract of service running five years at most (so-called limited executive assignments). In 1975 the regional director's job was again changed, and to attain his goal the careerist had to leave the career service and accept what then became a political appointment.[9]

PATTERNS OF IMPROVISATION

No elaborate political theory is required to explain the variegated lines between what are formally political and civil service jobs. Improvisation usually suffices. The improvisations, however, do fall into fairly regular patterns, and each has left its imprint on the executive structure.

"Blanketing-in"—the wholesale importation of formerly noncareer jobs into the career civil service system—occurs sporadically and has constituted the chief means by which civil service reformers in the past have sought to extend the merit system. Although having short-run drawbacks, this strategy has accomplished the reformers' aim of quickly and relatively painlessly covering more jobs under the civil service. As a spokesman for a career employees' union summed up thirty-five years of his reform agitation: "You've got to recognize you're blanketing in a number of political hacks, but it's the one way of getting the merit system extended." Toward the end of most presidents' tenures, somewhat less high-minded motives have also inspired a more limited form of blanketing-in, or "seeding," by which specific political appointments are converted into career jobs as an unwelcome bequest to the next administration.

Ambiguities in the line between political and career jobs are intensified by the predictable political reaction to blanketing-in, the "shake-out." The most blatant and troublesome seedings are likely to be transformed back into nontenured positions by a new administration.[10] In the process, what were thought to be new positions for careerists dissolve again, as in the department where a spokesman said that

> changes in the Democratic years blanketed political guys into career jobs, and well, even though they did it for the wrong reasons, it was a good thing

---

9. Executive Order 11839, February 15, 1975. The regional director's posts affected were those for the Environmental Protection Agency and the departments of Health, Education, and Welfare, Housing and Urban Development, Transportation, and Labor. Later in the same year the Commerce Department and the Small Business Administration were added.

10. But reports of individual cases of "un-blanketing" also need to be treated skeptically. According to one appointee, "You can get points back home politically by saying you were forced out by the new administration."

Figure 2-1. *Political and Career Executive Positions in the Department of*
June 10, 1974[a]

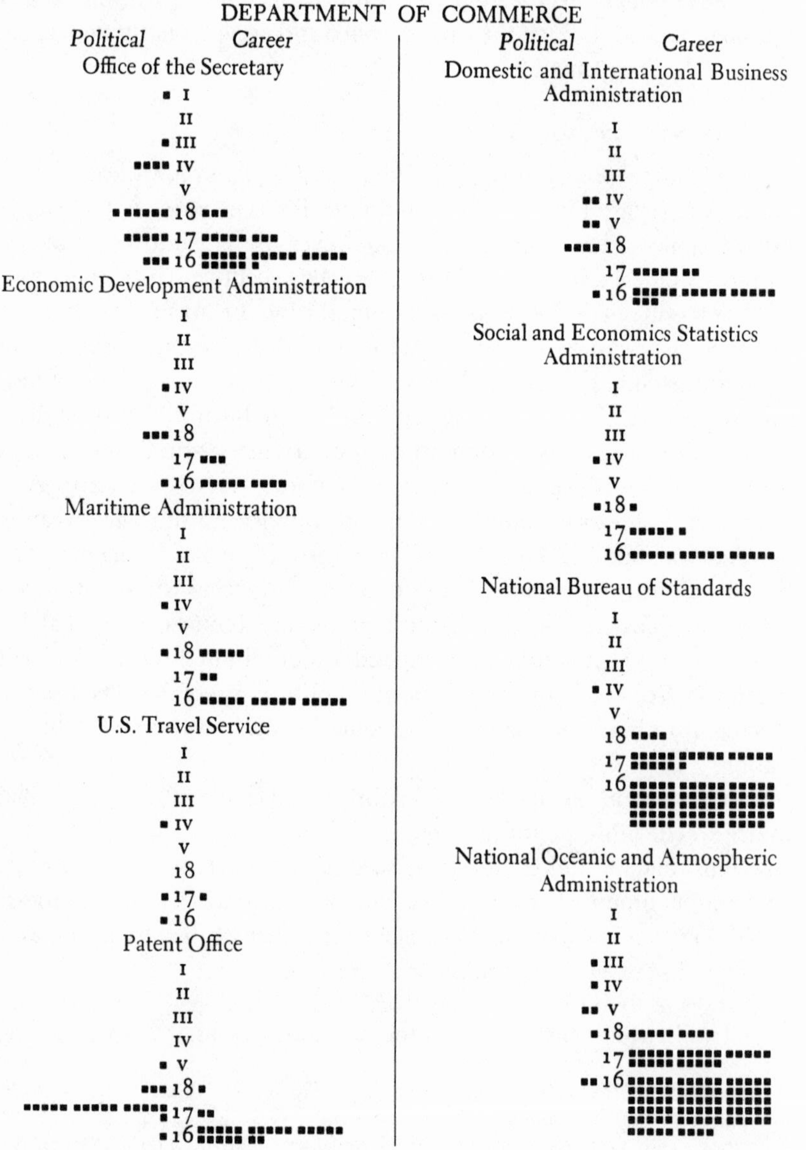

DEPARTMENT OF COMMERCE

Political	Career		Political	Career

Office of the Secretary

■ I
II
■ III
■■■■ IV
V
■ ■■■■■ 18 ■■■
■■■■■ 17 ■■■■■ ■■■
■■■ 16 ■■■■■ ■■■■■ ■■■■■

Economic Development Administration

I
II
III
■ IV
V
■■■ 18
17 ■■■
■ 16 ■■■■■ ■■■■

Maritime Administration

I
II
III
■ IV
V
■ 18 ■■■■■
17 ■■
16 ■■■■■ ■■■■■ ■■■■■

U.S. Travel Service

I
II
III
■ IV
V
18
■ 17 ■
■ 16

Patent Office

I
II
III
IV
■ V
■■■ 18 ■
■■■■■ ■■■■■ ■■■ 17 ■■
■ 16 ■■■■■ ■■■■■ ■■■■■

Domestic and International Business Administration

I
II
III
■■ IV
■■ V
■■■■ 18
17 ■■■■■ ■■
■ 16 ■■■■■ ■■■■■ ■■■■■

Social and Economics Statistics Administration

I
II
III
■ IV
V
■ 18 ■
17 ■■■■■ ■
16 ■■■■■ ■■■■■ ■■■■■

National Bureau of Standards

I
II
III
■ IV
V
18 ■■■■
17 ■■■■■ ■■■■■ ■■■■■
16 ■■■■■ ■■■■■ ■■■■■
■■■■■ ■■■■■ ■■■■■

National Oceanic and Atmospheric Administration

I
II
■ III
■ IV
■■ V
■ 18 ■■■■■ ■■■■
17 ■■■■■ ■■■■■ ■■■■■
■■ 16 ■■■■■ ■■■■■ ■■■■■
■■■■■ ■■■■■ ■■■■■
■■■■■ ■■■■

Source: Unpublished data from the personnel offices of the Department of Commerce and the Department of Housing and Urban Development.

a. Numbers in figure represent executive schedule grades I–V and general schedule grades 16–18.

Commerce and in the Department of Housing and Urban Development,

DEPARTMENT OF HOUSING AND URBAN DEVELOPMENT

Political	*Career*		*Political*	*Career*		*Political*	*Career*
Office of the Secretary			**Housing Production and Mortgage Credit**			**Legislative Affairs**	
■ I						I	
II			I			II	
■ III			II			III	
IV			III			■ IV	
■■ V			■ IV			V	
18			■ V			18	
■■ 17			18			■■ 17	
■ ■■■■■ 16			■■■■ 17			■ 16	
			16 ■■■■■ ■				
General Counsel						**Community Planning[b]**	
I			**Policy Development and Research**			I	
II						II	
III			I			III	
■ IV			II			■ IV	
■ V			III			■ V	
18			■ IV			18	
17 ■■			V			17 ■■	
16 ■■■■■ ■■			18			16 ■■■■■ ■■■	
			■■ 17				
			■ 16 ■■■■■ ■				
Housing Management						**Assistant Secretary for Administration**	
I			**Federal Disaster Assistance Administration**			I	
II						II	
III			I			III	
■ IV			II			IV	
V			III			V ■	
18			IV			18 ■	
17 ■■■			V			17 ■■■■■	
16 ■■■■■ ■■■■			■ 18			16 ■■■■■ ■	
			17 ■				
			16 ■■■■■ ■				
New Communities Administration						**Miscellaneous[c]**	
I						I	
II						II	
III						III	
■ IV						■■■ IV	
V						V	
■ 18						18 ■	
17 ■						17 ■■	
■■ 16						16 ■■■■■ ■■■	

b. Includes Office of Community Development and Office of Community Planning and Management.

c. Includes Office of Interstate Land Sales, Federal Insurance Administration, Office of Equal Opportunity, and Inspector General.

to do. They raised the places where a career man could go to a higher level.
. . . Now they've brought in a bunch of appointees with this administration
and we are retrogressing, putting career jobs back in political layers.

Interesting as these individual comings and goings may be, it is the
cumulative impact over the years that matters most for the working relations of political administration. If the reform strategy of blanketing-in
has proved a practical way of extending civil service coverage, it has also
played an important part in creating an atmosphere of suspicion. What
is good for extending the civil service system can be bad for individual
civil servants suspected of being carry-overs from a previous administration's plots. Most higher civil servants can expect to encounter such mistrust with the arrival of any new administration or agency head.

With the general civil service buffeted between blanketing-in and
shaking out, it is not surprising that specialized groups have felt a need
to complicate the picture further with separate career personnel systems.
Since World War II a typical response to any national emergency has
been the creation of an organization specifically designed to be outside
the general civil service system. The Atomic Energy Commission, the
National Aeronautics and Space Administration, and the Cost of Living
Council (and its predecessors) are prominent examples of agencies that
have organized all or part of their personnel systems outside the general
civil service; the same treatment was scheduled for Defense Department
scientists in the 1960s until more detailed study showed the major problems were not related to civil service ratings for scientists. It is especially
revealing that as a supposed aid in promoting the nonpartisan business
efficiency of the Post Office—to take mail services out of "politics"—the
department was separated from the regular civil service system and made
an autonomous public agency with its own competitive service at the end
of the 1960s.

The vagaries of political interest and events add more uncertainty to
the line between political and civil service positions. To political activists
in the White House, Congress, and interest groups, not all top posts in the
federal executive branch are of equal salience all the time. How far down
political appointments go in a given agency typically registers the degree
of political interest and controversy attached to the particular activities at
the time of its creation. The location of these political hot spots naturally
changes over time. In the Agriculture Department, for example, some
units (such as the Agricultural Stabilization Service) have traditionally
had a political head; other less controversial units, such as the Com-

modity Exchange Authority or Animal and Plant Inspection Service, have had a careerist in charge. When commodity dealing aroused new political interest in the 1970s, pressure grew to increase the role of political appointees (in this case by tying them more directly to Congress than to the department's secretary) and to reduce traditional reliance on a career administrator.[11]

Particular circumstances can also combine to change temporary political appointments into career posts. This is especially the case where scandals have arisen (for example, the transfer of almost all posts below the commissioner's into career jobs in the Internal Revenue Service after scandals in the Truman administration) or where the head of a newly created agency has become so closely identified with the organization as to acquire a kind of de facto career status (the best-known example being J. Edgar Hoover and his new Federal Bureau of Investigation after 1924). In any event, the explanation for why some high positions are formally designated as political and others as civil service usually cannot be found by reference to any grand design or clear criteria for the separation of policymaking and administrative duties. Typically, the explanation has to be found by looking at each particular agency's circumstances and the forces of expediency in play during its history.

Congress has had an increasingly important part in prescribing what career and noncareer posts are, despite the President's position as chief executive. By 1972 slightly over half (54 percent) of the executive positions exempted from the competitive civil service rules had acquired that status through congressional determination rather than through orders of the President or the Civil Service Commission acting under presidential authority. Such actions do not represent coherent congressional appraisals of executive manpower needs but rather a string of ad hoc enactments, typically seeking to ensure the influence of congressional committees over the agency affected. This came through in the comment of a man with twenty-five years' experience as a civil servant and seven years as a political appointee: "The decisions I make—money, people, timing—all involve issues of priority and so are to some extent political, but it doesn't take a political appointee to do my job. The reason this is a political appointment is, I think, mostly that Congress likes to have a say in who gets the position."

The struggle for influence, however, can just as readily be expressed by

11. This political pressure resulted in the passage of the Commodity and Futures Trading Commission Act of 1974, P.L. 93-463, October 23, 1974.

attempts to place a post within rather than outside the career civil service—the key point often being not the designation itself but who makes
it. Hence Congress frequently tries to continue a group of jobs in the
competitive service against administration efforts to exempt them and
vice versa. After one six-year struggle of this kind, a career personnel
officer said, "Look, whether they're career or political jobs, you're really
talking about who is going to control these guys. Everybody says that they
don't care what you call the jobs as long as they can appoint their own
people."

Obviously, formal designations for defining political and bureaucratic
interaction take one only a little way toward understanding the working
relations of these people in government. The overall environment is one
of uncertainty. Formal boundaries have varied as reorganizations, political maneuvers, and ad hoc improvisations during particular emergencies
have washed back and forth across the executive structure. Given these
forces and the fact that no modern president has treated overall reform
of the government personnel system as a serious priority, ambiguity is not
only possible but assured.

Informalities

Informal arrangements governing political and career jobs introduce a
wholly new dimension of ambiguity. The unwritten understandings and
practices among people in Washington, rather than formal numbers, tell
this story. The blurring comes from career bureaucrats serving in capacities of supposed political responsibility and from political intrusions into
what is ostensibly a nonpartisan civil service system.

CAREERISTS IN POLITICAL POSITIONS

Officials often have little choice but to take the place of absent political chiefs, for whom the turnover rate can be very high (see chapter 3).
At any one time during the past fifteen years, from one-tenth to one-third
of the presidential appointments to political executive posts have been
vacant; the corollary in most cases is a career employee in an "acting"
capacity while awaiting the next occupant of the head office. Some agencies are especially prone to interim government by stand-ins. The Domestic and International Business Administration, probably the unit most
central to Commerce Department purposes, is a good example. By 1933
its organizational equivalent had had eight political heads during the first

twenty-one years of the bureau's existence. Similarly, its "acting" head in 1974 could report having had five assistant secretaries in the preceding four years.

Moreover, a political appointment need not be unfilled to be functionally vacant; career officials can be found in charge where the supposed political leadership is uninterested or inept. As a former supergrade who had moved up to a presidential appointment said:

> In a department where there is a vacuum and only a series of transients, then the bureaucrats try to fill in the vacuum. Without malice, with the best intentions in the world, people trying to fill a political vacuum can adopt some pretty unique strategies . . . arranging special trips for congressmen or upgrading their own or other people's jobs.

Of course, careerists who are in line to take over may have their own interests in claiming that a political vacuum exists. How political leadership tries to cope with the situation and the broader question of its being "captured by the bureaucracy" is a subject more appropriately dealt with at length in a later chapter.

Custom also plays an important part in the informal mixture of political and civil service positions. Government agencies are not simply machines for turning out discrete policy decisions; they are also bundles of memory and practices that are inherited from a particular past and carried forward.[12] Since this cultural heritage is rooted in networks of mutual advantage between specific agencies and private groups and congressmen, it is not surprising that personnel appointments often reflect private and congressional interests.

The formal law frequently states that the heads of particular bureaus are to be political appointees; left unstated is the customary expectation in Washington that these top positions will be filled by careerists promoted from within or from related specialized networks. The Bureau of Prisons, Weather Service, and Bureau of Standards are long-standing examples, and similar expectations surround other less technical political appointments dealing with education, labor, agriculture, and minorities and other group interests. Locating the particular point of contact between bureaucratic and political leadership therefore depends on these customary practices and indulgences that persist through time, as well as on the formal personnel designations or the political pressures surrounding the subject matter.

---

12. A number of examples are discussed in Harold Seidman, *Politics, Position, and Power* (2d ed., New York: Oxford University Press, 1975), pp. 121–60.

Even when agency culture plays little part, high-level civil servants often leave their careers to take political appointments, particularly as the exempted posts grow in number and require more specialized knowledge. At the end of the Johnson presidency 45 percent of presidential executive appointments were filled by people who had spent the preponderance of their working lives in government career jobs (both domestic civil service and foreign service). This was an admittedly high level compared with that of every recent administration save Truman's, but the overall picture of career recruitment to political jobs is what matters most for present purposes. Since World War II, anywhere from one-fifth to two-fifths of every president's top political appointments have come from the ranks of federal bureaucrats, the proportion being somewhat higher in Democratic than in Republican years.[13] Career officials are also more prominent in presidential appointments toward the end of every administration, partly it seems, because it becomes harder to recruit outsiders and partly because there is more confidence in such officials by this time.

Somewhat lower down from these top executive positions, political appointments at the supergrade level tell a similar story. Usually one-third to one-half of the 600 noncareer executive assignments (i.e., GS 16–18) are filled by former career civil servants, not by outside political appointees or in-and-outers to government. These political appointee–bureaucrats fall into two distinct groups. The largest number are careerists who are near retirement and are willing to leave the security of the tenured civil service system; they have usually been in government at least twenty years, rarely have moved outside their agencies, and are actually older than most personnel in the career supergrades. The other group consists of young officials in their late thirties and early forties who have risen rapidly, are against the top of the career ladder, and are willing to take risks to mover further ahead. Hence even the noncareer posts mixed into the top of the civil service structure are filled by people who are a mixture of insiders and outsiders.

As a result of these informal arrangements—civil service stand-ins, agency cultures, and ad hoc promotions—no one scanning the number of

13. Laurin L. Henry, "The Presidency, Executive Staffing, and the Federal Bureaucracy," in Aaron Wildavsky, ed., *The Presidency* (Little, Brown, 1969), especially pages 547, 548, 555. The Johnson years in particular are discussed in Matthew B. Coffey, "A Death in the White House: The Short Life of the New Patronage," *Public Administration Review*, vol. 34 (September-October 1974). Figures given in the text include the major political executives in the federal executive branch and exclude ambassadorships.

career-exempt, so-called political positions should assume that he will necessarily find in these jobs a "true" nonbureaucratic political appointee or even an in-and-outer who continually mixes government jobs with work in the private sector. Both critics and defenders of the United States' politically accessible and changeable layers of political executives often overlook the extent to which the filling of top executive positions is dependent on people who have a relatively permanent attachment to the executive branch. Without anyone planning it, bureaucrats have become an important component of "political" leadership in the nation's executive branch.

POLITICAL FINGERS IN THE CIVIL SERVICE

The reverse, however, also holds: informal practices in Washington are such that no observer should assume that what is ostensibly a career civil service job is necessarily filled by a government careerist, at least not by one who has come to the job free from the machinations of the higher political levels. In every administration within living memory this influence has existed to some degree and has taken three forms: political displacement, political placement, and political clearance in career civil service jobs.[14]

Given civil service rules and the possibilities of disclosure, outright displacement—removing a tenured civil servant and substituting a politically favored person—is the most drastic and infrequent technique. But it is not unknown. Experienced careerists in staff positions who have no commitments to particular programs are often willing to move on to similar positions in other agencies when it becomes clear they lack the confidence of their political supervisors. Without such voluntary departures, however, so much political capital may be expended in displacing an entrenched careerist that none is left to ensure support for the intended successor.[15]

Wary of such Pyrrhic victories, politicians have more commonly influenced top career jobs by trying to place people in vacancies or in new

14. For a free-ranging discussion of officials' experiences in many agencies over a number of years, see *The Bureaucrat*, vol. 4 (January 1976). The reality of personnel politics in Washington has been documented as never before in the 1,500-page volume *Final Report on Violations and Abuses of Merit Principles in Federal Employment Together with Minority Views*, Subcommittee on Manpower and Civil Service of the House Committee on Post Office and Civil Service, Committee Print 94-28, 94 Cong. 2 sess. (GPO, 1976).

15. Several well-known cases are described in Laurin L. Henry, *Presidential Transitions* (Brookings Institution, 1960), pp. 647–51.

posts, sometimes building a shadow organization to bypass those out of favor. However haphazard and unreliable the arrangements, both Republican and Democratic administrations have used particular political appointees—sometimes dubbed "political commissars"—in the departments to process political appointments, to handle the large numbers of congressional requests, and to transmit political referrals for all sorts of government jobs.[16]

Frequently, the day-to-day political patronage work of the commissars spills over to include preferential treatment and placements in career positions. What starts as a referral for a political appointment can easily end up being perceived as an injunction to arrange a job—civil service or otherwise. This is especially likely if a powerful political figure is backing the request or if officials receiving a referral see an advantage in ingratiating themselves. Sometimes political intrusions into the civil service develop because these transient political middlemen have little real understanding of the government's complicated personnel process and at other times because they understand the system only too well. A young law school graduate's description of his personnel activities as a former appointee in the Department of Health, Education, and Welfare is an example of one of the more extreme cases during the Nixon administration:

> It took us some two years to get the hang of the system. . . . We first relied on [a senior personnel official's] expertise in political leanings [of employees] and his knowledge of how to get the job done. . . . We had learned how to outsmart the Civil Service Commission, we virtually could make whatever appointments we wanted, we could get rid of anyone. . . . Thinking about it now, we were really a bunch of juveniles with incredible power, a power that never should have been entrusted to us.[17]

Political clearances are less obvious than outright political placement, and they constitute by far the most common means of informally mixing

16. The use of such political commissars has a long lineage. After the 1892 election, for example, a messenger (who later rose to be chief clerk—a very high civil service position at the time) described the Treasury Department arrangements: "Secretary of the Treasury Carlisle placed a small political scout in the janitorship of the bureau. It was his business to get acquainted, spot the jobs beyond the pale of the civil service —and send the names of the incumbents to headquarters. No place was too unimportant to be overlooked. . . . When the 'janitor' finished his clean-up job he was made a chief of division in the same bureau." (Quoted in Arthur W. Macmahon, "Selection and Tenure of Bureau Chiefs, Part II," *American Political Science Review* vol. 20 [November 1926], note 50 on p. 801.) By the 1970s the term "janitor" was out of fashion, but strong parallels existed in the work performed by some special "management" advisers.

17. Stuart Young, quoted in *The Federal Times*, January 19, 1976.

political interests with career service positions. "Clearing" has covered a range of political purposes by serving as both a way to positively favor individuals with presumed loyalty and as a more passive veto system designed to ensure that a job candidate culled by regular civil service procedures will offend no vital political sensitivities. The procedures for politically scrutinizing civil service appointments have varied from deadly systematic efforts to the farcical.[18] Clearing has usually meant checking with congressmen from the relevant district, selected state party officials, and the White House. Typically, the candidate's party registration will be obtained on the dubious assumption that party labels can be a reliable guide to policy preferences and personal loyalties.

For present purposes the detailed procedure used is not as important as the overall tone that persists at the interface of political and civil service leadership. Traditionally that tone has been one of tolerance for what the formal rules and regulations would label—at a minimum—as improprieties. Coming as they do from a variety of inside perspectives, the following comments on political placement and clearance capture the general atmosphere better than any history of particular cases:

A Civil Service commissioner during Republican years:

[A White House assistant] would recommend people for jobs whether they could be filled in or out of the civil service. Our office tried to show some flexibility, and where a person was qualified and competent he would very likely get placed. . . . If you knew a job was opening up they might be interested in, you would get in touch with [the White House assistant]. . . . Supergrades or below had some political clearance some of the time.

A Civil Service commissioner during a Democratic administration (when for the first time in the commission's history all three commissioners were former civil servants):

It is clearly illegal for someone to be appointed on the recommendation of a congressman or political big shot, but everyone knows that there are ways of getting around these legal requirements and not directly violating the law. . . .

Normally, political clearances haven't caused much trouble in the past: first, because they haven't been blatant; second, because they haven't been based solely on grounds of partisan political affiliation; and third, because most people know how to handle these things with finesse. . . . Finesse means, for example, that you do your clearance within the department more often than having some campaign type sitting in the White House

18. In the latter category was the choice of a bureau director (Smith) from among three qualified candidates "because someone noticed from the résumé that his father's name was Grover Cleveland Smith, so we thought there was some presumption he'd be a good, responsive Democrat."

doing it. Or, to take an example, if there's someone in the regional office getting an appointment because he's a party chairman, you'll eliminate a lot of the trouble if at the same time you make a straight-out career appointment of a good civil servant with a lot of zip into a similar post. They'll tend to cancel each other out. The commission finds it difficult to get evidence in part, at least, because these things tend to be handled with finesse.

A White House official who bridged the administrations of both parties for over a decade:

Political clearance of career jobs didn't change much between administrations. . . . If there was a vacancy or appointment coming through, there was somebody identified from the secretary's office in the department who would check [with a White House aide] who had a card file. They would check to see if Mr. X, who was being considered for the job, had a card on him which would show who had recommended him politically. If there wasn't a card on him, the [White House] aide would look to see if there was someone who had been recommended and might be qualified for such a job. The file was essentially a compendium of political recommendations and endorsements.

A career personnel officer with experience in three departments:

At least since I've been in charge of personnel operations [over ten years in 1973] there has been considerable collaboration on supergrade positions prior to any Civil Service Commission action. A lot of times appointments didn't get approved until there were discussions at the White House on the person or at least on some general guidelines from the White House personnel operations. . . .

How do I know this? Because I had phone calls from people in the White House personnel office checking on people that we had sent to the commission and on which they hadn't acted yet.

While political clearance of career jobs has normally been a haphazard arrangement incapable of dealing with all the thousands of personnel changes in the upper levels of the civil service, it has occurred regularly enough and with enough impunity that most experienced participants—careerists and political appointees alike—have been inclined to accept at least some restrained form of it as a fact of life. Generally a so-called rule of reason has been applied, to the effect that unless the clearance process is used indiscriminately to deny all nonpolitical qualifications, it is legitimate to factor in political acceptability in filling high-level career jobs. In some places, such as the President's Office of Management and Budget, or in highly technical and professionally specialized agencies, this norm of acceptance does not usually exist, but in general there is tolerance, or at least resignation. A supergrade who had moved from OMB to a responsible position in an operating agency expressed the prevailing attitude:

> It would bother me if it happened at OMB, but it doesn't here, where people are committed to particular subject matters and programs. . . . As long as it's reasonable, I mean not keeping topflight people out . . . and being done on the basis that "all other things being equal we'd rather have an administration supporter in this job than someone else," then I can live with it. . . .
>
> I don't know the criteria, but I assume my appointment will be coming up for political clearance—if not this promotion, then the next one. I assume I am going to be treated the way you hear other people are being treated.[19]

Where major shifts in established programs are intended, there may be good reason to seek some reassurance about basic agreement with administration aims. The real question is whether the civil servants involved are initially assumed to be loyal or disloyal to political leadership and whether the political appointees' fairly blunt clearance techniques offer any reliable basis for judging career bureaucrats, much less holding them accountable to civil service norms.

Most of these informal arrangements high in the bureaucracy are unlikely to be detected by checking to see if formal civil service procedures have been followed. The more effectively a political clearance system operates, the less observable it becomes—particularly if it is used only to disqualify rather than to favor selections. Those considered bad risks will be unlikely to apply or to be sought out as realistic applicants; hence grievance cases will rarely develop. Often one incident will be sufficient to establish the point, as with the selecting official who said, "I learned my lesson from that one. Thereafter I didn't propose any people for appointment who would be unacceptable." Investigators from the Civil Service Commission also recognize that while positive endorsement may produce tangible memos about "must hires," negative clearance may simply mean that the papers do not come back from the head office; it is, therefore, much harder to prove.[20] Likewise, political placements can

19. The extreme in tolerance (or, if one prefers, retribution) was expressed by a civil servant ousted from a technical agency during the Nixon administration:

I don't know; I suppose it would be better if you didn't have political clearances, but I don't think it is so important. . . . It's been going on for a long time. . . . My wife has been active in [a local suburb's] Democratic party. When there was a Democratic administration in power she used to do some checking on names sent to her—on their general registration and whether they had voted in the Democratic primary.

20. See *Violation and Abuses of Merit Principles in Federal Employment*, Hearings before the Subcommittee on Manpower and Civil Service of the House Committee on Post Office and Civil Service, 94 Cong. 1 sess. (April 10, 1975), pt. 1, p. 149.

easily be obscured when the same personnel office processes political appointments and makes referrals for career positions. In investigating the Office of Special Projects (OSP), where the previously quoted "juvenile" commissar at the Department of Health, Education, and Welfare was employed, Civil Service Commission officials could find little evidence of wrongdoing.

OSP has not systematically or deliberately conducted inquiries into the political affiliations of candidates for competitive positions [violating Civil Service Rule 4.2].

But the report's qualifications were more revealing than its conclusion:

OSP conducts political checks on candidates for noncareer positions in close conjunction with its other function of referring candidates for competitive [career] positions. Under existing arrangements it would be virtually impossible to detect deliberate violations or to prevent inadvertent violations of Civil Service Rule 4.2. For example, OSP may conduct a political check on a candidate who is presumably a candidate or potential candidate for a non-competitive position. Later, OSP may refer that same candidate for a competitive position. . . . OSP has the discretion to either make the referral directly and follow up on placement efforts, or to forward the application . . . for relatively more routine handling.[21]

The practical result of all the informal political practices is this: knowing who is who in a department's bureaucracy involves, among other things, knowing who are in fact career civil servants and who are the figures associated with particular White House, congressional, or other patrons. A common situation was described by a career official (responsible for much of a department's management) to an undersecretary intent on "shaking up" his bureaucracy:

The undersecretary came in complaining: "Look, we gotta have more people. These bureaucrats under me are incompetent, brainwashed." So I said, "Here's a piece of paper; give me a list of the incompetents, and we went through it name by name, one, two, three." Almost invariably, these were people brought in by his predecessors. "That's just it," I said, "your fair-haired boys are going to be the next bums that your successor is going to want to get rid of. You are going to bring in your own hard-chargers and in an earlier incarnation they are exactly the kind of people you're complaining about now."

This is not to suggest that political placement efforts in the career service invariably meet with success or are equally intense at all places

21. U.S. Civil Service Commission, Bureau of Personnel Management Evaluation, "A Report on Alleged Potential Influence on Personnel Actions at the Department of Health, Education, and Welfare" (July 1975; processed), pp. 3–4.

at all times. But the blurring of political and civil service lines is a customary and persisting part of the executive setting.[22]

Taken as a whole, the informalities begin to suggest something of the personal quality of government high in the executive branch—the real influence of trust and suspicion, individual loyalties, and personal networks. The same informal understandings can of course also be read in other ways:

—That the traditional spoils system is alive and well in Washington.
—That practical men who must work with the world as it is must also inevitably compromise rather than strictly adhere to abstract principles.
—That any distinction between political and civil service roles is basically irrelevant.

Such quick, unidimensional judgments are not particularly helpful to understanding executive politics. To be sure, ample evidence can be found in Washington to show political spoils, compromised principles, and an intrinsic mixture of political and administrative roles. But before readily accepting any final verdict, it is worth pausing to ask what larger trends lie behind the jagged, blurred, and variable boundaries between career and political executive personnel. There is of course the all-pervasive fact of separated legislative and executive branches sharing powers, but this alone does not explain why tendencies so evident to scholars in the thirties should remain not only unfulfilled but largely reversed.

Trends

It has become commonplace to observe that the fundamental change in American government has been growth—growth in the complex tasks it undertakes and in the size of the government machinery used to per-

22. Naturally, some officials have a clearer sense than others about the political–civil service demarcations. At the urging of one of the few careerists to have worked any length of time in the White House, the Ford administration issued an unprecedented order to presidential staff, admonishing them to avoid any involvement in filling career jobs. (White House Order, October 5, 1975.) A year earlier the White House Personnel Office had begun sending to the departments political referral forms that were specifically limited to noncareer positions, stating that the referrals should not be furnished to appointing authorities "if it subsequently develops that this candidate will be considered for a career position." (GPO form 566.663.)

form them. Yet what has occurred in the political administration of official Washington is not simply a blowup of an earlier small-scale image. Imagine a clerk—employed, say, by the Reclamation Bureau in the Interior Department—traveling through time from the pre–World War I era of starched collars, high-button shoes, and a six-day government workweek to the Washington of today. No doubt he would first notice the growing size of staffs and programs. As he watched government in operation, however, he would perceive somewhat deeper differences.

Organizational Abundance

If he could find his old offices, the time-traveling clerk would discover not only a larger number of people but, more important, people organized in more layers higher in the department and divided into more specialized divisions with each layer. The two trends are of course related. More specialized activities have been accompanied by more attempts at higher-level integration, which in turn has contributed to the creation of intermediary units. Whereas in all likelihood the bureau clerk's chief reported to a department head who had at most one or two ad hoc assistants, today there is a luxuriance of intermediating organizational layers—assistant secretaries and deputies, specialized staff assistants, and what in Washington jargon are termed "shops" for management analysis, policy evaluation, automatic data processing, auditing, budgeting, and many more activities.

Few accurate data are available with which to trace in detail the changes in top executive manpower, but some rough approximations are possible. In 1907 during Theodore Roosevelt's presidency, the bureau clerk would have operated in an executive branch where there were perhaps 165 heads of departments, independent offices, and bureaus.[23] This Census Bureau figure, however, refers to formal titles rather than to actual duties. According to a more accurate survey in 1919, the clerk would have looked up toward a top administrative and supervisory structure of about 600 persons.[24]

23. U.S. Bureau of the Census, *Statistics of Employees, Executive Civil Service of the United States,* Bulletin 94 (GPO, 1907).
24. In addition to the top political appointments as department secretaries and commissioners, this figure included assistant secretaries, bureau and office heads, assistant bureau heads, and head clerks and their principal subordinates. For a detailed description, see U.S. Joint Commission of Reclassification of Salaries, *Report,* H. Rept., 66 Cong. 2 sess. (1920), pp. 196 ff. Otherwise unpublished statistics from the

Certainly many more important officials might have been included in this classification, but still, as he traveled toward the New Deal, this old-time bureaucrat might not consider the numbers particularly large. He might recall, for example, the semiannual meetings held under the Republican presidents of the 1920s, where for the first time in history presidents had addressed the entire "Business Organization of the United States." ("Management" was not yet a fashionable term.) The 2,000-seat Interior Department auditorium sufficed to hold the secretaries, bureau chiefs, budget office heads, and all the other lesser officials of the executive branch who came to hear the appeals for government economy. Figure 2-2, which shows the organization of the clerk's bureau then and now, conveys better than words how top organizational structures have proliferated in the past fifty years.

The New Deal and World War II obviously added a great many new activities and organizations to government. Knowing who was who had no doubt become more difficult, but many bureaucratic old hands were close to the center of things and could help coordinate the government's wartime effort in personnel as well as materials. In the President's Bureau of the Budget (BOB) for example, Director Harold Smith used his agency's information on how other government organizations were being run in order to recommend the recruitment and dismissal of political executives. Another official on the administrative side of the BOB might have had the Bureau of Reclamation clerk (probably now called an administrative specialist) on one of his 3 x 5 cards. In this informal network for higher civil servants, a few central officials tried to keep track of "good, broad-gauged people" who could be used in new agencies or programs. As one of the officials involved explained:

> You were always getting calls about names to suggest for all kinds of responsible positions, but we didn't have good information. . . . so I went around talking to senior types around town, finding out how people were working, who they thought looked promising for new assignments which had to be filled. From this we developed a little file with pretty frank and private opinions and when there was a call you'd go through these cards and bring out some name. . . . It sounds hit and miss, but things were much simpler then, and people tended to know one another. Now there's no central system for this kind of personal evaluation by people who know each other. It really is hit and miss.

Even by 1952 the top three grades of the civil service general schedule

Joint Commission are given in Lewis Mayers, *The Federal Service* (Appleton, 1922), p. 15, and app., table III.

Figure 2-2. *Management Organization of the Department of the Interior,*
1924 and 1976[a]

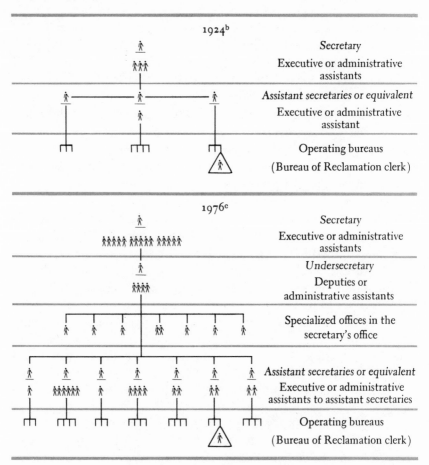

Sources: Information for 1924 is adapted from George Cyrus Thorpe, *Federal Departmental
Organization and Practice* (West, 1925), pp. 276–78; and the *Congressional Directory,* 69
Cong. 1 sess. (GPO, 1925), pp. 268–70. Information for 1976 is from *United States Government Policy and Supporting Positions,* House Committee on Post Office and Civil Service,
94 Cong. 2 sess. (GPO, 1976).
　a. Covers only political executive positions located in Washington, D.C.
　b. Excludes offices concerned with the administration of U.S. territories.
　c. Excludes special or confidential assistants below the level of GS 14 and all private
secretaries.

Table 2-2. *Postwar Growth of U.S. Congressional Staffs*

	Senate		House		
Year	Personal staff	Committee and subcommittee staffs	Personal staff	Committee and subcommittee staffs	Total
1947	590	222	1,449	182	2,443
1957	1,115	371	2,441	348	4,275
1967	1,749	448[a]	4,055	506[a]	6,758
1975	2,600	1,120	6,114	952	10,786

Source: Adapted from Harrison W. Fox, Jr., and Susan Webb Hammond, "The Growth of Congressional Staffs," in Harvey C. Mansfield, Sr., ed., *Congress against the President*, Proceedings of the Academy of Political Science, vol. 32, no. 1 (1975), p. 115.
    a. Figures are for 1965.

numbered only 581 persons, all but 32 of whom worked in Washington. By 1972 there were 4,384 supergrades, of whom 1,162 worked outside Washington.[25] This almost eightfold increase at the top bureaucratic levels occurred while total government employment over these two decades continued relatively stable between 2 million and 3 million people. The time-traveling clerk might reflect that when he started his trip early in this century the political and bureaucratic leadership of the executive branch was scarcely larger than the 550-member Congress.

But Congress had also changed. To be sure, the number of congressmen had not increased significantly as the years passed (only five states had been added in the twentieth century), but congressional staff had grown with its own tempo of bureaucratization. Before World War I there were 72 personal staff employees for 96 senators; by 1975 there were 2,600 for 100 senators. Staff employees for congressional committees had increased their numbers more slowly since first appearing in the last half of the nineteenth century, but following World War II they too made up for lost time, growing from about 260 in 1924 to 400 in 1947 and to 2,070 by 1975. Taking personal and committee employees as a whole, the congressional staff grew from probably between 1,000 and 1,500 during the normalcy of the 1920s to almost 11,000 by the mid-1970s. (See table 2-2.) In addition there were over 20,000 employees in the other components of the legislative branch (Congressional Research Service, General Accounting Office, and so on).[26]

    25. Data provided by the U.S. Civil Service Commission, Manpower Statistics Division.
    26. For a fuller discussion, see Michael J. Malbin, "Congressional Staffs—Growing Fast but in Different Directions," *National Journal*, vol. 8 (July 28, 1976), pp. 958–65.

As this growth has occurred, internal legislative leaders have been less able to organize Congress and congressional committees for consultation and bargaining with politicians in the executive branch. A cabinet secretary and longtime Washington observer described how

> in the 1940s you could talk to five or six congressmen (Lyndon Johnson used to call them the Whales) and you'd know what Congress would do. Now you can't be sure—no matter how many you talk to. There isn't an effective focus for consultation in Congress that a cabinet officer can rely on. The Whales are gone, and it's bucket of minnows. If nothing else, this greatly complicates your relations with the President.

Uncertain about the political counterweight in Congress, political executives find it more difficult to calibrate their own relations with each other and with the bureaucracy.

Abundant Rationales

Not all of this luxuriance in government occurred because no one knew or cared about what was happening. The topside layering and specialization throughout Washington is in part the fulfillment of several generations of conscious effort by well-intentioned reformers and reorganizers. One of their basic aims has been to strengthen "staff" capabilities, and to a large extent they have succeeded. By the first decade of the twentieth century, staff units in government agencies were already present in embryo, usually in the form of a chief clerk for each department.[27] After World War I, the concept of general staff functions was copied from the German military organization, instituted in the U.S. War Department, and gradually elaborated in such departments as Agriculture, Treasury, and Interior. New Deal programs intensified this trend for expanded staff activities, as did new bursts of enthusiasm from the experts reporting in the first Hoover Commission's studies on government organization. Between 1923 and 1973 the birth rate of staff units rose while line units were falling off sharply: in one sample of government organizations the ratio of pure line to staff units fell from 2.25 to 1 in 1923 to 1.5 to 1 in

27. Unfortunately there is no modern analysis of the chief clerk's role in Washington. Before their submergence under layers of political appointees, these early bureaucratic generalists apparently were often figures of considerable administrative power, sometimes sitting in as acting secretary, serving as chief executive officer of the department, distributing incoming correspondence to the few assistant secretaries and others, and supervising all outside communications from the department. See John Philip Hill, *The Federal Executive* (Houghton-Mifflin, 1916), pp. 68, 71.

1973.[28] Over time, even the staff concept itself became differentiated between pure staff (such as planners and personal advisers) and auxiliary staff services (organizational maintenance functions such as supplies, personnel, and so on).

Public administration experts had good theoretical reasons for arguing that the expansions of staff capabilities in the executive branch were not creating a more fragmented and layered system of intermediary units. Unity of command was not being diluted because staff services were only advisory to the responsible top leadership; the power of operating units was not being made incommensurate with their responsibility, because directives did not come from staff units in their own right but only as extensions of the top executive. In practice, however, staff units could normally be expected both to advise and to become heavily involved in operational decisions.[29]

A more subtle difficulty lay in the imported notion of strengthening staff units in government. The obvious justification for reform was the need to integrate the agencies' information, plans, and services with operating realities in particular bureaus. But another equally important if overlooked justification for the original staff concept in Germany and other European nations had been the desire to constrain as well as to aid the top leadership. In a European setting strong staff units could serve as a corrective to the uninformed and often capricious exercise of autocratic power. In the United States they were more likely to constitute yet another force for partitioning an already deeply divided public authority into more self-contained technical and organizational specialties.

More staff was what reformers wanted; staff and more layering of officialdom is also what the government's expanding demand for technical expertise has seemed to require. One retired official remarked that in the old days "the major concerns involved filling jobs rather than conducting programs and contracts. . . . Now you're dealing with questions of birth control, medical care, income maintenance, environmental protection, and questions of safety that go far beyond our original notions of injuries to workers' health."

28. Herbert Kaufman, *Are Government Organizations Immortal?* (Brookings Institution, 1976), p. 39. One of the most influential arguments for staff units was in the *First Report of the Commission on the Organization of the Government*, H. Doc. 55, 81 Cong. 1 sess. (1949), pp. 31–40.

29. Peter Self, *Administrative Theories and Politics* (University of Toronto Press, 1973), pp. 122–45; and Herbert A. Simon, Donald W. Smithburg, and Victor A. Thompson, *Public Administration* (Knopf, 1950), pp. 280–91.

As the federal government has become more active in the domestic policy of a highly industrialized society, it has required not simply more people but more highly trained specialists. In 1970 government employed almost two-fifths (38.3 percent) of what the Census Bureau categorized as "professional, technical, and kindred" workers; excluding teachers the proportion was still as high as 24 percent.[30]

Technical specialization has been accompanied by the growth and division of overhead managerial labor. The 1960s, for example, witnessed a new surge of activity in domestic and scientific policies. One of the clearest expressions of these new activities lay in the expansion, not of government employment in general, but of those in the upper and upper-middle levels of the bureaucracy—officials who could be expected to be intermediaries between top decisionmakers and those close to actual operations. (See figure 2-3.) About half of the remarkable increase in mid-level executives since 1963 has been research scientists, many of whom combine some managerial responsibilities with their scientific specialties.

Another expression of the same phenomenon is the tendency over the years for the average rank of federal government employees as a whole to escalate. This so-called grade creep seems to have occurred to about the same extent in private industry as in government. Both public and private sectors are affected by the upward push of specialization in management (higher ratios of supervisors, administrative assistants, etc., to operational portions of the work force) and formal skill certification (higher status "credentialing"). Case studies in the mid-1960s found, however, that most of the grade escalation in government then could be traced specifically to new or expanded programs requiring more high-grade technical skills and supervisory levels (e.g., growth in specialist engineers vis-à-vis general engineers, insurance claims administrators vis-à-vis claims examiners).[31]

One might conclude that in its increased layering and professional specialization, the federal government has simply been involved in a general social trend toward ever more division of labor and specialization of skills. This conclusion would be correct as far as it went. Experienced

30. U.S. Bureau of the Census, Census of Population, 1970 Detailed Characteristics, Final Report, PC(1)-D1, United States Summary (GPO, 1973), table 225, p. 1-749. On professionalization, see Frederick C. Mosher, Democracy and the Public Service (New York: Oxford University Press, 1968).

31. "Strengthening Control of Grade Escalation," Report of McKinsey and Company, Inc., to the Bureau of the Budget, June 1966 (Office of Management and Budget Archives; processed), vol. 1.

Figure 2-3. *Index of the Growth of Mid-Level Executive Positions and Federal Civilian Employment, 1961–74*

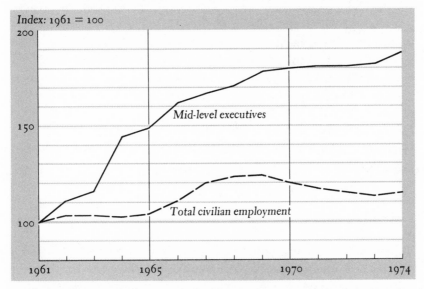

Sources: Mid-level executive positions here include GS 16–18 positions and their Public Law 313 equivalents; data are from U.S. Civil Service Commission, *Executive Manpower in the Federal Service* (GPO, 1974), table 2, p. 9. Civilian employment covers total end-of-year employment in the federal executive branch; data are from *Special Analyses, Budget of the United States Government, Fiscal Year 1976*, table H-4, p. 136.

wielders of bureaucratic power also know that such an explanation seriously neglects a political dynamic that has been at work for many decades. Just as general blanketing-in has been used to expand civil service coverage, so the division and elaboration of technical specialties has provided a major strategy by which particular pieces of the bureaucracy can protect themselves from outside control by nonspecialists in Washington.

Four decades ago an experienced personnel director went to the heart of the matter:

Many persons who have worked closely with the national government for the advancement of personnel administration have secured a measure of success through convincing the legislators or the political administrators that the positions demanded scientific and technical competence. . . .

Repeatedly during the past quarter of a century old agencies have been reformed by what is often called the professionalization of the service. If the only qualification is "a good administrator," then the door is open to the campaign contributor or his friends.[32]

32. Lewis Meriam, *Public Personnel Problems: From the Standpoint of the Operating Officer* (Brookings Institution, 1938), p. 317. Meriam's examples are taken from the 1930s, but they could easily have come from any recent administration.

Bureaucratic leaders have not been oblivious to the value of generalists, men and women who may be knowledgeable in one field but who
are also able to move across overlapping specialties to judge the broader
situation as a whole. Bureaucrats, however, have also recognized that any
explicit acknowledgment of a generalist administrator's value would be
an open invitation to outside intrusions—fair game for anyone, as one
bureau chief put it, "who had ever run anything, from his brother-in-
law's bank to a political campaign." Without doubt all specialized groups
of human beings seek to become self-controlling. The Washington setting, with its uncertain and informal crosscurrents of power, has only
heightened incentives for functional specialists to acquire a dominant
position in political administration.

Results

Increased staff units, professional specialization, bureaucratic strategies for self-protection—all carry important implications for relations
between political executives and bureaucrats. Bureaucratic power is likely
to become more insulated within particular sectors of government activity. Less evident but equally important is what is likely to happen (or
more accurately not happen) outside the specialized units. As both political appointees and civil servants work more and more on smaller and
smaller pieces of government activity, the networks among political and
civil service generalists are apt to become attenuated.

Externally, government presents a less united front to the larger number of groups making claims on it. Internally, different parts of the government machinery are less able to take realistic account of each other's
intentions and actions. People who do not know each other across the
fragmented top layers are less likely to be able to coordinate operations
(who does what), information (who knows what), planning (who fore-
sees what), or any of the other working relations in government. Even
with goodwill on all sides, it can become vastly more difficult to arrive
at mutual understandings and to agree on courses of action for the executive branch as a whole—which is also to say, for purposes with a presidential perspective.

If these results seem obvious, others are less so. What happens as the
search for political leadership winds its way through the executive mélange? And what are the consequences for the basic idea of civil service?

The paradox is that political levels can be bureaucratized at the same time the career bureaucracy becomes politicized. A closer look suggests that each of these developments is under way and is reenforcing the other.

Bureaucratizing Political Leadership

Bureaucrats worry about the prerogatives of their bureaus, congressmen about the strength of Congress, scholars and would-be presidential advisers about the state of the presidency. Almost no one, it seems, has a vested interest in worrying about the general health of the political executive system—certainly not the appointees themselves who come and go with the administrations and seasons of Washington. For its own part, the White House has normally confined its interest to selecting political personnel and subsequently complaining about the tendency of these department appointees to be captured and "go native."

Anyone surveying the trends discussed earlier might sympathize with the belief of various administrations that their political forces in government—far from being too large—have been so few as to be overwhelmed by the number of bureaucratic officials near the top of government. Compared with the thousands of career executives in the bureaucracy, any growth and layering at the political levels seems ridiculously small. Yet the significance is strategic rather than numerical. For people who are supposed to be in politically responsible positions, problems of coordinated control, decisionmaking, and mutual understanding rise more than proportionately with increases in their numbers. In a government bureau one more career supergrade may simply mean another pair of hands to do the work. For purposes of political leadership, another political appointee means one more person with a potential for setting directions and subdividing responsibility for what is happening. Of course, if the political figures constituted a coherent group, growing numbers could indicate a stronger capacity for leadership. But teams of political executives are fragile and short-lived. In these circumstances the bureaucratic growth of political appointments—their increased numbers, the division of labor, and hierarchical layering—invites bureaucratization. Political leadership is likely to be subordinated to, or at least circumscribed by, the self-interests of its particular bureaucratic setting.

The modern White House is the most familiar example of the general trend in political appointments, but it is far from unique compared with the political layers in government departments. What is revealing about political bureaucratization is not simply the growth in absolute numbers but the subdivision and specialization at the intermediate and higher levels. To return to the Bureau of Reclamation, here is how the arrival of big government affected the number of noncareer appointees higher in the department (*excluding* confidential aides, attorneys, lower-level assistants, and private secretaries):

	1933	1973
Secretary	1	1
Undersecretary	...	1
Deputy undersecretary	...	1
Executive assistant	3	6
Special assistant	...	16
Office director	...	9
Associate office director	...	2
Field representative	3	7
Assistant secretary	2	6
Deputy assistant secretary	...	7
Special assistant	...	11

A governmentwide perspective can be gained by contrasting the current and past situations for one particular type of political executive. Assistant secretaries are the men (and occasionally women) who have traditionally constituted the second echelon of political appointees and the group in most direct contact with government bureaucrats. At the end of the nineteenth century and during the first quarter of the twentieth century, between one dozen and two dozen people filled these positions at any one time. Only two departments, State and Treasury, had any superior positions other than the department secretary himself. With very few exceptions, it was "painfully apparent" to scholars that the outstanding feature of the assistant secretaries was the "political considerations" behind their selection. These were "secondary posts in the scheme of national patronage" filled by men whose "careers were a miscellany of party assignments and political posts."[33] Assistant secretaries had little technical expertise and were dropped into the departments from the outside to cover a broad and confusing range of functions. Whatever their personal qualities, these political executives were not bureaucratic in any sense of that term.[34] In other words they demonstrated a minimal division of

33. The political considerations are summarized in Macmahon and Millett, *Federal Administrators*, pp. 59–60, 94, 290–92, 295, 302.

34. Indicators of bureaucratization are discussed in Parker Frisbie, "Measuring the Degree of Bureaucratization at the Societal Level," *Social Forces*, vol. 53 (June 1975), pp. 563–73.

labor, little specialized training, and only the most meager ordering into layers of superordination and subordination.

In many respects the current situation is quite different. The one hundred or more assistant secretaries (or their equivalents) are in every case arrayed below a department undersecretary and often one or more deputy undersecretaries; most assistant secretaries also have their own deputies and special assistants. Less than half of these political executives in recent administrations have had any significant record of party political activity, and very few have had anything like the miscellany of party assignments characterizing their predecessors.

While experience across several departments is still at a premium among assistant secretaries, now the most common route into these jobs during the course of an administration is from lower political appointments, suggesting a superior-subordinate political ladder almost unknown in earlier decades. Typically, the "politicians" filling these posts are "program rather than President or party-oriented."[35] Most are assistant secretaries "for" something and thus are easily identified with a specific, fairly limited set of government activities. The generalist who is not an assistant secretary for rural development, housing management, fish and wildlife, or some other program area is likely to claim a professional management specialty far removed from any party or political identification and agenda. "I'd be offended to see these management techniques used for overtly political purposes," a politically appointed management expert said. "I mean, my personal feeling is that all politicians should have the same objectives and differ on the amount of resources and means to achieve them."

The changing nature of the political executive jobs to be filled has generally favored those with specialized technical abilities rather than those with broad political experience. In the process the traditional resources for party patronage in lower-level government jobs have been replaced with high-level executive positions (or part-time work on advisory commissions, committees of experts, and so on). In 1933, for example, at least one of every two presidential appointments could be classed as involving low-level, routine positions; by 1976 probably less than one in five were at a comparable level.[36] More than ever before, the presidential ap-

35. See Henry, "The Presidency," p. 534, and the various studies cited therein.
36. The indicator used here is the proportion of presidential appointments at or below the level of U.S. attorneys and marshals. In both 1933 and 1976 these positions were at a point on the salary scale somewhat less than half the highest executive

pointment of people who are ignorant about complex policies for which
they are responsible (e.g., energy, space, environment, economic management, and so on) can mean that important decisions are mishandled
or devolve to bureaucrats below. In the past forty years the social base for
recruitment may have broadened, but the skills of political executives have
become more narrowly specialized. Moreover, electoral swings in party
control of the White House have had little effect on this trend.[37] The
result appears to be a growing distance between the electoral coalition with
which a president wins office and the executive coalition with which he
must try to govern in the bureaucracy.

The important pressure generated by the bureaucratization of political
leadership is not within the agencies, where both officialdom and the
relevant interest groups can find it useful to have a new assistant secretary
to run political interference. The major counterpressures are created in
the White House. Presidents have fewer old-style patronage jobs to dispense and more highly qualified political executives to recruit. Yet the
very competence and specialized clienteles of political appointees can
produce layers of officials who are indistinguishable from the organization
men of the bureaucracy. The more appointees talk about "their" programs and agencies, the more a president may worry about controlling government actions that will go down in history under his name. It is not
surprising, then, that as political levels have become bureaucratized, incentives have grown for the White House to politicize the bureaucracy.

Politicizing the Bureaucracy

How is it possible to speak of politicizing the bureaucracy when every
historical study has demonstrated the relentless extension of the civil
service system ever since the day President James Garfield was assassi-
nated by Charles Guiteau?[38] By the middle of the 1960s, 85 percent of
all federal employees were under the classified civil service, a proportion

salaries. See *Positions Not Under the Civil Service*, S. Doc. 173, 72 Cong. 2 sess.
(GPO, 1933), tables I and II, pp. 1 and 19; and *United States Government Policy
and Supporting Positions*, Committee Print, Senate Committee on Post Office and
Civil Service, 93 Cong. 1 sess. (GPO, 1973).

37. Kenneth Prewitt and William McAllister, "Changes in the American Executive
Elite, 1930–1970," in Heinz Eulau and Moshe Czudnowski, eds., *Elite Recruitment
in Democratic Polities* (Wiley, 1976).

38. Invariably termed "a disappointed office seeker," Guiteau was seen to symbolize
the need for civil service reform.

that some experts considered to be about the practical limit of further extension of the civil service system. Nonetheless, there are several reasons for speaking of politicizing the bureaucracy.

One (suggested earlier) is a concern for informal practices as well as for formal designations. The more formal requirements there are to block unjustified political intrusions, the more political pressures are likely to take indirect, informal channels.

Another is that spoils politics and civil service protections have traditionally concentrated on the total quantity rather than the quality of job favors: how many jobs for how many party workers? Relatively less attention has been devoted to the much smaller number of jobs at the higher career levels where political and bureaucratic leaders must actually deal with each other. Satisfaction with combating gross spoils in government jobs can easily obscure the importance of strategic politicizing at these higher levels.

Finally, reformers seeking to expand civil service coverage have generally focused on incursions by political parties into government hiring. Parties, however, are only one possible politicizing agency. The distinction noted in chapter 1 between political and civil service roles depended on the kind of responsibilities placed on public officials, not on the presence or absence of party activity. The more officials' jobs become dependent in practice on commitment to particular people or programs, the more the system takes on the attributes of a political mode of administration. The more responsiveness depends on institutional standards rather than on personal preferences, the more one may speak of a civil service role. Government officialdom may become politicized not only by the spoils patronage of political parties, but by any agent seeking to treat public offices as private property—whether through the crony network of bureaucrats themselves, or the charisma of a brave new leader, or ideological loyalty to specific policies and management doctrines. Personal or programmatic politicizing are no less dangerous to the integrity of government institutions than party politicizing. Ultimately, they all imply a system of government machinery that must be dismantled and restaffed every time a new political representative is installed to exert leadership and take responsibility for setting directions.

The basis for talking about politicizing the bureaucracy lies, therefore, in a threefold concern: (1) for informal practices rather than formal descriptions, (2) for those in the higher posts rather than the gross sum of job favors, and (3) for "political" influences in the broad sense rather than in only the party-related sense. What then can be said about politicizing the bureaucracy in terms of this bundle of factors?

Making such assessments is particularly difficult in Washington. Unlike most other industrialized nations, the United States has developed the highest levels of its career service in the form of a few selected peaks in scattered parts of the federal establishment rather than as a coherent top layer throughout the national government. These strategic "promontories" for civil service careers have provided such focus as exists for governmentwide institutional continuity above and across the separate power centers of particular bureaus and programs. Moreover, other bureaucrats in charge of program bureaus have traditionally operated in a highly charged political atmosphere at the interstices of congressional, presidential, and interest-group pressures. The renowned influence of U.S. bureau chiefs is one indicator—not necessarily that the American bureaucrats are far more powerful than their foreign counterparts—but that they must play a more visible and active political role to survive in a complex political setting. Hence a politicized bureaucracy can seem more a constant fact of life than a trend in the United States.

Nevertheless, important changes do appear to have taken place in political influences within the bureaucracy. Understandably, these involve some of the informal practices cited earlier. Those engaging in such practices, however, have left few records, and their verbal recollections are likely to be particularly self-serving. The most reasonable approach in these circumstances is to compare the experiences of many participants whose views can be expected to be self-serving in conflicting directions. From both political and career officeholders, Republicans and Democrats, a certain consensus does seem to emerge.

A number of recently retired officials can recall the system operated by Franklin Roosevelt's chief patronage dispenser in which application forms for federal jobs came in three colors: one color meant "this fellow has such great political connections that he has to be found a job"; another, that the applicant had to get a letter from a congressman; and the third, that no special preference would be given. For the most part, this system applied to the host of new agencies created in the 1930s that provided abundant opportunities for using people who were strong supporters of the New Deal programs and approach, as well as good Democrats. And many stayed. A man who had been a top administrator in two departments said:

In the 1950s when I became personnel director, I was amazed to see in the records whole sets of political referral files on our employees. . . . They showed that extending all the way back into the 1930s and 1940s there were very close ties between personnel actions and the Democratic National Committee. . . . Mostly these were for exempted positions when they first occurred, but then over time the people in the exempted positions got blanketed into the civil service.

A crucial aspect of these activities was that the 1930s were years when federal employment was growing rapidly so that adding rather than replacing officials was the main focus of political attention. These times of mass unemployment also meant that to a large extent the federal government could pick and choose among a variety of qualified persons needing work. Moreover, both the Roosevelt and Truman administrations continued a tradition of "negative clearance"; that is, nursing political referrals and clearing official appointments in order to placate those political leaders in Congress and in state, local, or other organizations who might otherwise take exception. One higher official who spent thirty years working near the top executive levels explained what seems to have been the usual process:

> The selectors would ask themselves if there was anybody who would object to this person's being appointed. . . . In my own case, my father was a prominent Republican and this could have stood against me. But the clearance that took place essentially raised the issue of whether or not there would be a congressman or someone who would object to appointing this son of a Republican. . . . The answer came back, no, there were no strong objections, and so my government career began in 1936.

Without too much exaggeration it seems reasonable to say that throughout all the New Deal and Fair Deal years, political patronage was used more as a means of managing potential political conflict than of building a network of presidential loyalists throughout the executive branch. In 1949, for example, the important step of creating a new layer of supergrade positions provided few new opportunities for political intrusions.[39] According to a senior political adviser to President Truman:

> There wasn't much room to play politics with these jobs. If there had been room, we might have tried it, but the fact is we were creating a system in the midst of people already in their jobs. . . . Few jobs fell vacant, and mostly we were promoting from within. . . . Now there are a lot more jobs at this level, a lot more room to play politics with them.

The Eisenhower administration combined the precedents of former

39. In fact, of the 400 supergrade positions, only 12 were filled by persons from outside government. See Ismar Baruch, "The Super-Grade Story, 1949–1952" (Ismar Baruch Collection, U.S. Civil Service Commission Library, Washington, D.C., n.d.), vol. 2, p. 153.

years with a renewed and intense desire on the part of Republican party leaders for government jobs to dispense to the faithful. As might be expected, available job favors fell far short of the needs for traditional party patronage. Largely as a response to these unsatisfied pressures, certain White House aides constructed and began operating an elaborate system for political manipulation of the civil service. This so-called Willis Plan would have organized a complex pseudoscientific reporting system between government departments with civil service or political job openings, on the one hand, and the Republican National Committee and Congress on the other.[40] What matters more than the details of the plan is that, however ill-advised, it aimed only at a refinement of the customary desire for party spoils rather than at strategic presidential control over the executive establishment. Equally important, these politicizing efforts were not the product of a monolithic White House staff system, and other factions of presidential aides could and did strongly counter the plan. In the end, opposition from within and publicity from without (leaks to the press occurred when letters describing the plan were inadvertently sent to Democratic congressmen) combined to scuttle what in the later Watergate period would be termed "overzealousness."

Subtle but important changes occurred in the 1960s. The Kennedy administration certainly recognized the importance of the traditional party deferences and some degree of political clearance in the bureaucracy, but there was also a desire for more active and positive control by the President. "There was the idea of being tough," said an official over whose desk passed most of the personnel files of career executives, "... of getting clearances and control of the civil service, implementing it through [White House aides]." Observing many of the chief actors at close range, a Civil Service commissioner, now retired, saw that

> there was more activity and White House effort to find recruits compatible with Kennedy views—young people in the eastern universities, campaign volunteers. Kennedy was not so much interested in existing programs and personnel as in looking for people to fill key spots in new agencies and programs—say, in the upper quarter of GS grades.

Officials in ongoing programs might catch some of the enthusiasm, but the main emphasis was on people with new blood, with a common New Frontier philosophy, to be brought into new jobs. On a considerably

40. Details of the plan (named after Charles Willis, the White House aide who is said to have originated it) are described in *Administration of the Civil Service*, Report to the Senate Committee on Post Office and Civil Service, Committee Print 2, 85 Cong. 1 sess. (GPO, 1957).

smaller scale, the Kennedy administration enjoyed advantages similar to some of those in the Roosevelt years, that is, using the personal charisma of the President and opportunities for filling new jobs (notably in the Peace Corps, Alliance for Progress, and Agency for International Development) to bring new sources of loyalty and energy into the government service. Here and there, as the following comment shows, the price of this new vigor was the sacrifice of the basic civil service concept:

> They got special reduction-in-force legislation through the Congress and some 800 employees were put out on the street. . . . The first week I was in the personnel director's job I was called to the White House and told [by a presidential aide] of the White House concern about the Foreign Aid program and the fact that they had all these "must" cases, and that my job was to find jobs for persons that the administration wanted in there. My response to him, looking out over the Rose Garden, was, "as long as they're competent people I will do what I can to place them. When they're not, you and I are going to have trouble."
>
> We had trouble. Within a month, an agent was placed in the personnel office of AID with the assignment to handle such special cases.

The Johnson administration had little chance of drawing on presidential charisma or a New Frontier esprit de corps as spurs to bureaucratic responsiveness. What the Johnson White House did have was the Rooseveltian ingredient missing during most of the Kennedy period: programs. The White House could and did try to build a loyalty based on presidential program commitments—the Johnson education program, the Johnson antipoverty program, the Johnson housing program, and a host of others. Indicative of this shifting emphasis was one of the more ambiguous procedures informally adopted to "welcome" new supergrade officials. To its White House sponsors, a small get-together in the White House with forty or so new career supergrades at a time represented an extension of the Johnson personality—a "massaging operation," a way of "making them feel part of the family" and of recognizing that "these were the people that made the machine go . . . people working for you and making the administration and its programs a success." To the skeptics, including a number of bureaucrats who had received the Johnson treatment, White House welcomes were more likely to convey the message that "you got where you are because of us, and we're keeping an eye on you." Some rightfully wondered whether the LBJ embrace occurred only after the fact or earlier as part of the civil service selection process.[41]

41. See *Civil Service Commission Merit Staffing Review Team*, Hearings before the House Committee on Post Office and Civil Service, 94 Cong. 2 sess. (GPO, 1976), pp. 237–317.

Whatever the intentions of the Kennedy and Johnson administrations, there were enough indicators to fuel the intense suspicions about the bureaucracy that were already present in the new Nixon administration. By now the specific abuses of the Nixon years have become well documented in the public record—political referral units in the departments, attempts to bend procedures in order to "get" enemies, political clearances and placements in key civil service posts, and many others.[42] Usually these efforts to politicize the bureaucracy have been interpreted as rather isolated cases of misconduct stemming from the personal failings of top officials—abuses reminiscent of the worst of spoils patronage in the public service. At this point it is worth asking: were the Nixon efforts an aberration or a culmination, a deviation from or codification of existing behavior?

Certainly there was a legitimate consensus among people working in government between 1969 and 1974 that political intrusions into the civil service had become more systematic and widespread than ever before. Elaborate organization and reporting procedures on political placements were similar to the Willis Plan's flow chart. But now there was an unprecedented degree of White House centralization, a search for monolithic power that would tolerate none of the internal opposition greeting the Willis Plan in Eisenhower's White House. Likewise, experienced bureaucrats were thoroughly familiar with ways of increasing their maneuverability on personnel by working around and through civil service rules. Yet a manual in the Nixon White House for training political executives in the manipulation of the merit system was also something different, even though each practice cited had a precedent in former administrations.[43] Never had these individual practices been deliberately gathered together into a White House–sanctioned code of conduct for political executives. There was a difference (Democrats could later protest) between organized and unorganized crime.

Yet the plans of the Nixon White House were also a culmination of sorts. Organized crime—if that is the analogy—rarely occurs spontaneously but grows out of a climate of acceptance. Over the years the informalities of the system had become so accepted by Washington participants that few were sensitive when changes occurred and more

42. All the details, with voluminous documentation, are set out in *Final Report on Violations and Abuses.*

43. The manual is reprinted in *Presidential Campaign Activities of 1972*, vol. 19: *Watergate and Related Activities: Use of Incumbency–Responsiveness Program*, Executive Session Hearings before the Senate Select Committee on Presidential Campaign Activities, 93 Cong. 2 sess. (GPO, 1974), pp. 8903–9041.

systematic efforts at political clearances, seeding, and referrals began. Taken as a whole the Nixon efforts did carry forward the three basic characteristics of the recent trend toward politicizing the bureaucracy:

1. Far from being a return to the spoils of party patronage, the Nixon efforts bypassed the claims of the Republican party regulars as much in government political appointments as in the 1972 Campaign Committee to Reelect the President.

2. Unlike the old-style negative clearance, politicizing centered on positive attempts to create a system of team-playing loyalists in the bureaucracy. Such efforts could in fact be expected to create controversy rather than to serve the traditional function of defusing political conflict.

3. Attention had shifted from dispensing job favors as such, except where a few key placements could be used to build support from a minority voting bloc. Instead, emphasis was put on high-level career positions important to operational control in the executive branch. The attempts of the Nixon White House to politicize the bureaucracy followed the basic trend already under way in the 1960s—away from old-style job patronage and toward a yearning after strategic means of presidential control outside the bounds of traditional party organizations.

In the case of the Nixon administration, neither presidential charisma nor a multitude of new jobs and program commitments were available to help. If anything, the Nixon domestic program (emphasizing cutbacks in categorical grants, budgets, and federal domestic involvement) could be seen to threaten many existing positions and programs in the bureaucracy—not to add new ones. Faced with these constraints and an opposition Congress, the reaction of the Nixon men after 1970 was to turn to a strategy that was less than ever based on party, more depersonalized compared with the Kennedy strategy, and essentially indifferent to Johnson-type program commitments: it was a strategy of management control.

Old-time government officials might have thought that they knew that management meant businesslike administration, but they were in for an awakening. The end in view for the Nixon White House was not so much administrative economy and efficiency as it was comprehensive managerial control of the executive branch under the President.[44] However apolitical the management concept might seem in theory, operating

44. Richard P. Nathan, "The Administrative Presidency," *The Public Interest*, no. 44 (Summer 1976), pp. 40–54.

in the government context of Washington it could be nothing but political. What was being created was a control mechanism based on loyalty to one particular president—a machine that would have had to be taken apart and reconstituted with every subsequent political transition in the White House.

Watergate upset many things, including the Nixon experiment in management control. But it did not cancel or necessarily imply an end to the broader politicizing trend. Relations between political and career executives have become increasingly blurred as political levels have become bureaucratized and presidents have tried to gain control—especially in the higher career ranks and without the political orientation provided by old-style party ties. Yet this situation damages the basic idea of a civil service far more than it threatens bureaucratic self-interests. Caught up in a politicizing trend, career officials have every incentive to neglect civil service norms of objective responsiveness and instead to survive by relying on their own buddy systems or by showing they can be as unquestioningly loyal as any personal aide who might be brought in (with the added asset of knowing how to work the system). In this sense, bureaucratized power can become more entrenched while the broader concept of a civil service declines.

What then has happened to the promontories for civil service careers above the particular bureau and program levels? How have the preceding trends affected the traditional idea of using a few strategic top spots to institutionalize the values of governmentwide civil service? Two good examples are the assistant secretaries for administration and the Office of Management and Budget.

ASSISTANT SECRETARIES FOR ADMINISTRATION

The post of assistant secretary for administration (ASA) within the departments emerged as a result of gradual and little-noticed changes in American government between 1936 and 1953. To the public administration reformers in these years, the reasoning was straightforward: government had become large and complex; if the huge departments were to function properly, professional management as well as political leadership was required. Both the first and the second Hoover Commission on executive branch reorganization recommended the creation of senior departmental posts filled from within the career service and responsible for ongoing administrative duties (budget, personnel, procurement, etc.).[45]

45. See especially *First Report of the Commission on Organization of the Executive Branch of the Government*, H. Doc. 55, 81 Cong. 1 sess. (GPO, 1949), pp. 37–38.

The reformers recognized the need for managerial discretion and suggested that the civil servants in these top posts be appointed, and if need be replaced, by the political department heads. But the intention was also clear: though individuals might be changed, these top administrative posts were to be filled, and continuity in government management assured, by choosing ASAs from among the career civil service rather than by temporarily appointing outsiders. Such top career posts would also provide worthwhile targets for the ambitions of young civil servants on their way up.

In response to the Hoover Commission proposals, reorganization plans were approved by Congress in 1950 for the departments of Commerce, Justice, Labor, and Treasury. The political heads of the departments—with the approval of the President—were to appoint administrative assistant secretaries "under the classified service." In subsequent years comparable posts were added in Agriculture (1953), Health, Education, and Welfare (1960), Housing and Urban Development (1965), and Transportation (1966). Civil service values of continuity and experience lay behind both the unwritten expectation that ASAs would come from the career ranks and the legal requirement that appointees had to have or be given civil service status at the time of taking up their office. With the exception of the Commerce Department, a civil service background remained the general rule for ASAs throughout the Eisenhower years.

Erosion of the career concept for these jobs accelerated markedly after 1969, but there were initial steps in the same direction during the Kennedy and Johnson presidencies. Wary of playing an active role in management, some ASAs concentrated on routine operations and were left outside the mainstream of department decisionmaking. Others who saw the relation between administration and policy became politically identified with particular political figures and found themselves distrusted by the next set of department appointees. Gradually the tendency grew to give outsiders career status as a formality in filling the ASA positions. The Civil Service Commission might warn that a particular appointee could not in good conscience be given career status and that public outrage would result from making an overt political appointment to what was ostensibly a career post. But after the first year of the Nixon administration there was very little public comment, much less outrage, about such incidents. The Civil Service Commission did resist White House efforts to transform ASAs into normal political appointments,[46] but sub-

46. See testimony by White House Personnel Officer Robert Davidson, in *Violations and Abuses of Merit Principles in Federal Employment*, Hearings before the

sequent developments were an object lesson in how the same results could be achieved by informal means.

In the nineteen years from 1950 to 1969, twenty-three men held jobs as ASAs; during that time, three new departments were added to the federal government. In the five years from 1969 to 1974 no new departments were created, but about twenty men served in these same posts. By the beginning of 1974 three-fourths of the incumbents had been on the job for less than a year. Table 2-3 shows how the political-bureaucratic profile of ASAs changed. The new-style "political" appointees generally came from the private sector and possessed technocratic skills but little prior experience in either government or politics. In 1976 almost all the career ASAs had been replaced by men with little or no government experience, and the experiment in top-level administrative continuity was, for all practical purposes, a dead letter.

OFFICE OF MANAGEMENT AND BUDGET

Traditionally, the old-time Bureau of the Budget (BOB) was a second promontory for the concept of a top-level career civil service—this time at the presidential rather than the departmental level. Throughout most of its fifty-year history, the bureau aimed to be a politically uncommitted institution serving each particular president and also supporting the presidency as a continuous office. Within its own analytic perspective (that is, as a budget pruner), the bureau as an institution could be expected to offer its best independent judgment to any president on the pros and cons of issues and to reflect in turn its understanding of any president's wishes when dealing with the agencies. The bureau director and two or three aides with no direct supervisory responsibilities were normally the only political appointees in an organization otherwise composed entirely of career civil servants.

Changing the bureau's name in 1970 to the Office of Management and Budget symbolized a number of important changes in that original and historically serviceable tradition of neutral competence.[47] One of these changes was the introduction of a new layer of political control in the agency—the program associate directors (PADs). Unlike the former political assistants who served largely as staff aides to the director on ad hoc

---

Subcommittee on Manpower and Civil Service of the House Committee on Post Office and Civil Service, 94 Cong. 1 sess. (GPO, 1975), pt. 2, pp. 195–214.

47. See Hugh Heclo, "OMB and the Presidency," *The Public Interest*, no. 38 (Winter 1975), pp. 80–98.

Table 2-3. *Previous Government Experience of Incumbent Assistant Secretaries for Administration, Selected Years, 1954–74*

Number of years of previous experience	Number of assistant secretaries for administration					
	1954	1958	1962	1966	1970	1974
In the executive branch						
0–1	0	0	0	0	4	6
1–2	0	1	2	2	1	1
2–5	1	0	0	1	0	1
Over 5	6	6	5	5	4	1
Total[a]	7	7	7	8	9	9
In the departments[b]						
0–1	2	1	0	3	6	8
1–2	0	1	2	1	0	1
2–5	0	0	0	1	0	0
Over 5	5	5	3	3	3	0
Total[a]	7	7	5	8	9	9

Source: Compiled by the author from department records and press releases.
a. Excludes Post Office, State, and Defense departments.
b. At time of appointment as ASA.

assignments, the PADs are political appointees who head the permanent examining divisions and are responsible for line operations. This change is significant because the examining divisions in the BOB and in the OMB have always been a key—perhaps the most important—locus of enduring power at the government center. Since they control budget-making, a process that is of vital interest to almost all other agencies, they possess sanctions and access to information that few other government offices can match. Formerly, career division chiefs headed these examining groups in the bureau; now a layer of political line officers is in charge. Significantly, though, these "political" appointees as a group have been distinguishable by nothing so much as their common lack of experience in party politics, their unfamiliarity with agency programs, and their general protectiveness of their own organizational jurisdictions. All have been managerial or subject matter experts well-fitted to the trend of more bureaucratized forms of political leadership.

There have been other changes. Directors of the agency have increasingly performed as personal advisers to the President. The OMB has become identified more as a member of the President's own political family and less as an institutional supplier of independent analytic services regardless of who is president. While the BOB carefully shunned public visibility and policy advocacy, since 1971 the OMB has become more prominent in bargaining with Congress and in lobbying with the other executive agencies in order to sell the administration's policy. However well intentioned many of these efforts have been, the agency and its staff have become politically identified as they have become visibly connected with given political bargains and acts of public advocacy. One OMB official contrasted the current situation with that of the BOB, which he had joined in the late 1950s:

> Frankly, it tends to make this agency an extension of the party in power. . . . I guess we've always been that, but we're also supposed to be more than that. It's hard to achieve in practice, but there's something of value in the idea of serving the presidency, as well as each particular president.

As these changes have occurred, it is understandable if others in government—including Congress and the White House—have failed to make the distinction between the OMB's governmental authority as an institution of the presidency and its partisan political power as the President's personal staff. The Nixon administration showed how once the OMB was redefined from a career institution into the President's loyal advocate and "lead agency," there were likely to be people in the White House who expected it to follow with a minimum of questioning.

The correlate of these tendencies has been a decline in the experience and continuity that had been among the most important assets of the Budget Bureau. A persuasive case could be made that the old BOB was in serious need of more political positions to reduce its reliance on civil servants for important policy decisions. At the same time, these changes to heighten the political profile of the OMB could easily become counterproductive without equal attention to the possible costs of undermining the civil service role performed by BOB/OMB as a continuing institution of the presidency. These costs have grown considerably in recent years.

Compared with a personnel turnover rate in the teens or lower during much of the 1960s, over one-quarter of the professional, full-time staff (i.e., GS 9s and above) separated from the OMB for one reason or another during fiscal year 1973. Those who were left were relatively inexperienced in their jobs, in their own agency, and in government at large. Table 2-4 highlights some of the declines in experience that have occurred in the past twenty years. Of the heads of the major offices and examining divisions in 1960, nearly three-quarters had six or more years' experience in BOB/OMB and nearly half had been in their current posts for six or more years. Of the comparable group in 1974, only a quarter had six or more years' experience at BOB/OMB, only 13 percent had been in their

Table 2-4. *Government Experience of Bureau of the Budget/Office of Management and Budget Executive Personnel, 1953, 1960, and 1974*

	Percentage of BOB/OMB executive personnel with government experience								
Number of years	In current post			In previous BOB/ OMB post			In another federal agency		
	1953	1960	1974	1953	1960	1974	1953	1960	1974
Heads of major offices and divisions[a]									
0–1	22	9	63	22	18	63	22	18	50
2–5	44	45	25	11	9	13	11	36	38
6 or more	33	45	13	66	73	25	67	45	13
Total	100	100	100	100	100	100	100	100	100
Principal staff under office and division heads[b]									
0–1	16	15	64	0	6	21	36	36	49
2–5	60	49	28	48	6	21	28	42	32
6 or more	24	36	8	52	88	59	36	21	19
Total	100	100	100	100	100	100	100	100	100

Source: Compiled from unpublished BOB/OMB records. Figures are rounded.
a. Includes heads of examining divisions and offices of budget review, legislative reference, and management.
b. Includes all deputy heads, assistant division chiefs, and branch chiefs, but not budget examiners.

current posts for such a period, and almost two-thirds had one year's experience or less. Essentially the same tendencies characterize the main subordinate officeholders in the agency. While such figures may tell nothing about important questions of behavior within the organization, they are nonetheless important—especially when it is recalled that practical government experience and continuity are among the chief assets that any civil service is supposed to contribute to policymaking.

Summary

With rare exceptions the changes described in this chapter have been subtle shifts in premises and climates of activity—differences in emphasis rather than dramatic realignments in government machinery. Few trends in Washington's kaleidoscopic system are apt to be clear or fully accomplished. Nor has any participant lived long enough, observed closely enough, or remembered disinterestedly enough to identify for sure what has changed and the directions of movement. But there are sufficient indications to suggest a few plausible conclusions about the setting for executive politics.

Founded well before any concern with modern bureaucracy had developed, the American constitutional structure left the question of the national bureaucracy open, which is to say, vulnerable to fits of improvisation and neglect. To the jagged and variable contours of the formal structure, informal arrangements have added their own considerable ambiguity, blurring demarcations and mutual obligations between political executives and civil servants. Seemingly small things, a political referral here, a clearance or special exemption there, have reenforced an overall tone of permissiveness. Each new group of Washington actors has been tempted to ask itself: if sharp practice can make personnel procedures work for our predecessors, why not for us?

If anything, the long-established ambiguities have increased in recent years. Political appointments to positions of executive leadership (once the domain of party men) have taken on more of the enlarged, specialized, and layered characteristics of bureaucracy. Old-fashioned patronage influences in the civil service have been augmented by increased attention not only to controlling the bureaucracy but to identifying the higher civil service with the particular policies and purposes of the White House. The few promontories of a higher career service have become less distinct and more dependent on political rather than institutional loyalties.

The dynamics at work seem, in fact, to be producing self-reenforcing and unwholesome cycles. Political appointees trying to "get in deep" and control increasingly complex government agencies are likely to take more interest in directing the day-to-day work of bureaucrats. But such appointees themselves are apt to be molded in conformity with the intricate administrative organizations of which they are a more integral part. More layers of technocratic political appointees may well reduce rather than increase bureaucratic responsiveness to broader political leadership by the President and department heads: this in turn increases incentives for the White House to politicize the civil service by trying to build an executive team of loyalists throughout the political and higher career levels. Protectors of the civil service can react by well-tried techniques—more emphasis on functional specialties in the bureaucracy, closer ties with clienteles, more extensive civil service coverage, rules and regulations—but this will probably only remove self-interested bureaucracies further from the reach of political leadership.

Hence the central problem comes down to this: whether through overzealousness, or ignorance about the civil service rules, or for whatever reason, attempts to debureaucratize political appointees and create a responsive team of political loyalists are likely to spill over to threaten the higher civil service. Trying to depoliticize civil servants often creates more personnel restrictions and incentives for circumvention, more massed expertise, and more insulated centers of bureaucratic power with which erstwhile political leaders in the executive branch are ill-prepared to cope. Debureaucratizing threatens the civil service. Depoliticizing menaces political leadership. What helps on one side of the equation may well exacerbate undesirable consequences on the other.

In this complex and highly interdependent setting, anyone's solutions can easily become part of the problem. Reorganizations or other changes need to be looked at from the viewpoint of political executives, of civil servants, and of the working relationship between them. Trying to provide this threefold perspective on their world of practice is my task in the succeeding chapters.

CHAPTER THREE

Political Executives: A Government of Strangers

If, on the one hand, public bodies [are] partial to their members, on the other they [are] as apt to be misled by taking characters on report, or the authority of patrons and dependents. All who had been concerned in the appointment of strangers on those recommendations must be sensible of this truth.
—James Madison, *Constitutional Debates*, June 23, 1787

To SPEAK of political appointees in Washington is obviously to embrace a wide variety of people and situations. Political appointments cover everything from the temporary file clerk recouping a campaign obligation to the cabinet secretary heading a department organization larger than many state governments or the national administrations of some foreign countries. Table 3-1 shows the number and types of what are considered to be the most clearly political appointments in the executive branch.

My focus in this chapter is on the political executives at or near the top of government agencies. Volumes could be devoted to describing the maze of special circumstances in which these roughly 700 men and women find themselves. Here, however, attention will be given to some important points of common reference—the political executives' recruitment problems, inexperience, transience, disunity, and—not least—their strategically vulnerable position. Despite the large variety of government agencies and types of appointment, the most interesting thing is how much U.S. political executives actually have in common.

The Political Executive System

From the outset political executives share one broad feature: all hold an ambivalent leadership position in what might loosely be termed the American "system" of public executives. To appreciate the peculiarity of their political situation, one must return to the basic rationale for having

Table 3-1. *Full-time Political Appointments in the Executive Branch, June 1976*

Schedule	Political officials				
	Presidential appointments with Senate confirmation	Presidential appointments without Senate confirmation	Schedule C appointments	Noncareer executive assignments	Miscellaneous[a]
Executive schedule					
I	12	...	...	...	...
II	61	10	...	...	...
III	109	4	1	...	1
IV	311	12	27	...	3
V	113	3	66	...	12
General schedule supergrades					
18	30	13	6	178	20
17	36	1	6	184	19
16	49	4	14	171	38
(16–18)[b]	...	18	...	...	24
General schedule lower grades					
15	10	2	282	...	15
14	36	...	98	...	16
13	54	...	63	...	20
12	1	...	75	...	14
11 and below	1	...	500	...	126
Total[c]	823	67	1,138	533	308

Source: Compiled from official estimates and sources.

a. Includes certificated White House staff, some Veterans Administration personnel, and others.

b. The grade level is administratively determined within this range and in a few cases can include executive schedule V.

c. Excludes a number of positions that are exempted from civil service examinations (although insiders argue about whether they are or are not "political" jobs). Thus the table does not include schedules A and B mentioned in chapter 2 or 162 noncareer positions that fall under the Foreign Assistance Act.

a number of nonelected political appointees in the executive branch in the first place. According to the Founding Fathers' design, power for the legislative functions of government was spread among the various representatives from states and congressional districts; for the executive function, power was deliberately unified in one elected chief executive. A single president to nominate and supervise the principal officers of the executive branch would promote the unity and vigor of executive operations, while requiring the Senate's consent to make appointments final would safeguard against any presidential abuse of the appointment power and would stabilize administration.[1] Theorists of party government later elaborated on what some of the Founders only hinted at—that competition in the electoral marketplace would result in choices between alternative political teams and policies.[2]

The idea of a single chief executive entering office to promote his measures through a band of loyal political supporters in the executive branch is an easily understood model. It fits well with the media's desire to focus on the central presidential personality, and the notion of undertaking public service at the call of the President attracts many new political appointees to Washington. Astute scholars have pointed out that in reality the President's formal power as the single chief executive is often illusory, that even within his own executive branch he must persuade others and calculate his power stakes rather than cudgel his minions. This revisionist view, however, has not altered the customary concentration on the President and, like the standard constitutional or party government models, it relegates the bulk of political executives to a secondary, derivative role in the executive branch.

As noted earlier, the problem with relying on such president-centered models of executive politics is that they all depend on a tenuous political chain of events. The links of this chain are unlikely to hold from a pre-election formulation of intentions, through an election contest giving a clear mandate to a particular president and his measures, to the installation of his team of executives in positions of control over government actions, to faithful administrative implementation of the promised policies. Nevertheless, there is an underlying psychological validity to the president-centered models. In good times and bad the President *is* the focus of national political attention. His popular following and public stature give him resources for bargaining and leadership that no political executive in the departments can hope to match.

1. For the political appointment process and the decision against a plural executive, see Arthur Taylor Prescott, *Drafting the Federal Constitution* (Louisiana State University Press, 1941), pp. 544–646; and Alexander Hamilton, James Madison, and John Jay, *The Federalist*, Max Beloff, ed. (Oxford: Basil Blackwell, 1948), nos. 70, 72, and 76. There is some question about how far the Founders actually intended the President to function alone or with the cabinet and Senate as a semicollegial group.

2. Alexander Hamilton contended that after an election, "the person substituted is warranted in supposing that the dismission of his predecessor has proceeded from a dislike to his measures, and that the less he resembles him, the more he will recommend himself to the favor of his constituents. These considerations, and the influence of personal confidences and attachments, would be likely to induce every new president to promote a change of men to fill the subordinate stations. . . ." (Ibid., no. 72, p. 370.)

Hence even if one disregarded all the policy challenges and personnel trends discussed in the first two chapters, U.S. federal executives would still find themselves in an extraordinarily difficult political situation. In theory political executives are supposed to provide departmental leadership and to work together under the President. But there are no "natural" political forces bolstering such expectations. Where, after all, does the political strength of these executives lie?

In elections? Departmental appointees are supposed to be helping the President make and carry out public policies affecting millions of lives, but no one has elected them. Typically, in fact, they will have played little part in the election responsible for their presence in Washington. Can ties to the President supply political strength? The President's closest companions are those who have followed him—not necessarily the party—and they will often have done so throughout the long march to the White House. Knowing the source of their power, they usually prefer proximity as White House aides rather than isolation as executive appointees somewhere "out" in the departments. And in any event a president who calculates his own power stakes is unlikely to let department executives borrow heavily on his political resources. Might political executives look for strength in their managerial authority? Hardly. Their second-hand mandate from the President competes with the mandates of elected congressmen who call the hearings, pass the enabling legislation, and appropriate the money. What about interest groups and clienteles? Obviously they have power, and many new political appointees do arrive in office closely tied to one or another such group.[3] But if this is the executives' exclusive source of political backing, any leadership role will be severely constrained. A public executive's responsibility is supposed to entail something more than advocacy for private groups.

Since these are "political" appointees, can strength perhaps be derived from political parties? As this chapter will show, new political executives may be outsiders, but they are not outsiders who have been linked together politically during periods of opposition. Whatever central campaign machinery there is belongs largely to the individual president rather than to a set of national party leaders. At the vital state and local party level, those ambitious for their own elective careers know they must pre-

3. See for example, *Appointments to the Regulatory Agencies*, Senate Commerce Committee, 94 Cong. 2 sess. (GPO, 1976); and Common Cause, *Serving Two Masters: A Common Cause Study of Conflicts of Interest in the Executive Branch* (Washington: Common Cause, 1976; processed).

pare their true political bases back home rather than in the Washington bureaucracy. Political parties are in no position to reward appointed executives for their successes or punish them for their failures.

On all of these counts, Washington's political executives have as few incentives to pull together as they have resources to stand alone as political leaders. Like the President, they must persuade rather than command others, but they lack the President's preeminent position to improve their bargaining power. The glare of White House attention may occasionally sweep across their agencies' activity, but for most political executives the President's traditional handshake and photograph will be his way of saying both hello and goodbye. In the constitutional structure and in the public eye, they are distinctly secondary figures to the single chief executive, yet the President's limited time, interests, and fighting power will make him utterly dependent on them for most of what is done by the executive branch. That they exist in such a twilight zone of political leadership is the first and primary fact of life shared by political appointees.

The Selection Process

Unlike the United States, most Western democracies need pay little explicit attention to finding political executive manpower. Not only are there relatively fewer political appointments vis-à-vis the bureaucracy, but these political systems generally produce combinations of potential executives as a natural by-product of forming governments out of the parliamentary parties. American political executives are unable to count on such an automatic recruitment system; rarely in fact has there been any system at all for acquiring the manpower for political leadership in the executive branch.

Yet presidents and department heads make few choices that are more important than those concerning the type of people who will serve with them in the administration. In affecting the everyday work of government, these hundreds of personnel selections add up to a cumulative act of choice that may be at least as important as the electorate's single act of choice for president every four years. Although many politically appointed positions require certain formal qualifications, this is one area where political calculations can have full play. "Who's going to argue," a civil service personnel officer asked, "if the secretary wants someone who isn't particularly qualified in an exempted position? It's really none of your business. They aren't going to be around long any-way." Moreover, while an ineffective performance in government can stultify policy and weaken an administration's record, it may have little effect on the personal careers of appointees, for whom "political leader-ship" is likely to have been a strange interlude. "I started as an assistant secretary," said one departing executive, "and leave as an undersecretary, and I don't think the people back home know whether that was a pro-motion or demotion."

Political recruiters soon learn that the academic advice to appoint good people offers little help. The first problem, a Johnson aide said, is "how to create some kind of staff system for identifying good people, getting reliable information on them, getting them doing their job." Every recent administration has struggled anew with the problem—never to anyone's complete satisfaction. Insofar as there can be any system, it is a system more of art than of science, blending information on individuals, job requirements, and the political realities at stake.

Organization

Each postwar administration has tried to develop some rational process for managing the creation of political executives. In the Truman White House, an Ivy League consultant was hired because, as the President's political headhunter said, "We wanted to reduce the whole political appointment thing to more of a science, to get the best brains. I had to conclude it couldn't work because of the political facts you have to deal with. Appointing this guy will displease Senator X or we need to do something else for Mr. Y in the House."

At the outset of the Eisenhower administration and again in 1960, private consultants prepared comprehensive studies advising the new President on the major control points in the executive branch and the nature of the job requirements.[4] Few participants can recall these studies being used very much in either administration. "Maybe they were too technical or maybe no one was interested in getting comprehensive con-trol," said a former White House adviser, "but the fact is a lot of these jobs were and are going to be filled by relying on Tom, Dick, and Harry; by going to the interest groups and so on; by asking who makes sense in a job like this."

4. These studies are described in Daniel Guttman and Barry Willner, *The Shadow Government* (Pantheon Books, 1976), pp. 98–101; and in Laurin L. Henry, *Presidential Transitions* (Brookings Institution, 1960), pp. 644–51.

In the 1960s the growing demand for competent political executives
was being reflected in more White House attention to positive recruitment rather than to just selecting among political applicants. The Kennedy administration spread a small network of evaluators around the
country to suggest names and offer confidential evaluations of the qualifications of candidates for political appointments. Kennedy supporters
also made new attempts to reach out for "action intellectuals" who
would be unlikely to surface through the normal political recruitment
channels. Naturally these efforts also overlapped with more traditional
methods of selection—the intricate political networks of friends and
friends of friends throughout the country. Thus while some sought to recruit nonpartisan talent, other White House aides maintained the patronage files (eventually numbering upwards of 5,000) containing political referrals, endorsements, and—as a Kennedy aide put it—a "motley
collection of information on who had scratched whose political back.
White House recruiters could go to the President, but so would everybody else to get personnel decisions."

Kennedy's evaluation process was greatly expanded and systematized
after 1964, so much so that the last half of the Johnson administration
constitutes one of the few examples of a relatively successful attempt to
organize the recruitment of political executives.[5] At least this seems to be
the case if success means a procedure that served to fill vacancies as they
occurred, provided relevant information on a candidate's qualifications
as well as political constraints, and was found to be of use by the President without undermining the responsibility of department heads.

It is worthwhile pausing to ask why something in the field of political
appointments actually worked. The heart of the success was not—as
many outside observers have assumed—a computerized talent bank of
personnel information in the White House. Such computers have typically provided little more than a sophisticated cross-indexing system that
could be no better than the quality of information fed in by the White
House staff. Compared with personnel operations in other administra-

5. The Johnson personnel operation is described in John W. Macy, Jr., *Public
Service* (Harper and Row, 1971), pp. 222–31. For a broader discussion of political
recruitment in recent administrations, see Calvin Mackenzie, "The Appointment
Process: The Selection and Confirmation of Federal Political Executives" (Ph.D.
dissertation, Harvard University, 1975); and *Study on Federal Regulation*, vol. 1: *The
Regulatory Appointments Process*, Senate Committee on Government Operations, 95
Cong. 1 sess. (GPO, 1977), pp. 95–160.

tions, the Johnson personnel system was different in four significant ways that seem to account for its usefulness.

First, information put into the computers was not simply the normal biographical information or vague personal endorsements but frank, confidential reports from the evaluators around the country. These reports were recorded verbatim over the telephone, often without the respondents' knowledge, and then were analyzed, compared, and summarized. In lieu of a "natural" political community, the recruiters in effect created their own word-of-mouth networks for taking readings of people who might be potential executives.

Second, the system departed from the usual White House personnel clearinghouse (in which presidential aides on personnel matters often find choice jobs for friends or themselves) and was organized more as a professional staff service. Summaries of evaluations and qualifications were prepared in a politically sensitive but impartial way that left the political judgments to the President.

Third, a president well versed in the programs and intricacies of Washington was usually able to set out his concept of the major job requirements *before* the recruitment effort began. "If you write the job description," said a personnel aide, "you're in control of who's getting the job. We were usually successful in getting the President to describe what he wanted in an appointment and so could feel pretty confident in the candidates we'd put up to him."

Finally, and most important, this political personnel organization was one of the few that worked because there was a presidential commitment to making it work. The top personnel officer was a senior official with direct access to the President. The President in turn insisted on a disciplined use of White House personnel channels. A Johnson aide who consulted with Kennedy, Nixon, Ford, and Carter personnel offices concluded:

> It happens in every administration. If the personnel people have to filter their information through a staff member short of the President, that guy is going to start picking his own people. . . . The key is having the President's support. Johnson didn't undercut his own personnel operation. When another staff member wanted to sell someone to the President directly, he would say: "You've got to go to the head [of the personnel office]. That's their problem."

These four conditions have rarely been met during any administration and then only briefly. Most political appointees can expect to be selected against a much more confusing interplay of political forces. Sev-

eral presidential aides, officially designated as the White House personnel office, will be found struggling with mixed success to make their voices
heard and to have their procedures followed amid the din of other interested parties. Prominent among these contenders will be congressmen
intent on preserving their particular power stakes, local supporters seeking the rewards of loyalty, pressure groups concentrating on their vital
points of access, and other presidential aides building personal lines of
credit. The attention of selectors and would-be selectors is likely to focus
on the "Plum Book," a convenience prepared at the request of Congress
after every presidential election that lists the appointive jobs exempt
from competitive civil service rules.[6] Applications invariably exceed the
positions available.

Within the White House any organization of the political appointment process usually occurs as an afterthought and is assigned to someone
who ranks below the level of top presidential aides and whose qualifications for work as personnel adviser are not carefully screened. A host of
other advisers also help inform the President on personnel matters, often
informally but sometimes, as in the Carter administration, through formally constituted panels. In any case, rarely is there any in-depth analysis
of what specific organizational and policy needs should guide the filling
of a given vacancy. And never has the White House had a procedure for
systematically following up on the performance of its appointees once
they are on the job.

Changes in recent years have, if anything, increased the difficulty of
organizing executive recruitment. At least until the 1960s well-established political figures in Congress, in party organizations, and on the
perimeters of presidential power seem to have provided fairly clear reference points to help reduce the uncertainties. Linked to a president
through common party ties, they offered him what Richard Neustadt
terms "familial advice" based on long-lasting loyalties and shared readings on familiar people. Neustadt observed: "What makes the instability
of presidential staffing seem so stark today is that this stable context now
has all but vanished, part of it declining with our party organizations, all
the rest suspended by persistent ticket-splitting."[7] The progressive disinte-
gration of old political networks in the selection process is apparent in the

6. U.S. House of Representatives, Committee on Post Office and Civil Service,
U.S. Government Policy and Supporting Positions, 94 Cong. 2 sess. (1976).

7. Richard Neustadt, *Presidential Power Revisited: The Politics of Leadership,
with Reflections on Johnson and Nixon* (Wiley, 1976), p. 60.

comments of aides who worked in the White House personnel offices during three different administrations. To the man handling political applicants and endorsements in the Truman years:

> Patronage is essential to governing. It's a way a President can get leverage, rewarding people and things like that. . . . We broke the country down geographically and by the type of political endorsement given the man. You wanted sectional spread and you wanted to keep track of who'd already gotten what by way of patronage; maybe the Banking Committee chairman in Congress already had a lot. We paid a lot of attention to the partisan coloring, not so you ended up with someone from the wrong factions. . . . You had to do the fieldwork to find out who the guy is—get the opinion of other knowledgeable people around the administration and Washington. The Democratic National Committee was more effective. . . . I don't know how I'd do the same job today.

Thirteen years later Kennedy political recruiters reported that they "started out by holding regular weekly sessions between top White House staff and the Democratic National Committee. . . . There were also the patronage files on applications and endorsements." But often those applying and endorsed did not fit the New Frontier image. More active recruitment methods reached out to the external evaluators "who had broad involvement in their local community. We were specifically not looking for politically partisan people." As recruitment progressed, Kennedy and Johnson aides sought "mainly to go out and try to find people outside the normal political channels."

The Nixon White House not only encountered the perennial problem of Republican administrations (i.e., trying to recruit people interested in government), but it saw less value than ever in relying on political and party organizations. A White House personnel director explained:

> The way our system works every party politician has some people he's beholden to. . . . You'll get a certain number of these cases where the support you need depends on getting something that this politician needs to maintain good relations with his supporter. A few of these are key issues, but only for keeping guys from jumping off the ship. Patronage isn't that important for positively building anything or managing the government.

In its modern guise the spoils system has often become a matter of dressing up the old ethnic patronage with a new minority-group image.[8] The White House official continued:

8. See *Presidential Campaign Activities of 1972*, Executive Session Hearings before the Senate Select Committee on Presidential Campaign Activities, bks. 18 and 19: *Watergate and Related Activities: Use of Incumbency—Responsiveness Program*, 93 Cong. 2 sess. (GPO, 1974).

The uses of incumbency for the '72 election were a lot more limited than we'd thought. About the only way you can positively use patronage is with the minority groups, and we tended to do this. There aren't that many jobs, but a few key appointments (a black at Health, Education, and Welfare; a Spanish-American at the Mint) . . . probably do swing some votes.

After the 1976 election Jimmy Carter carried the same tendencies somewhat further in his transition arrangements. Acting earlier than any new administration had before, Carter and his staff both renewed and extended the procedures developed in the Kennedy-Johnson years, using some of the same personnel recruiters. They formed largely nonpartisan panels of outside evaluators who solicited names, coded qualifications, and hurriedly prepared lists of possible appointees, first for the 312 top presidential appointments and then even more frantically for almost 2,000 lesser positions. As usual, these supposedly objective efforts produced a few obvious choices and a host of chancy compromises as their goals became blurred under personal, political, and interest group pressures. Shortly after taking office President Carter allowed himself a rare expression of frustration:

> I have learned in my first two and a half weeks why Abraham Lincoln and some of the older Presidents almost went home when they first got to the White House. The handling of personnel appointments, trying to get the right person in the right position at the right time is a very, very difficult question.[9]

But Carter's difficulty was hardly as simple as Lincoln's and the earlier presidents', whose chief struggle had been to satisfy political party claims for relatively unimportant jobs. The new President's frustrations with the political personnel system merely once again reflected the absence of a political community that could evolve and test potential leaders to fill hundreds of highly important executive positions.

The implications seem clear. Fragmentary national party organizations in the United States have always been an uncertain source of political manpower for managing the executive branch. In recent years, as the demand for more high-caliber political executives has increased, the capacity of established political networks to provide such personnel has declined even further. The White House can, of course, try to take a positive lead in organizing its own recruitment process, but this demands

9. Press conference, February 8, 1977, reported in the New York Times, February 9, 1977. A description of the Carter administration's initial personnel process is in Joel Havemann, "Carter Is Taking Pains in Picking His Plums," National Journal, no. 47 (November 20, 1976), pp. 1650–54.

exceptional discipline and competence on the part of the President, his personnel office, and the rest of the White House staff. In the end the problem of recruiting and controlling "his" political appointees is a major worry to a president because it is a nonexistent problem to the party he ostensibly leads.

Divided Loyalties

The selection process for political executives is therefore not so much an organizational process as it is a social-political melee that turns around several axes. One zone where conflicts usually arise is between the White House on the one hand and congressional sponsors (often allied with interest groups claiming certain positions) on the other. The more any administration tries to enforce its own preferences and bypass the traditional claims of party favoritism and interest-group representation, the more conflict can be expected. Almost by definition these sponsors of a particular candidate are less interested in weighing alternative recruits and their qualifications and more interested (for whatever reason) in delivering on the appointment of a given applicant. A congressional staff member and veteran of many personnel skirmishes said he had found

> that White House people are generally quite sincere when they say they want good people. They tend to realize—to a greater or lesser extent—that the success of their administration depends on getting high-quality people. . . . Frankly, some of the biggest problems come from Congress and local political types. Naturally they've got far less interest in the caliber of these people because they don't have to work with them.

The other well-worn channel of conflict on political appointments is between the White House and its own top appointees in departments. Not surprisingly, the former will claim a continuing presidential stake in subsequent appointments to the departments. Department heads are likely to claim—also not surprisingly—that if they are responsible for running the agencies, they need a free hand in picking their staffs.

The inevitable result is a great deal of skirmishing and a few pitched battles between the White House and agency heads. Best remembered are the extreme cases: Kennedy's appointment of a lower political official before the secretary of state was chosen and several secretaries in the Eisenhower and Kennedy years who insisted on complete discretion in choosing their political subordinates. The normal pattern, however, is for a negotiated settlement between the agency's head office and the White

House.[10] The one generalization that is possible is that usually neither side will win or lose all the time and for very good reasons.

Why shouldn't the agency head always win? As one presidential adviser put it, "Look, some of these top people get appointed as a pure political favor. Give them a free hand and they are going to appoint a string of incompetent people below them." There is some basis for this complaint because political executives are often poorly equipped to organize a reliable political recruitment process for their own agency. Of course, every top appointee has personal preferences for filling some subordinate positions, but he usually has too few willing acquaintances to fill the large number of political appointments in a government department. Even if he had, the recruitment machinery would have to be organized anew by each succeeding department head. Hence political recruitment within the departments is apt to be a haphazard arrangement. Frequently a trusted assistant to the cabinet secretary will find himself assigned the role of political recruiter and will have to cope as best he can. "It was a nightmare, really," said one aide. "I'd never done any executive recruitment. What I eventually did was call up a friend who had done some personnel work to come to Washington and help me."

What commonly evolves out of the departmental search for political manpower is a small personnel office somewhere near the agency head (the political "commissars" mentioned in chapter 2). These offices will usually process the customary political referrals but do little to find and recruit qualified candidates who might not otherwise apply. Here is how one participant described the typical procedure:

> The referrals often come from a congressman or senator to the secretary. And there are always some from the White House and [interest groups]. Sometimes there are ten or more a day, so everyone can't be given priority. . . . If the sponsor has a lot of political clout, there will be a personal interview or you telephone the applicant. Otherwise, you write a letter saying he is being given every consideration and send a copy to the sponsor.
>
> An applicant without political backing just gets placed in the inventory for noncareer jobs. The important thing is not to make anyone mad and show you're trying to help. . . . For guys who look good there'll be an affili-

10. Typically, the operational responsibilities are divided, with the White House personnel office doing all the staff work on presidential appointments and the departments choosing candidates for the other political positions and clearing their selections with the White House. The White House in turn will clear the names by checking with relevant congressmen and party organizations. In 1976 this meant that the White House had direct recruitment duties for 900 presidential appointments and clearance responsibilities for about 2,000 political appointments in the departments. See table 3-1.

ation check to see if they are supporters of the administration. That takes three or four phone calls to the state party organization, or maybe the governor's office. Several days later, they'll usually call back and say how the candidate is registered. Then you clear it on the hill by calling the Senate and House offices from the candidate's home area and asking if they have any objections. That's the way it works.

Dissatisfaction with such traditional procedures often prompts the White House to make more positive efforts to recruit political appointees who are in tune with the President's own particular position. But there are also good reasons why the White House personnel office must usually settle for negotiated decisions rather than domination over the selection process. A cabinet secretary without control of key political appointments will be able to exert little influence on the semiautonomous fiefdoms that make up most departments. Consistently losing to the White House will destroy his standing in the department, for as one experienced personnel director said, "Word really filters down that you've got a weakling at the top and it creates a feeling no one really cares about the department." Equally important, the successful candidates themselves are likely to find that a decisive White House victory on their behalf spells disaster for their leadership position within the department. It is worth emphasizing this point with some recent history.

The Nixon administration eventually went further than any other in trying to clarify the lines of allegiance by placing White House loyalists in key department positions. Yet well before the Watergate controversy began weakening the administration, experience was beginning to show why some division rather than a monopoly of loyalties has usually been found to be more satisfactory to all sides concerned with the political selection process. After 1970 management experts appointed to strategic positions in the departments soon found that too close identification with the White House restricted the very effectiveness that had motivated their appointment in the first place. One of the Nixon aides responsible for these placements expressed the inevitable dilemma of overcentralization: "I didn't think this would be much of a problem but it was. For the guy to be worth controlling, he has to know what is going on in his department. If he knows what's going on there, he's less likely to be amenable to central control."

Soon the loyalists placed in the departments were trying to distance themselves from the White House.

Eventually some other assistant secretaries in other departments and I had talks with the [White House] aide and we said, "Look, we want to discontinue these meetings. We don't want it to look like we are going to be the dancing girls for [a presidential office]. We've got to make it clear that we are the secretary's man."

In short, to be of use to the White House, appointees had to be of use to the departments. Their effectiveness depended on a selection process that permitted divided loyalties, or at least room to maneuver as both the President's man and the department's advocate.

The homiletic advice, then, is to appoint only strong, well-qualified people at the top of government agencies and to make them responsible for choosing effective political subordinates. The practitioner's response is likely to be that—in the first place—there are rarely any organized political processes to accomplish these ends in Washington. In the second place, such advice assumes the politics out of political appointments. Because politics has to do, among other things, with fashioning compromises and repaying debts, a president or department head may not be able to come within hailing distance of his first choice for a political appointment. The more appointing officials have to settle for something less than their first choice in one position, the more incentives they have to fight about subsequent selections. In the third place, any neat management design for political recruitment dissolves from science to art because of power calculations.

To an outsider, all this intricate, often tedious maneuvering over political personnel can seem absurd—particularly since many of the political positions fought for so strenuously are often not expected even by the combatants to make any real difference to government agencies and their extremely complex policy choices. What an outsider is unlikely to appreciate is that these personnel struggles have to do not only with a product but a process. The process of filling jobs is an important facet of political interaction because of its symbolic significance in the mutual calculations of political power. Each new appointment is another test case in the struggle within, across, and outside the political layers of the executive branch, each participant preserving or yielding up his prerogatives in choosing the personnel below him. Observers of the Washington selection process are as interested in who stands behind the person appointed as in the person himself.

All of this has operational significance for political executives. A new appointee can easily get in trouble because the selection process often creates a number of political minefields. A newcomer may not notice the dangers until some misstep upsets a hitherto hidden understanding that was implicit in his selection. Moreover, the selection process deemphasizes operational goals, making an appointee's journey through the Washington minefields into something of a random walk. If he is not entirely sure of what is expected of him, it is not surprising; in many cases neither are his selectors, many of whom are more interested in the process of getting their way than in the executive's eventual output. The selection process also puts a premium on free-floating adaptability. Unlike congressmen in committees, political executives are not normally part of a well-tried self-selection process by which they can seek to match their interests with their working assignments.[11] In most cases adaptation will have to occur in whatever the job happens to be.

Thus the Washington selection process leads political appointees into a variety of situations that, if impossible to predict individually, are important to understand in general from the outset. Some executives will arrive as if by accident, such as the assistant secretary who said, "I tried to look into it and as far as I could tell my name fell out of a White House computer, largely because I'm a woman and had just been elected president [of a national professional society]."

Others will take office only too well aware of their specific patrons in the executive branch, Congress, interest groups, or some other combination of forces to whom the placement is owed. Yet even those most clearly oriented may find they do not know all that went into their appointments, like one incautious presidential selection who said, "I only found out considerably later that I'd gotten the job by a strange maneuver. . . . I started out in the department with one strike against me and didn't even know it."

Most political appointees are neither complete accidents nor the property of particular patrons but the result of a variety of known and unknown compromises in the selection process. They probably are involved, at least implicitly, in some divided loyalties and will need to move back and forth across the lines of confidence among the department, White House, Congress, and interest groups. The selection process may have facilitated or prejudiced the appointees' chances of doing so and thus will have helped or hurt their chances for political leadership in the bureaucracy. Selection creates the initial network of debts and credits a new appointee brings with him, but it is a tentative network. Allegiances, like the appointees themselves, can change quickly.

11. See Richard Fenno, *Congressmen in Committees* (Little, Brown, 1973), p. 1.

Characteristics of Political Executives

Although reliable information about political executives' behavior is lacking, a surfeit of data exists concerning their biographical characteristics. These data add up to a description of a statistical elite—statistical because there is little evidence of a self-conscious group seeking agreed upon goals and screening out other entrants; elite because political appointees in the federal government are consistently drawn from the most socially and economically advantaged portions of the population. With a degree of certainty rare in social science, political executives can be predicted to be disproportionately white, male, urban, affluent, middle-aged, well educated at prestige schools, and pursuers of high-status white-collar careers. They are unlikely to be female, nonwhite, wage-earning, from a small town, or possessors of average educational and social credentials.[12]

Work Experience

These socioeconomic data, however, reveal little about the kind of experience political executives gain on the job. For this type of information, researchers have examined job tenure and mobility in hopes of describing the government executives' opportunities to learn about their working environments. Such information does not entirely support several commonly held assumptions about the characteristics of political appointees. One is that the top political layers are filled with newcomers to government—politically imported outsiders credited by defenders with introducing a fresh view of government operations and labeled by detractors as ignorant intruders. Another common view (and one of the chief justifications for the extensive use of political appointments in government) is that those in the top strata resemble the Founding Fathers, in that they are "in-and-outers," that is, people who periodically interrupt their private careers to move in and out of the public service. Qualifying, if not entirely dispelling, each of these assumptions leaves behind a more realistic picture of the public careers of political executives.

Compared with the government experience of civil servants, that of the men and women coming to top political positions naturally seems

12. See David T. Stanley, Dean E. Mann, and Jameson W. Doig, *Men Who Govern* (Brookings Institution, 1967), pp. 9–36; and Thomas R. Dye and John W. Pickering, "Governmental and Corporate Elites," *Journal of Politics*, vol. 37 (1974), pp. 913–15.

Table 3-2. *Political Executives' Years of Experience in the Federal Government*, 1970[a]

Percent

Years of government experience	Presidential appointees	Noncareer supergrades	Career supergrades
Less than 2	69	40	3
2–5	19	7	11
6–10	6	14	9
Over 10	6	39	77
Total	100	100	100

Source: Reproduced with the permission of Joel D. Aberbach and the Comparative Elite Project at the University of Michigan. The project is a comparative study of the attitudes of high-level administrators and elected officials in Western Europe and the United States. More information on the American portion of the study can be found in Joel D. Aberbach, James D. Chesney, and Bert A. Rockman, "Exploring Elite Political Attitudes," *Political Methodology*, vol. 2 (1975), pp. 1–28.

a. Figures refer to years of continuous or noncontinuous experience at the time of the survey (1970) and therefore overstate the amount of experience in government enjoyed by these officials (17 presidential appointees, 43 noncareer supergrades, and 64 career supergrades) at the time of their appointment to executive positions.

meager. Table 3-2 shows that in 1970 the highest political executives (presidential appointees) had the least experience in the federal government, the next echelon of political appointees (noncareerists in the supergrade range of GS 16–18) had somewhat more, and higher civil servants had the longest experience of all.[13]

It is worth emphasizing the general point evident in such data: unlike the situation in most private organizations, in the U.S. executive branch those in the top positions of formal authority are likely to be substantially less familiar with their working environment than both their civil service and political subordinates.

But as foreshadowed in chapter 2, this relative inexperience at the top does not mean that political executives are complete novices to government. One bureaucratic-type feature of the layers of political executives is the tendency (particularly after the early days of a new administration) for recruitment to occur from subordinate to superordinate political positions. Studies of top political executives from the Roosevelt to Johnson administrations have shown that the large majority had some previous experience in the federal government. During those years 29 percent of the senior appointees (cabinet secretaries, undersecretaries, assistant sec-

13. Nixon political executives in 1970, however, had somewhat less government experience than those in previous administrations, including Eisenhower's.

retaries, general counsels, administrators, deputy administrators, and commissioners) had previously held high political positions in the same agency and 11 percent in other agencies; 24 percent had held lower-echelon political appointments (special assistants, personal aides, etc.) in the same agency and 37 percent in other agencies. All together about two-thirds of the top political executives had federal administrative service before their appointment by the President.[14] Lower-level political appointees, i.e., noncareer executives in the supergrades, also are often recruited from among people with narrow experience inside government. During 1974, for example, over three-quarters of noncareer vacancies were filled from within the same agency, 11 percent from other agencies, and only 13 percent from outside government.[15]

These statistics, however, should not summon up images of a top government layer peopled with men of public affairs who, like modern counterparts of Cincinnatus or George Washington, repeatedly exchange private lives for public offices. While prominent examples of such men do exist (Nelson Rockefeller, Clark Clifford, Averell Harriman, etc.), true in-and-out careers are much less common than usually thought. Such careers would presumably show a periodic interchange of public service and private employment, possibly with several appointments in different administrations. In fact, these characteristics are uncommon. Between 1933 and 1965 nine out of ten top political executives had no more than two government appointments. Four-fifths served only one president and while most appointees reported their principal occupations to be in the private sector, seven out of ten held government rather than private positions immediately before their presidential appointment. Since nine out of ten of these top political executives served in only one agency, it is also difficult to see how the in-and-outers can be thought to supply anything like a general, governmentwide capability for political leadership in the bureaucracy. Similar tendencies are evident in the lower-level political appointments, i.e., the noncareer executive assignments in the supergrade range. Very few of these noncareer executives have repeated spells of government service and rarely have they worked in more than one agency. In 1975 noncareer supergrades actually had somewhat less experience outside

14. Stanley, Mann, and Doig, *Men Who Govern*, table 3-5, p. 45, and table E-5, p. 137.
15. U.S. Civil Service Commission, *Executive Manpower in the Federal Service* (GPO, September 1975), table 15, p. 19.

their agency than did the relatively immobile career bureaucrats at the same grade level.[16]

In sum, political appointees are generally people who will move in and sometimes up. They will cope as best they can and move out without returning. The few top executives with continual government experience may be extraordinarily valuable, but as a former civil servant said, "What most people don't realize is that an in-and-outer usually ends up staying an outer." The conventional image of Washington in-and-outers erroneously suggests a political team of utility players, when what actually exists is a one-time sequence of pinch hitters.

Birds of Passage

The single most obvious characteristic of Washington's political appointees is their transience. While most take up their appointments with somewhat more government experience and have a more terminal government career than is usually assumed, political executives are not likely to be in any one position for very long. The standard figure quoted is that the average undersecretary or assistant secretary remains in his job for about twenty-two months. More detailed breakdowns show this average to contain a large number of very short tenures; about half the top political executives can expect to stay in their jobs less than two years. (See table 3-3.) The Nixon administration provided an extreme example of the general tendency when its personnel office in 1970 (*before* large-scale purges by the White House) found there was already an annual turnover rate of 27–30 percent in presidential and executive-level appointments to the departments and agencies. The tenure of cabinet secretaries declined from a previous average of forty months to eighteen months during the Nixon administration.

Again, those in the lower rather than in the higher political echelons have a better chance to acquire job experience. Unlike the high political executives just mentioned, noncareer supergrade appointees have an average tenure of fifteen years in the federal service. But as noted in chapter 2, up to one-half of these "political appointees" are in effect

16. Information on presidential appointees between 1933 and 1965 is from Stanley, Mann, and Doig, *Men Who Govern*, pp. 6, 8, 34, 50. Data on noncareer supergrades in 1975 is in unpublished tables prepared by the U.S. Civil Service Commission, Bureau of Executive Manpower.

Table 3-3. *Tenure of Political Executives, 1960–72*
Percent

Type of executive	Months on the job		
	Less than 12	12–24	Over 24
Cabinet secretaries	16	25	59
Undersecretaries	16	35	49
Assistant secretaries	22	32	46

Source: Arch Patton, "Government's Revolving Door," *Business Week*, September 22, 1973, p. 12.

former career officials. One year after the Johnson-Nixon transition about 90 percent of these civil-servant-type appointees were still in their jobs, and the turnover rate was in line with what could be expected of comparable civil servants. As for the other half (the 300 or so younger outsiders), two-thirds were no longer in their jobs a year after the Johnson-Nixon transition.[17]

Much more important than the experience or inexperience of political appointees as individuals is their transience as a group. Cabinet secretaries may bring with them a cadre of personal acquaintances to fill some of their subordinate political positions, but in general public executives will be strangers with only a fleeting chance to learn how to work together. This characteristic is worth examining in a little more detail.

One of the most persistent themes in comments from political executives of all recent administrations is the absence of teamwork characterizing the layers of appointees. This absence of unifying ties is foreordained, given the fractionalized, changing, and job-specific sets of forces that make up the selection process. But it is not only methods of selection that put mutually reinforcing loyalties at a premium. Rapid turnover intensifies all the other problems of political teamwork.

In many ways what matters most is not so much an individual's job tenure as the duration of his executive relationships. Those in superior positions need to assess the capacities of their subordinates; subordinates need to learn what is expected of them. Political appointees at the same hierarchical level need to learn each other's strengths, weaknesses, priorities, and ways of communicating. Normally the opportunity to develop these working relationships is even shorter than the time span for learning

17. U.S. Civil Service Commission, Bureau of Executive Manpower, "Non-Career Executive Assignments" (July 1975; processed).

a particular job. As the following percentages show, during the Kennedy, Johnson, and Nixon administrations, almost two-thirds of the undersecretaries and four-fifths of the assistant secretaries worked two years or less for the same immediate political superiors:[18]

	Under 12 months (percent)	12–24 months (percent)	Over 2 years (percent)
Same undersecretary– cabinet secretary relationship	29	34	37
Same assistant secretary– undersecretary relationship	39	38	23

The effects of this group instability are reflected in countless ways, all expressive of the fundamental point that a political executive in Washington must operate amid kaleidoscopic sets of interpersonal relations. These situations are predictable only in the sense that they are likely to arise in unexpected ways to affect the chances for political leadership in the bureaucracy. For example, with one set of personalities and circumstances, a cabinet officer dealing with an assistant secretary may bypass an undersecretary but create little difficulty. An undersecretary who found himself in this position said, "It was something I knew [the cabinet secretary] was interested in. I was made to feel welcome if I wanted to get into it, so why should I be upset?" Later, with other people and in other circumstances: "There was [the undersecretary] from the California crowd. [The cabinet secretary] had no trouble with that because he simply outflanked him by bringing in his own man as assistant secretary. So there was poor old [the undersecretary] between the hammer and the anvil." But within another two years turnover in the assistant secretary's slot brought a new constellation of forces. "[The new man] made it clear he wasn't going to perform the same sort of hatchet job on the undersecretary. He was going to be strictly nonpartisan, and you could see things becoming more politically sanitized." One political appointee found that the cabinet secretary regularly used meetings to alert him that he "was being torpedoed by [a political colleague] who was always cutting deals on his own." Another man formally in the same position found himself "going to meetings, and people would want to know why I was there."

18. See Arch Patton, "Government's Revolving Door," *Business Week*, September 22, 1973, p. 13.

The Larger Picture

The unstable teams within departments are positively collegial when compared with the attenuated relations of political appointees across departments. At least within departments there may be the shared need to protect and promote a common set of agency programs. Weighed against this territorial imperative, political appointees elsewhere can seem like alien tribes.

Few political appointees are likely to be united by bonds of party loyalty, the academics' favorite prescription for overcoming political incoherence in Washington. Though they may be in broad agreement with the President's general approach, political executives usually will not have been active members of his party and only a small minority will have struggled together against common opponents in electoral campaigns. Civil servants are identifying a fundamental characteristic of executive leadership in Washington when they report that they have worked for many political appointees but rarely for a politician.[19] Most would probably agree with the assistant secretary who said, "As far as I can tell, in this town a political appointee is simply someone whose career isn't in this department."

None of this inexperience necessarily means a lack of partisanship in "nonpolitical" political appointees. Quite the opposite. Many of those eventually known as the most partisan of Nixon's appointees came from backgrounds with a minimum of party-political experience. "I came to Washington with absolutely no party or political background," one of them said. "I had a naive idea of managing as in private enterprise but quickly learned political factors are all pervasive."

The record of the Nixon White House demonstrated in a number of cases how those least politically experienced can be susceptible to developing more extreme personal partisanship than those accustomed to regular political interaction and its inevitable compromises. Often the zealousness of the new convert to Washington politics can make effective political teamwork that much more difficult. One official summed up his experience in four administrations by observing: "Inexperienced peo-

19. Although data are not entirely comparable, certainly less than half the political executives in all recent administrations had any record of political party activity, if by that is meant experience as campaign or party officials, convention delegates, elected officials, or political candidates or their staff members. See Stanley, Mann, and Doig, *Men Who Govern*, table E-1, p. 132; and Dean E. Mann, *The Assistant Secretaries* (Brookings Institution, 1965), table A-9, p. 295.

ple tend to lack the political instinct. . . . Sometimes the political instinct means the best politics is no politics. And it knows where that's true, it's not pure partisanship."

Lacking any larger political forces to help unify political executives, the lines of mutual interdependence normally run vertically down the departments and their loosely related programs—not horizontally across the layers of political leadership in various departments. Insofar as top political executives need each other (as opposed to needing the President's support or endorsement) the needs are temporary and issue-specific, not enduring. Even at the height of public criticism concerning the placement of Nixon loyalists in the departments, many of those placed recognized the lack of any workable horizontal contacts. As one appointee said: "For all the talk about teams, I have no contact that amounts to anything with other appointees outside the department. The few lunches we have aren't of much use for getting business done. There is no strong mechanism for getting political appointees together. As a group there's no trust."

It would be a mistake, however, to conclude that political executives are averse to creating alliances. At any given moment, informal communications and networks do exist throughout the political levels and across the departments in Washington. But as participants and issues change frequently, so do the nature and location of these relationships. Some political appointees will have enough common objectives and mutual knowledge to create fairly close informal groups. "There are me and six other assistant secereteries from other departments," said one such man. "We've got some management techniques we want to move on." A year later two of these executives were left in government. Another appointee was trying to draw his counterparts into monthly meetings but recognized "the problem is how to get continuity and institutionalize this sort of thing to keep it going." A year later, he too was gone and his group largely dismantled.

Equally revealing of the flux confronting any outsider is the fact that the last man quoted was like many resigning political appointees. He did not depart for reasons bearing any relation to the substance of what he was doing in government but because his own political patrons were leaving. While resignation for reasons of conscience or policy are relatively rare,[20] the chancy circumstances that create political executives in

20. See Edward Weisband and Thomas Franck, *Resignation and Protest* (Penguin, 1976), especially pp. 121–63 and fig. 1, app. B, p. 201.

the first place can just as easily lead to their departure. Political executives and their particular sets of relationships with each other not only fade, but fade fortuitously. Even a close observer of these political comings and goings is likely to pick up confusing signals about whether an executive personnel change is a case of tactics, accident, or grand political strategy.

In recent years greater efforts have been made to formalize cross-departmental ties, with the hope of institutionalizing more permanent and general-purpose relationships than those that usually prevail. The Undersecretaries' Group, begun informally toward the end of the Johnson administration, is a good example. Formal organization occurred in 1968–69 at the urging of Bureau of the Budget officials and mainly, as one of the founders described it, "to get more political weight behind some procedural reforms we were pushing."[21] Nixon's advisers attempted later to broaden the scope of the Undersecretaries' Group and to establish regular meetings of a governmentwide team identified with the administration as a whole. According to one of the plan's promoters:

> It was something we should have done a lot earlier in the administration. We started monthly meetings, even had an executive order. We had a weekend session at Camp David with the wives along. The undersecretaries got to know each other. We talked about where we should be going and had some very thought-provoking sessions. . . . I think these people at this level are interested in things bigger than the department. I think they realize their success is measured by the success of the President.

Unfortunately, sociability and big thinking could not provide a foundation for serious working relationships. After one year, another presidential aide more closely connected with the activities of the group concluded:

> I didn't get the feeling they were acting like prima donnas, [but] it's just generally hard to get their attention, even concerning the federal regional councils, if they don't feel it's important to their departmental operations. . . . They just weren't interested in talking about these broader issues.

Where they'd had a problem, they'd already met to settle it informally. Undoubtedly every administration could help itself by doing more to exchange information and create understanding across political levels. But governmentwide teamwork is another question. One undersecretary, generally recognized as a leading member of the group, went to the heart of the matter:

21. These procedural reforms are described in Joint Administrative Task Force, *Reducing Federal Grant-in-Aid Processing Time: Final Report*, An Interagency Report to the President (GPO, March 1968).

You can't build a governmentwide executive team through artificial structures like the Undersecretaries' Group. It's a group in search of a mission. You can't build an executive team by pressing issues that aren't particularly relevant to people just for the sake of having everybody in on them. You can't do it by bypassing people to get to another layer. [Insofar as there is going to be a team] it has to begin at the top and use the cabinet secretaries.

Yet if there were to be such a serious effort at decisionmaking by enduring teams of political leaders across the top of departments, the U.S. presidency would look far different than it does today or ever has. In such a system cabinet secretaries would need each other as a group more than they would need their departmental identifications and more than they would need any individual member, including the President. Presidents may be advised that they need more collegial help and reactivated cabinets, and they may with good reason even take such advice, at least for a while. But barring any profound institutional and structural changes, no modern president can be expected to be like a foreign prime minister, merely the first among equals. He needs the particular colleagues in his cabinet too little; his colleagues need him too much and each other too little for that to happen. No public executive short of the President has a vested interest in coordinating political leadership in the executive branch as a whole. Political appointees out in the departments and agencies can expect to remain in their twilight zone.

Because the executive branch has a single head, its political leadership is inherently noncollegial—except for a sharing of some executive powers with Congress. That is the way the Founders designed it. That is the way it functions. But "single" does not mean unitary. The political executives' very lack of coequality—no one is the President's peer—means that their successes are likely to be expropriated by the President, their failures left behind in the departments with little effect on the appointees' real vocations outside government. Since there is only one chief executive but many sources of political support and inspiration, top political appointees do not necessarily hang separately if they fail to hang together. *E unibus plurum.*

A Summary and Look Forward

Any commitment to democratic values necessarily means accepting a measure of instability in the top governing levels. Democratic elections are, after all, "a political invention to assure uncertainty of leadership, in what are deemed to be optimum amounts and periods of time."[22] But to the inherent electoral changes, the American executive political system adds a considerably greater range of nonelectoral uncertainty to political leadership. This system produces top executives who are both expendable over time and in a relatively weak, uncertain position at any one time.

The number of political executives is small vis-à-vis the bureaucracy but large and fragmented in relation to any notion of a trim top-management structure. To the normal confusions of pluralistic institutions and powers in Washington, the selection process contributes its own complexities. White House personnel efforts have rarely been effectively organized. Political forces intervene from many quarters, and their interests in political appointments often bear little relation to presidential needs or to qualifications required for effective performance by public executives. White House efforts at political recruitment can be effective, but the organizational requirements are difficult to master. A White House operation that veers too far in the direction of centralized control can easily become self-defeating by overlooking the need for political executives to balance their responsiveness to the President with their usefulness to the departments.

While political appointees are more experienced in government than might be assumed, their government service does not usually provide continuity of experience, either through periodic spells of officeholding or long tenure in particular jobs. This is especially true at the higher political levels. Hence without a very steep learning curve, political appointees are likely to find that their capacities for effective action have matured at just about the time they are leaving office. As one assistant secretary said, "You're given this particular situation for one moment in time ... you've got to get on your feet quickly." The entire process does not produce long-suffering policymakers who realize their major changes will come gradually through persistence. Most political appointees are more impatient. Any civil servant who offers the standard and often sensible bureaucratic advice to watch, wait, and be careful can expect to arouse more than a little suspicion.

All these tendencies are vastly intensified by the instability and uncertainty of working relationships among political appointees as a group. Over time, changes in the Washington community, particularly the de-

22. Dwight Waldo, *Perspectives on Administration* (University of Alabama Press, 1956), p. 14.

clining role of parties, have provided even fewer points of political reference to help orient leadership in the executive branch. Despite the conventional models, political interaction is less like regularly scheduled matches between competing teams of partisans (President versus Congress, Republicans versus Democrats) and more like a sandlot pick-up game, with a variety of strangers, strategies, and misunderstandings. Such working relationships as exist are created and recreated sporadically as the political players come and go. Each largely picks up his lore anew—how to make his way, look for support, and deal with officialdom. It is circumstances such as these that lead many civil servants and experienced political executives to echo the words of one presidential appointee (in fact a Nixon placement in the supposedly enemy territory of the Department of Health, Education, and Welfare): "In my time I've come to the conclusion you can't say it's the damn bureaucrats. With some exceptions, that's not the problem. What's lacking is the political leadership." Political executives have no common culture for dealing with the problems of governing, and it is seldom that they are around long enough or trust one another enough to acquire one.

Weaknesses among political executives lead inevitably to White House complaints about their "going native" in the bureaucracy. The image is apt. To a large extent the particular agencies and bureaus *are* the native villages of executive politics. Even the most presidentially minded political executive will discover that his own agency provides the one relatively secure reference point amid all the other uncertainties of Washington. In their own agencies, appointees usually have at least some knowledge of each other and a common identity with particular programs. Outside the agency it is more like life in the big city among large numbers of anonymous people who have unknown lineages. Any common kinship in the political party or a shared political vocation is improbable, and in the background are always the suspicions of the President's "true" family of supporters in the White House. Political appointees in the larger Washington environment may deal frequently with each other, but these are likely to be the kind of ad hoc, instrumental relations of the city, where people interact without truly knowing each other.

Yet the political appointee's situation is not so simple that he can act as if he is surrounded by a random collection of strangers outside the confines of his agency village. Everywhere extensive networks of village folk in the bureaucracy, Congress, and lobby organizations share experiences, problems, and readings on people and events. An appointee may or may not be in touch with people in these networks, but they are certain to be in touch with each other independently of him. In sociological terms his networks are thin, transient, and single-stranded; theirs are dense, multiple, and enduring. Among public executives themselves there is little need to worry about any joint action to enforce community norms, because there is no community. In dealing with outside villagers who know each other, however, appointees can find that reprisals for any misdeeds are extraordinarily oblique and powerful. The political executive system may be a government of strangers, but its members cannot act as if everyone else is.

Now one can begin to see the real challenge to the political executives' statecraft in Washington. They must be able to move in two worlds—the tight, ingrown village life of the bureaucratic community and the open, disjointed world of political strangers. A public executive in Washington needs the social sensitivity of a villager and the political toughness of a city streetfighter. It is an increasingly unlikely combination. Despite all the resources devoted to more topside staff, new management initiatives, more elaborate analytic techniques, and so on, there remain few—probably fewer than ever—places where political executives can look for reliable political support in any efforts at leadership in the bureaucracy. Political appointees in Washington are substantially on their own and vulnerable to bureaucratic power.

CHAPTER FOUR

Bureaucrats: People in the Machine

. . . a government ill executed, whatever it may be in theory, must be, in practice, a bad government.
—Alexander Hamilton, *The Federalist*, no. 70

NEARLY A CENTURY AGO the civil service joined the other American political institutions largely as an afterthought. It has continued into the present era with much the same status. Americans have long expressed impatience with red tape and Washington bureaucrats, but few of the heavy demands they make on the federal government can be satisfied without some form of organized bureaucratic activity.[1] Sometimes more and sometimes less intense, this ambivalence is a persisting—if poorly defined—influence on the work of all civil servants.

A relatively small fraternity ("establishment" would be too strong a term) of specialized Washington participants concerns itself with the actual workings of the civil service—its rules, pensions, pay, organization, and well-being. Normally these overseers include the Civil Service Commission, government employee unions, several congressional subcommittees, a few civic groups such as the National Civil Service League, and an occasional aide in the Executive Office of the President.

1. Public opinion polls show, for example, that the overwhelming majority of Americans agree that the federal government should control inflation; avoid depression; assure international peace; regulate (but not run) private business; and see to it that the poor are taken care of, the hungry fed, and every person assured a minimum standard of living. But a comparably large majority also agree that the federal government is so "big and bureaucratic" that it should return more taxes to subnational governments and count mainly on the states to decide what programs should be started and continued. See *Confidence and Concern: Citizens View American Government*, Committee Print, Subcommittee on Intergovernmental Relations of the Senate Committee on Government Operations, 93 Cong. 1 sess. (GPO, 1973), pt. 2, tables 026A, p. 111; 026, p. 117; 027, p. 118–19; 070A, p. 238.

While public criticism of big government and bureaucracy is often remote from the day-to-day realities of administration, the practitioners' efforts are often narrowly focused on the nuts and bolts of administering civil service procedures without much attention to the bureaucratic system as a whole. Often those critical of bureaucracy and those concerned with the civil service seem to be living in two different worlds, and in a sense they are.

In this chapter I assess the role of higher civil servants from a viewpoint midway between the two extremes, a perspective more detailed than stereotypes about the bureaucracy but more general than descriptions of particular programs and procedures. In fact, "the" bureaucracy can hardly be said to exist as a collective entity in Washington. Instead, a number of subbureaucracies are linked by what are best thought of as similar predilections. These tendencies could be discussed in many ways. Here, my emphasis will be on bureaucratic careers, protections, and dispositions. By trying to put ourselves in the shoes of higher civil servants, we will be able to understand something more about their power and the price it extracts from those who would use it.

The Higher Career System

Over the decades reformers' efforts have left behind a series of arrangements that combine to produce the civil service version of people in government. Taken as a whole the U.S. federal bureaucracy appears open and broadly representative of the American population in education, income, and social status (as indicated by father's occupation).[2] But the higher their civil service rank, the more U.S. officials approach the statistical elite qualities observed among political executives. For example, in 1975 almost one-half of higher civil servants, compared with 14 percent of the general population, had fathers who were professionals or business executives. Almost two-thirds of GS 14–18 officials, compared with only one-third of the general population, assessed their parents' situation to have been middle class. In fact, the degree of unrepresentativeness suggested by these social class indicators seems to be about as great for the higher U.S. civil service as it is for the supposedly elitist British administrative class.[3]

2. James Fesler has compared the socioeconomic characteristics of bureaucracies in several countries in "Public Administration" (Yale University, 1975; manuscript).

3. Kenneth Jon Meier, "Representative Bureaucracy: An Empirical Analysis," *American Political Science Review*, vol. 69 (June 1975), tables 1 and 2, p. 534, and figures 5 and 6, p. 535.

This and similar information casts considerable doubt on the frequently discussed suggestion of relying on demographic sampling to assure democratic responsiveness in the bureaucracy. The theory of "representative bureaucracy" implies counting on civil servants who are a cross section of the general population to mirror the many values of society. The simple fact is that such conditions do not apply at the highest, most influential levels of the federal bureaucracy and are even less likely to occur at the top of each separate government bureau. Moreover, without arbitrary quota requirements it is difficult to see how all top positions in the bureaucracy could ever encompass the many dimensions of social representation, which are as varied as social life itself.[4]

There is little need here to concentrate on the demographic data about civil servants since, as noted for political executives, it is a long and tenuous route from such background characteristics to actual behavior in office. Talking with two budget officers, one of whom is from a working-class background and the other from the middle class, a researcher is likely to find more similarities than in talking with two working-class bureaucrats, one of whom is a budget officer and the other the head of a spending program. Large and immensely complex social systems that they are, government agencies have their own ways of incubating bureaucrats and particular dispositions on the job.

The term "bureaucrat" camouflages the lack of any strong group identity among federal civil servants as a whole. In a way this is not remarkable, given the astounding variety of jobs (over 2,000 different occupational categories) throughout the federal civil service. Even at the highest ranks, where bureaucrats have less specialized jobs and should presumably have more in common (commiseration and mutual protection if nothing else), there is little evidence of a common identity with anything that

---

4. This does not mean that affirmative action programs are undesirable—only that efforts to increase one dimension of demographic representativeness for a particular group of jobs will inevitably increase unrepresentativeness along other dimensions. For example, only 4.5 percent of civil service jobs GS 14 and above are filled by nonwhites, a figure far from representative since nonwhites constitute 14 percent of the population. But women, who hold only 3 percent of GS 14 and higher-grade jobs, are even more underrepresented. Yet these women in government are still less representative of the social class backgrounds of the general population than male bureaucrats are. Who, then, should have priority? Increasing representation for one combination of these dimensions (e.g., nonwhite women from poor backgrounds) will decrease it for another (nonwhite men from poor backgrounds). The various points in the debate on affirmative action and merit principles in the civil service can be traced over the last several years in the *Public Administration Review* and in Harry Kranz, *The Participating Bureaucracy* (Heath, 1976).

could be termed a governmentwide civil service. Instead, the senior officials interfacing with political appointees are usually de facto members of different civil "services," depending on their agency or professional specialty. The retired winner of a distinguished award for civil servants suggested a fundamental characteristic when he said:

> I've never thought of myself as a career civil servant. . . . Ask a civil servant who he is and you'll probably find he'll say he is an economist who works for the Treasury Department, a manager for the Housing Department and so on. What he's *not* likely to say first is that he's a civil servant.

A much younger man who had recently entered government work gave a timeless quality to the older man's words. "It's a great place to influence policy. . . . I hadn't planned on becoming a bureaucrat. I was joining the bureau, not the civil service."

Typically, effective direction over civil service careers is not located at the department level and only rarely in the major subdivisions within the department. The normal source of control over the development of career executives is centered in the bureaus and other subunits that lie below the department or agency level. In each case there is a particular culture or subculture associated with life in the bureau, and those tied together in this culture generally develop the bureaucratic leaders of the future from among their own kind. According to one personnel expert:

> The ordinary civil servant comes into government being hired by a particular person in a bureau and right away he's got a sponsor. Then he'll probably have a training program and a set of promotion possibilities laid out in the bureau and pretty soon he's walking down the hall almost as if he had a badge out in front of him saying, "I'm a Bureau X man," or "I'm a Bureau Y man."

Immobilities

It is at the bureau level that the real day-to-day management occurs over both government operations and civil service personnel. It is there that civil servants' careers are typically "tunneled through narrow organization tubes with the managers at the top husbanding and hoarding their best talent for the benefit of their part of the organization."[5] The bureau and office heads who are in effective charge of bureaucratic careers worry about homegrown talent that might become so visible as to gain

5. William A. Medina, "Factors Which Condition the Responses of Departments and Agencies to Centrally Mandated Management Improvement Approaches" (Ph.D. dissertation, American University, 1976), p. 202. See also pp. 203–04, 211–12, 217–18.

promotions elsewhere and are skeptical about outsiders from other parts of the bureaucracy who have not grown up learning about the bureaucrats' organization and its ways.

Such impressions gained in talking with higher civil servants are borne out by information on mobility, tenure, and the filling of career jobs. Since 1967 the newly created Bureau of Executive Manpower in the Civil Service Commission has gathered executive personnel data that generally confirm the findings of previous studies—any evidence of a governmentwide civil service is marginal.

Looking first at movement within the executive branch, it appears that the bulk of career executives (i.e., the supergrade group that is mainly involved in direct dealings with higher political appointees) falls into one of two patterns. In 1975 approximately two-thirds could be termed non-mobile in the sense of having always worked in the same agency since reaching grade 13 in the general schedule or its equivalent (the threshold between middle and higher ranks). On the other hand, only 12 percent of supergrade executives were generalists in that they had worked in three or more agencies since grade 13.[6] Moreover, the small minority of higher career officials who do change their organizational home can usually expect salary increases that are well below the average for all supergrades in general and the less mobile supergrades in particular.[7]

Another way to look at the immobility of bureaucratic careers in Washington is to consider how vacancies in career executive positions are filled and why they occur. Before the 1967 reforms mentioned in chapter 1 went into effect to improve the situation, the Civil Service Commission chairman complained about career immobility in these terms: "Of 1,072 classification actions covering positions in the top three grades in a recent year, 964 (90 percent) were promotions or reassignments of agency personnel. Only 19 (2 percent) were transfers from other agencies! And only 39 (4 percent) were new hires."[8] Table 4-1 shows that civil service careers remain as agency-centered as ever. Similar conclusions hold if one considers how vacancies are created. In general it remains only a little more likely

6. These are the definitions of generalist and nonmobile used in U.S. Civil Service Commission, Bureau of Executive Manpower, *Executive Manpower in the Federal Service* (GPO, 1972), table 22, p. 21. Data for 1975 are unpublished figures supplied by the Bureau of Executive Manpower.

7. Thomas E. Scism, "Employee Mobility in the Federal Service," *Public Administration Review*, vol. 34 (1974) p. 252.

8. John Macy, "Assurance of Leadership," *Civil Service Journal*, vol. 7 (October-December 1966), p. 3.

Table 4-1. *How Career Executive Positions Have Been Filled before and after 1967 Reforms*
Percent

Period	Career executive positions		
	Filled from within agency	Filled from another agency	Filled from outside government
Before 1967 reforms	90.0	2.0	4.0
1971	88.5	5.0	6.5
1972	91.5	3.7	4.8
1973	88.9	7.9	3.2
1974	92.6	3.8	3.6
1975	92.4	4.7	2.9

Source: U.S. Civil Service Commission, Bureau of Executive Manpower, *Executive Personnel in the Federal Service* (GPO, 1976), table 17, p. 17.

that an executive vacancy in the civil service will be created because the incumbent has moved to another agency (the reason for 7 percent of career executive vacancies in 1971) than because he or she has died in office (3 percent of vacancies in that year). Some officials would almost seem to prefer the latter over the former.

One study revealed that the organizational immobility of higher civil servants is roughly equivalent to a "term of office" of seventeen to twenty-five years, compared with about two years for assistant secretaries, five years for foreign service officers and, of course, eight years for a reelected President.[9] The only other participants in Washington with organizational attachments to match the higher civil servants are Supreme Court justices and seniority-rich congressmen; in 1975 House committee chairmen had an average tenure of 23 years and Senate chairmen 21 years.

Mobility between the bureaucracy and private sector is also not as great as one might expect, considering the commonly held beliefs about "in-and-outers" and about government offering an "open opportunity for all Americans to compete for all positions at all levels in the Federal civil service."[10] Only about 18 percent of the career supergrades are what the Civil Service Commission terms in-and-outers—executives who entered public service at various grade levels but left and returned one or more times to the executive branch. Even for these careerists the breadth of experience is restricted because only a minority of this minority work in

9. Eugene B. MacGregor, Jr., "Politics and Career Mobility of Civil Servants," *American Political Science Review*, vol. 68 (1974), p. 24.
10. John Macy, *The Public Service* (Harper and Row, 1971), p. 46.

more than one federal agency in the course of their in-and-out careers (i.e., internal and external mobility are not often combined). Since 1970 the Civil Service Commission has conducted a formal program to provide more opportunities for career executives to take positions in the private sector and for private executives to spend a year working in government jobs. Again, almost all civil servants return to their home agency, having been mainly interested to learn new management techniques in their own field. For the businessmen who participate, the main motivations appear to be to understand how government works and to increase the scope of their contacts. Defenders of the program point out the value of better understanding between government and the private sector. Critics suggest that it gives a further advantage to corporate enterprises, accentuating the tendency for private and public spheres to interpenetrate and develop vested interests in particular government activities.[11]

On the basis of available data, there is little reason to change the observation made by a leading analyst of the public service over three decades ago: "Historically the component parts of the federal administrative mechanism have tended to remain somewhat apart from each other. With respect to inter and often intradepartmental employment opportunities, each employee has been on his own." Experts writing in each succeeding decade have reported the same theme, namely, the absence of any governmentwide career structure for civil servants.[12]

Thus the openly competitive, in-and-out image of Washington's permanent government can be misleading. That image is due, not to mobility in the civil service itself, but to those filling exempted positions, particularly the one-half to two-thirds of noncareer executive appointments that are not filled by de facto career-type employees. (See chapter 2.) The confusing array of positions outside the competitive civil service system (presidential appointments, noncareer executive assignments, schedule Cs, and so on) does bring a large number of new people into government. Bringing in new categories of people, however, does not change the narrowness of civil service careers themselves. If there is a

---

11. For a favorable evaluation, see President's Commission on Personnel Interchange, *Evaluation of the President's Executive Interchange Program, 1970–73* (GPO, 1974), especially table 1, p. 4. A more critical approach is in David Guttman and Barry Willner, *The Shadow Government* (Pantheon Books, 1976), p. 104.

12. The quotation is from Paul Van Riper, *History of the United States Civil Service* (Row and Peterson, 1958), p. 434. For more recent but similar appraisals, see David Stanley, *The Higher Civil Service* (Brookings Institution, 1964), p. 38; and Macy, *The Public Service*, p. 44.

strategy involved in all this, it is that of the deodorizer rather than of the open window—a design for covering up rather than for refreshing the stale air inside.

Mechanics of the System

Given that circulation is rare in the bureaucratic atmosphere, how does the higher careerists' personnel system actually work? In large part it is a shadow process that does not appear in the five-foot shelf of instructions and guidance known as the *Federal Personnel Manual*. In formal outline the personnel process is threefold and simple: applicants and their qualifications; a job and its requirements; and a matching of the two through a competitive examination of the applicants' qualifications for a particular job. But despite all the references to examinations, scores, ratings, and so on, the fact is that for those seeking civil service positions at the middle level or above (i.e., GS 9–18), usually no examination in the sense of a written test is scored. Instead, the applicants' education and work experience is evaluated in a judgmental process with procedural rules that are complex and arcane to insiders as well as outsiders.

The starting point is the job. Specific qualifications required in a position are laid down by the supervisor doing the hiring, but a trained classification official in the agency or (for supergrade positions) in the Civil Service Commission will already have classified the job as having duties at a particular grade and pay level. At first it is difficult to understand the emphasis placed on the extraordinarily complicated technology of job classification in the civil service.[13] The answer lies in history. A detailed evaluation of the skills needed in a specific position were thought essential to the traditional idea of an open competition for all jobs; this in turn was bound up with the nineteenth century effort to replace political favoritism with selection based on merits. Thus in Washington's domestic bureaucracy, rank and pay are attached to a particular job, not to the civil servant.

Once a particular job has been created and classified, how do civil service procedures affect its being filled? An applicant who already has status in the competitive civil service can simply be offered the job as long as it is below the supergrade level. If for no other reason than to

13. For a detailed critique, see Jay M. Shafritz, *Position Classification: A Behavioral Analysis for the Public Service* (Praeger, 1973), pp. 13–34.

avoid the cumbersome personnel procedures, it thus becomes much easier to hire a civil servant who is already known within the agency. In cases of a supergrade position or where applicants are outside the competitive civil service, the procedures differ somewhat but the theme is the same: an intensely bureaucratized process overlaying the highly personalized realm of executive politics.

For mid- and senior-level positions (GS 9–15), an "examination" (also termed a "rating schedule" in the personnel business) is devised by a Civil Service Commission examiner in conjunction with a request from the hiring agency for a list of candidates to fill a particular job. The commission assesses the various qualifications evident on a federal job application. Job seekers are then assigned a "rating" (that is, a rating as eligible for a particular grade level in the type of job sought in the application) and are put on a register containing the names of other applicants who are rated as eligible for that grade and occupation. A competitive match-up of people and jobs occurs when the commission receives a request to fill a particular job opening. The commission examiner assigns scores to applicants on the register by comparing their qualifications with the requirements specified for that particular job. The commission then "certifies" the three highest scorers to the hiring official in the agency. It is left to his or her discretion to choose among the three, except that a veteran cannot be passed over to select a nonveteran and an applicant from a state that is overrepresented in its share of federal jobs cannot be selected ahead of an applicant from an underrepresented state.

For career supergrade positions (GS 16–18) the process is even more complex and judgmental. Figure 4-1 shows the procedure for hiring a career supergrade official. Even this account simplifies the picture by assuming that a number of preliminary steps have already been completed—that authority for a supergrade position has been obtained from the Civil Service Commission quota (or special congressional authorization), that the commission has agreed to a given job classification for the work, and that it has accepted a set of qualifications for the job. After all this has occurred, the hiring process is basically one of requiring that a number of procedural rules are followed so as to search for candidates both inside the hiring agency and in other agencies, with an optional process for looking outside government.

Experienced bureaucrats recognize that the system operates far less automatically than it might seem to from the preceding formal outlines. The personal factor in personnel inevitably intervenes in a multitude of

Figure 4-1. *Procedures for Hiring a Career Executive*

HIRING AGENCY	CIVIL SERVICE COMMISSION
identifies job vacancy	
conducts internal search in accord with its merit promotion plan	approves each agency's merit promotion plan
prepares list of internal candidates / submits requirements for governmentwide search of Executive Inventory	approves requirements or, if requested by agency, can waive agency's obligation to search Executive Inventory
	"spins" Executive Inventory and prepares list of those meeting agency requirements
	if list is too long, cuts it by comparing mandatory versus desirable requirements for the job
evaluates names on internal and Executive Inventory lists, with additional option to conduct search outside government	
prepares plan for outside search	requires that any outside search follow procedures for an openly competitive examination of merit qualifications and cover all places applicants are likely to be found
constructs procedure to rate and rank applicants on their merits and in accord with veteran's preference requirements	
	approves rating and ranking plan in advance of any evaluations
compiles applications in accord with all preceding procedures	conducts "examination" on basis of job application, evaluates ranking, and certifies three highest scorers to agency
picks candidate from internal list, Executive Inventory list, or optional outside search list's top three	approves agency's selection after receiving all documentation, or can disapprove any qualified candidate if improper procedures have been followed

ways.[14] Three of the most common are in the areas of referrals for special attention, personalized recruitment, and preferential evaluations.

REFERRALS

In or out of government, people have a habit of tagging each other for special attention. This happens throughout civil service personnel work for both legitimate and illegitimate reasons. Often only a fine line separates a personnel action that is expedited to provide more effective management from one that uses preferential treatment as a means to curry favor. In either case personnel officials are in a position to treat something or someone as nonroutine. The paperwork moves faster; an otherwise worrisome hiring is facilitated. Usually it is not a question of one powerful figure coercing a weaker one to take action against the latter's will, but of people exchanging help with the procedures and thus making each other's lives a little easier. One of the most common operations is the sending and receipt of referrals for civil service jobs.

Personal referrals for federal career jobs are a legal, generally accepted part of the career personnel process, and they may or may not take on the politicizing overtones described in chapter 2. Political appointees, pressure groups, congressmen, other bureaucrats—in fact any citizen with knowledge of whom to contact—can recommend a job seeker to the attention of any government official. The *only* restrictions that apply are not on those doing the referring but on the examining and appointing officials. Since 1883 all executive branch officials with authority to take or recommend civil service personnel actions have been under presidential order (1) not to inquire into the political affiliations of job applicants, (2) to ignore such information if it is disclosed to them, and (3) to make civil service appointments only on the basis of merit and fitness without regard to political affiliation. In addition they cannot legally "receive or consider a recommendation of the applicant by a Senator or Representative, except as to the character or residence of the applicant."[15] In short,

14. A large number of examples involving the Civil Service Commission and others are documented in A *Self-Inquiry into Merit Staffing,* Report of the Merit Staffing Review Team, U.S. Civil Service Commission, for the House Committee on Post Office and Civil Service, Committee Print 94-14, 94 Cong. 2 sess. (GPO, 1976); and in *Final Report on Violations and Abuses of Merit Principles in Federal Employment Together with Minority Views,* Subcommittee on Manpower and Civil Service of the House Committee on Post Office and Civil Service, Committee Print 94-28, 94 Cong. 2 sess. (GPO, 1976), pp. 1–138.

15. 5 U.S.C. 3303. See also Civil Service Rules 4.2 and 7.1 of 5 U.S.C. 3301.

the entire responsibility for abiding by civil service rules is placed on those inside the system; it is not shared with outsiders who might seek preferential treatment.

Particularly for congressmen, inquiries about civil service jobs—up to 72,000 in a recent year—can be a valued link to constituents, even if it normally amounts to little more than the service of a public information bureau. But in practice congressmen can expect hiring agencies to do more than gratefully acknowledge their public information service. A congressman who writes a letter attesting to a job-seeker's character (and residence), according to Civil Service Commission officials, is entitled to a reply from the hiring agency, to a list of other positions for which the applicant might be qualified, and to the courtesy of an interview for the constituent.[16] Some hiring officials may understandably interpret such attention to job-seekers as going beyond the provision of neutral information, particularly if a sensitive position is involved or if the congressman has important leverage over the agency's budget and legislation.

Civil service procedures become similarly personalized by requests for special attention from political appointees or bureaucrats in the executive branch. To take a recent example (unusual only in that it is now part of the public record), between 1968 and 1974 the three Civil Service commissioners made at least thirty-five personal referrals to agencies on behalf of specific individuals seeking career jobs. In other cases the nonroutine interventions were more subtle, with a variety of commission officials involved in tagging some people for preferential treatment.[17] Of course, in all these instances it was the responsibility of the appointing officer in the agency to treat these and other applicants the same, whether they were commended by the chairman of the Civil Service Commission or the man on the street.

16. *Violations and Abuses of Merit Principles in Federal Employment*, Hearings before the Subcommittee on Manpower and Civil Service of the House Committee on Post Office and Civil Service, 94 Cong. 1 sess. (GPO, 1975), pt. 1, pp. 29–30.

17. See *Final Report on Violations and Abuses*, pp. 6 ff. The commissioners denied that there was anything improper in such referrals. Nevertheless, following publicity about the referrals in 1974, the same commissioners concluded that the propriety of such special actions might be "misunderstood" and adopted a new standard of conduct prohibiting commission officers and employees from making referrals or recommendations for job applicants "unless requested by an agency, or specifically part of his or her official duties." (U.S. Civil Service Commission, Employee letter A-375, January 31, 1975.)

PERSONALIZED RECRUITMENT

Outside referrals are only the most obvious and far from the most significant means of trying to personalize a supposedly automatic process of open competition and ranking of objective qualifications. Filling four-fifths of the 1,200 senior-level career vacancies each year has normally involved "name requests" by the hiring agency. This means that the Civil Service Commission, in preparing its lists of eligibles meeting the particular specifications of a job, is asked by the selecting official to certify a given individual as among those best qualified. At times, a chain of circumstances may suggest direct evidence of political intrusions—an outside referral, a name request for the same person, a highly specialized job description, and subsequently leaving the job unfilled if the name request is not certified.

Usually, however, more subtle questions of interpretation and motivation are involved. A name request combined with detailed job requirements laid down by the supervisor (so-called job tailoring) can mean that virtual preselection has occurred before any possibility of general competition could arise.[18] But a name request may also reflect the reality of how good people are found for high-level jobs. Traditional party spoils can undoubtedly be prevented by following anonymous procedures to process job applicants. However, to find high-caliber people for important bureaucratic jobs often requires a talent hunt, partly because such people are unlikely to be looking for jobs and filing applications and partly because capable professionals enter the job market by putting the word out among fellow professionals. Any efforts at active recruitment are likely to lead to name requests.

Thus there is often a fine line in the personnel process between helping a supervisor get the particular person he feels is needed and abusing the spirit of the civil service law with personal cronyism that is far more difficult to prove than political patronage. An experienced personnel director described how the doctrine of open competition for all jobs becomes diluted in practice.

18. Because of what were viewed as persisting abuses in this area, the Civil Service Commission in 1974 established new rules to restrict name requests and to require supervisors to certify personally that job descriptions accurately portray the duties to be performed. The commission's aim, as the chairman expressed it, was "to put somebody's neck on the line." *Violations and Abuses of Merit Principles*, Hearings, pt. 1, p. 69.

Managers and professionals tend to figure they can tell who is qualified for a job better than the civil service system. You can find you're working the system backwards, from the guy the manager wants to the job description to get him. I suppose I'm guilty of several hundred violations. It's not that you're putting unqualified people in, but neither is it quite the full, open competition required by the rules. . . . Go too far and you'll get into trouble because you don't necessarily know when, instead of an agency manager, some White House type or congressional administrative aide has slipped a name in. Then when it comes down to you it might seem like just the name of another guy the agency manager wants to hire, but it's actually a political hire.

EVALUATIONS

Finally, examinations to determine and rate qualifications for higher-level civil service positions are subject to various prejudices. In rating education and work experience outlined on job applications, commission examiners are compelled to make difficult, judgmental decisions with meager, second-hand information about both the candidate and the job. Yet such applications for mid- and senior-level jobs are assigned precise numerical scores and the three top-ranking candidates are certified to the agency for hiring. Typically, the sole source of information to be evaluated is the Personal Qualifications Statement, better known in the bureaucracy as form SF-171. Those who already know or are coached to use the right words and emphases in describing their experiences can go far in determining how their application will be evaluated by a harried examiner in the commission; others who do not know these folkways are at a disadvantage.[19]

Nongeneralist bureaucratic insiders have additional advantages in getting jobs. Despite all the civil service procedures, any evaluation of career personnel remains heavily dependent on the bureau's or agency's definition of what constitutes a civil service career. For outsiders trying to enter the higher career levels, "the thrust of the rating schedules . . . is on the specialized experience of the individuals."[20] Those already at work within an agency's specialized area are likely to have an advantage in gaining the particular experience in question, and the government careers of those selecting among the certified eligibles will also usually have fol-

19. A Self-Inquiry into Merit Staffing, p. 17. For GS 15 positions, the commission in 1975 began supplementing information on the SF-171 with questionnaires that are worked out between the agency and the commission and then sent to applicants before the examiner prepares a rating schedule.

20. Violations and Abuses of Merit Principles, Hearings, pt. 1, p. 127.

lowed the same specialized interests. For those who are already in the civil service and who are seeking positions up to the supergrade level, there is no requirement for the agency to look outside its own boundaries for hiring and advancing employees. The only outside evaluation will be a periodic inspection by the Civil Service Commission to see that procedures have been followed to provide a fair competition for jobs within the organization.

For all career supergrade positions there is, of course, the requirement for a search in other agencies, but few hiring officials depend very much on the lists provided from the commission's Executive Inventory. Any information provided by the commission is too sparse to count on in choosing people for important career jobs. The real evaluation process occurs by word-of-mouth among people who know each other, and such knowledge is naturally most likely among people within the same agency or subject area. What the commission evaluates is not people but whether or not a procedure has been followed. A seasoned bureaucrat with experience in the commission and several agencies accurately described the way things work:

> Executive searches through the inventory and so on may help a little, but your own man is always likely to come out a little bit ahead. There's no magic in the civil service procedures. Especially, there's nothing in them offering a straight-up evaluation of the man's strengths and weaknesses. For that, everybody trusts his own judgment above all. So the first place you look is to the workmates you've had with you. . . . If that doesn't work out, you'll call up someone you know and ask for suggestions. Then you'll check out the names with other people you trust.

None of the personalized referrals, recruitments, or evaluations mean that espousal of the merit system and the idea of civil service is empty rhetoric. It does mean that there is an inherent impracticality in the traditional mythology of an open opportunity for all Americans to compete for any civil service job. This is particularly true at the higher levels of the bureaucracy, where performance is almost impossible to measure and personal readings on people are all-pervasive. The rules and regulations of the competitive civil service do not, as some of their custodians like to suggest, constitute an impersonal system operating untouched by human hands, and those best able to lay their hands on it are those already operating from within. Given the extraordinary complexity of the rules, less experienced hands can quickly run into trouble from a Civil Service Commission jealous of its prerogatives. A personnel officer reflected on the recent case of a political executive who retired after having been charged with violating civil service regulations: "The trouble [with the appointee] wasn't that the people he wanted were unqualified but that he tried to ram it through and buck instead of use the established system. With patience he could have gotten everything he wanted."

Wider Horizons

The picture of a higher civil service based on agency career ladders needs to be filled in by three supplementary features: self-contained networks among bureaucrats in different agencies, occasional pockets of more mobile career development found in scattered parts of the executive branch, and non–civil service outlets for those at the top of their particular agency ladders. Considering these features as a whole, the senior officials' personnel system might be described as a system of parochialism tempered by accident.

NETWORKS

Some of the personnel networks that cross government bureaus are a function of what academics have termed the professionalization of the civil service.[21] Significantly, this is a phrase used to identify professionals who happen to find themselves in the civil service rather than a development toward the civil service as a profession. Horizontal contacts exist both informally and through organized associations among people identified with particular technical specialties—statisticians, economists, public works engineers, and a host of others. Members of these groups have a shared need to protect their professional perquisites and standards. Indeed their common identity as professional specialists goes far in defining what in fact are the standards appropriate to their work in government. Thus, for example, a study of an agency's failure to implement presidential orders may have reflected adversely on that agency, but to a man within it who regards himself as "a professional management analyst," the catalogue of "delays and mixed signals didn't reflect badly" on him and his peers. "That's what we're supposed to find out about," he said.

Bureau chiefs and other program supervisors do not often need each other because they usually operate under different statutes with their own distinct constellations of constituents, pressure groups, and con-

21. Frederick C. Mosher, *Democracy and the Public Service* (Oxford University Press, 1968), pp. 110–33.

gressional committees.[22] Cross-agency networks, however, do frequently develop among officials who have similar staff positions in different bureaus (e.g., budget controllers, personnel experts, public information officers, accountants, and so on). At the base of their common identity is a custodianship over procedures that cut across many different agencies. Mobility is therefore somewhat more feasible for those in staff positions. Even if they do not move, staff bureaucrats have an incentive to get together because the procedures under their control are the one thing that central agencies (Office of Management and Budget, Civil Service Commission, General Services Administration) are constantly trying to coordinate. Staff work actually is one of the few common denominators in the bureaucracy that facilitates some movement between the particular departments and the central agencies with a governmentwide (or sometimes even a presidential) perspective. But career development is also arranged on a hit-and-miss basis, and staff bureaucrats are likely to have at least as much interest in ganging up to resist central coordination as they are in using their staff expertise to lessen departmental parochialism.

A vast number of other networks depend less on professional or staff identifications and more on particular individuals who see advantages in building and using personal contacts elsewhere in the bureaucracy. These idiosyncratic networks are apt to include people frequently drawn into interdepartmental committee work, analysts trying to forecast outsiders' reactions or hoping to learn what "really" lies behind the formal memoranda from another agency, and many other varieties of bureaucrat. Like political appointees, these officials will feel a strategic need to look outside the village life of their particular agency. The difference is that the bureaucratic network-builders, unlike political appointees, can expect to be around much longer and to establish contacts on a more stable and slowly evolving basis. The comment of one thirty-year Washington veteran about his "people to people relationships" in the bureaucracy can stand for many of its kind:

> I need to be accepted over there [in another agency]. You have to go out, get introduced if necessary, so you know these people by name and who to contact. You need both the program and the budget people over there in order to get both sides of things. . . . Over the years it builds up. I joined this agency with Williams as my boss, and he had known his counterpart Miller over there, so we got used to dealing with each other with a lot of

22. Bureau chiefs do, of course, use intra-agency networks to meet their informational needs. For examples, see Herbert Kaufman, *Administrative Feedback* (Brookings Institution, 1973), pp. 33–37.

continuity—in fact from 1947 to 1960. Then both Williams and Miller left and I moved up, but so did Miller's legislative counsel, so there was no problem. . . . Later you had the new deputy secretary who I knew from the Truman and Eisenhower years. Then with Johnson there was the new secretary and comptroller, who I didn't know, but their chief aide was Hudson who I'd known since he was a GS 12. . . . Experience is a big help in this job.

POCKETS

The networks across agencies are complemented by intra-agency pockets of broader career patterns. As noted in chapter 1, a few officials in the Civil Service Commission and Office of Management and Budget have recently tried to encourage more mobile executive development. To date, the commitment of personnel and resources to these efforts has been meager. Moreover, as also noted earlier, the ambitious initial experiment with a governmentwide career development program has retreated to a strategy of encouraging the traditional power centers—the bureaus—to launch internal programs to develop executive talent for their own use.

As a result, any effort to identify promising executive talent and to plan broadening assignments for bureaucratic leaders of the future is haphazard and depends on the particular official in charge. One official who made the effort said, "I learned from my boss that if you're in charge you've got a responsibility to the organization to get good young people, give them as much responsibility as they can handle, and stretch them with assignments outside their usual field." Following political scandals, the Internal Revenue Service in the 1950s created one of the most effective programs to develop career executives; other agencies with a strong collective identity have done the same—for example, the National Park Service, U.S. Geological Survey, Soil Conservation Service, and Federal Aviation Administration, among others. But these programs are agency-centered, and in the domestic field only the Department of Transportation has anything approaching a departmentwide approach to planning civil service careers. Even here, where some success has been achieved in broadening career patterns, there is no mistaking the narrow interpretation of what is meant by a civil service career. As one of the officials in charge of the Transportation Department's program put it:

We train our own people so they have to serve in every section of the department. You can say this substitutes departmental for bureau parochialism . . . but I'm not training people to go to Health, Education, and Welfare or any other place. What interests me is this department.

The present personnel system does not preclude rapid advancement for some younger civil servants. Quite the contrary. When an agency is adding new duties or when it experiences rapid turnover in higher positions, the fact that rank is attached to a job and not the man means that younger specialists can advance quickly by moving into high-ranking jobs. Over two-fifths (44 percent) of civil service executives had attained their first supergrade position before they reached 45 years of age.[23] The point is that those who do advance quickly in the U.S. civil service can easily find that they have run up against the hazy ceiling dividing civil service and political appointments and that there is little chance to cross to the top of other agency ladders. One of the most widely respected and fastest risers in recent years described the decision facing such a bureaucrat:

> I was reluctant to take it [a political appointment], because it means I'll go when the administration goes, and I can't imagine anything in private business as interesting as government work. But when George Shultz offered me this job I looked at myself and at the people around here who had stayed on for a long time. At my age [38] I was at the top of my career. I had no place else to go.

Another department's personnel officer suggested why such dilemmas should be expected by young bureaucrats who "peak" early. "It is not unusual now to find a young supergrade in his late thirties or early forties who's gotten to the top of a GS 16 or 17. He's capped off his salary and in a way his career too. The question is where do they go for the next decade or so before retirement?"

OUTLETS

Obviously, there are outlets available in the growing congressional bureaucracy and in the particular interest groups operating close to the official's agency. As noted in chapter 1, within the executive branch a large number of political appointments are important sources of jobs for career bureaucrats. One-third to one-half of the 600 noncareer supergrade posts and anywhere from one-fifth to two-fifths of the higher political appointments are usually filled by career civil servants. That these outlets exist and are being used suggests mute acceptance of a significant role for bureaucrats in the higher reaches of the U.S. government.

For young bureaucrats confident of their own abilities, the insecure tenure may make little difference; for retiring civil servants with their government pensions assured, there may even be some advantage in a

23. *Executive Manpower in the Federal Service* (1972), table 16b, p. 17.

boost in retirement pay that is associated with the higher salaries of political executives. Yet it can hardly be called a strength of the bureaucratic personnel system that the price of mobility and challenge in government service is permanent exit from the civil service. The blunt fact is that officials who move into political appointments must accept the political reality that they are unlikely ever to return to a civil service job. One of the few who did move from career, to political, to career posts offered a fundamental lesson from his experience.

> It's not something that I can recommend. Your credentials are always doubtful, both to civil service associates you rejoin and the political types in the department. I always felt as if I wasn't quite trusted. There's also something of the feeling that you're coming back at a lower level, with diminished prestige. . . . The result is that to compensate for the suspicion you become too eager to please. There are a couple of instances where I now feel ashamed I didn't make a bigger fight.

For ambitious officials who want to remain civil servants and who do not happen to find themselves in a pocket of career development, what is the answer? Clearly there is little institutionalized help available when they want or need to move. The answer, once again, lies in the personalized networks that honeycomb the bureaucracy. The small minority of generalist civil servants who are mobile at the highest levels report essentially the same three features in their career patterns: far-flung personal contacts, a good reputation established within this network, and a large element of luck. Governmentwide career moves usually are worked out informally on a hit-and-miss basis by those who already know each other. Careerists in staff positions may be somewhat less constricted than line managers who have grown up with their programs, but even staff bureaucrats recognize the semifortuitous basis of their maneuverability. One imminent retiree described how there was "no systematic way of looking for other jobs" but added that

> being displaced in one place has helped me elsewhere. Troubles in the State Department made me look acceptable at Interior and later, when the new administration didn't want me there, there were people in Treasury who respected my work and so I ended up a director there. The ability to move and land on your feet depends mostly on who you know and your reputation, and happening to be in the right place at the right time.

A much younger bureaucrat who had just begun his career was drawing the same lessons early:

> There is a fraternity of people around in this field and you know you're going to have to continue dealing with each other. Reputation counts.

There are career people who can get a GS 15 or a supergrade slotted in with fifteen minutes of phone calls. So what they hear of me matters.

Obviously no generalized configuration can capture all the personalized relations that go to make up the higher civil service personnel system. What is generalizable is the lack of relationship among configurations—the fact that agency ladders, horizontal networks, and outlets often are self-contained components. The chemistry of the higher civil service is that of a mixture rather than a compound. However comingled they may appear organizationally, officials retain separate identities that are derived from the characteristics of particular subgroups and not from being part of a government—or event departmentwide—civil service. The very diversity of this mixture can be an important resource for political leadership. But political executives seeking to use it will have to look more for an amalgamation of ingredients than for spontaneous fusion into one loyal team.

Job Protection

Civil service arrangements are intended to provide protection as well as to fill jobs. How does the career personnel system function in this second area of responsibility and how much protection from political and personal influences should be provided?

Obviously answers to such questions are bound to differ depending on the time and circumstances. It does seem clear, however, that throughout the mass of civil service positions, outright job grabs by political parties have been greatly constrained in the federal government. Not only has the Civil Service Commission maintained its traditional interest in preventing massive patronage raids, but so too have the growing unions that represent middle- and lower-level federal employees. Writing merit principles into contracts can serve as a means of job protection, providing relatively open competition at entry into the civil service and a closed shop at the time of subsequent promotion. Congress also has shown itself particularly attentive to issues that concern the rank and file federal employees who constitute a large constituency with many union ties.

The protection of the higher civil servants dealt with in this book is another matter. Identified as they are with "management," these supergrade officials have little prospect of unionization, and the nature of their work is poorly suited to routine civil service procedures that rely on clear job classifications, unambiguous examinations, and the measurement of ability.[24] Since they operate at the extraordinarily difficult level where administration and policy and technical and personal judgments shade into each other, it seems reasonable that higher civil servants should face a more risky situation in the sense of being held closely accountable for their advice, judgments, and standards of behavior. Yet this ought not to imply an absence of any protection for such careerists. If the values of the civil service as a continuous resource for use by political leaders are to be maintained, an official's status as a civil servant would seem to deserve some protection, although not his hold on a given job.

In practice present arrangements emphasize just the opposite: top bureaucrats find it much easier to protect any specialized position than to safeguard their general standing as civil servants. Insofar as they cannot or will not defend their claim to the job that gives them their particular rank and pay, higher civil servants are thrown upon the casual networks described earlier for maintaining their government careers. For a number of reasons the individualized protections offered by congressmen, political executives, and the Civil Service Commission do not add up to protection of a career system for higher civil servants in Washington.

Protection at a Price

In its role as a protective check, Congress faces the inherent problem of being a collection of individuals and interests rather than a collective decisionmaker. Unless there is conscious discipline to the contrary, personnel matters, like budget matters, are likely to be handled on an item-by-item basis. Normally, a congressman's protective interests are dependent on the liaison between him and those bureaucrats operating within his areas of particular interest. Many civil servants have ample opportunity over the years to acquire such security, but never without a price. One supergrade described his move out of the Civil Service Commission to accept a major operating post elsewhere:

> My predecessor was very well wired [with the chairman of an appropriation subcommittee]. Several cabinet secretaries had wanted to remove him, but they were chopped down in the House, and eventually he just died in office. . . . When I came in, [the congressman] had hopes of establishing the same relations. He'd call and say, "What's wrong with those division directors? All I wanted was this or that. Why don't you get those guys off their butts?"

24. Macy, *The Public Service*, p. 221.

You see, he was giving me a chance to buy in with him. I was supposed to say, "Look, Mr. Chairman, you bring those issues to me, not them; I'll take care of you." It could have been very cozy. People here in the agency would know that if I didn't approve, Congress wouldn't, and he'd get his views reflected here and not look bad by having to make tough decisions in public.

Just as the executive branch has grown and become more differentiated, so the structure of Congress itself has contributed to further fragmentation in the consideration given to the higher civil service. Since the 1949 Classification Act, the respective Post Office and Civil Service committees of the two houses have gradually ceased to exercise general control over the distribution of supergrade positions, and increasingly the requirements for personnel have been written into the agencies' legislation by other committees. Agencies facing personnel difficulties recognize that it will be the budget and legislative committees that make the important decisions. Once involved in individual personnel questions, these committees and their staffs usually maintain a continuing interest, but only with regard to what happens within their special areas and not to the civil service as a whole.

As noted in the first chapter, those exceptional periods of congressional concern for the general career system arise sporadically and are usually triggered by larger antagonisms between President and Congress. This seems to have been the case, for example, in the Roosevelt, Eisenhower, and Nixon administrations. But such broader congressional attention has also often been too late and unsustained to provide continuous oversight, and Congress has never responded favorably to the many calls for basic reform in executive personnel management. Not surprisingly, the legislature's interest has lain in improving congressional rather than executive influence over bureaucratic behavior.

Political executives also play an important role in protecting higher civil servants from partisan abuses. This fact is not as paradoxical as it sounds, and the Nixon administration provided an instructive vignette. White House efforts to politicize the bureaucracy, particularly in the General Services Administration, the Department of Housing and Urban Development, and the Small Business Administration, during the Nixon years have been well publicized. Less attention has been given to what actually occurred in departments where political abuses were not as flagrant. In general, the success of political referral units and "must hire" directives varied inversely with the will of political executives receiving them to stand up for their prerogatives, which meant protecting their own agency's personnel procedures. The following comment of an assistant secretary gives some flavor of the political forces that were at work in many different departments:

> I never took any of the people that it [the White House personnel office] was trying to push on the department. I resisted simply by screaming like hell, complaining that it was going to foul up the agenda we'd agreed upon. Now if there were some old war horse the administration didn't want to throw out on the street, I would have followed orders and placed him if the President himself wanted it. But this was a bunch of crumby political advance men talking to each other. Eventually they just decided there was no point coming to me; I was more trouble than it was worth.

Relying on political executives in the departments for protection or improvements in the civil service system has serious weaknesses, however. The most obvious one is that political executives often lack the will or experience to stand up for their prerogatives in this way. But there are other more inherent limitations. Political appointees are rarely around long enough to offer sustained protection. Moreover, their main interest often is to achieve short-term goals for which they can take credit rather than to worry about the longer-term development of civil service careers. Above all, political executives, like Congress, focus their protective role, not on the career system as such, but on particular bureaucrats and positions.

Individuals protecting their agency prerogatives do not add up to general protection of a career system for one reason that all experienced bureaucrats recognize. The very fact of being protected by a particular political executive (or congressman) can itself become a mark of political vulnerability in Washington. A supergrade who was eventually forced out recalled:

> My staff and I spent a lot of time in the [presidential] transition period preparing briefings to tell new appointees what they needed to know about the department and programs. I made it clear to all my people they were to offer every ounce of possible cooperation. None of this helped me with the new appointees because they knew that [a secretary in a previous administration] had gone to bat for me when I'd helped him on some controversial things.

Protection by the Book

Whatever the informal role of Congress or political executives in the agencies, the Civil Service Commission is assumed to have the main responsibility for protecting the principles of appointment to public service on the basis of nonpartisan merit. The tools for carrying out this responsibility have changed in emphasis over time. During much of its history the commission has relied mainly on the collective structure of its leadership and its procedures to guard the "front door" with examinations for entry into the civil service. The original idea was that three commissioners (one a minority member of a different party) could not only watch each other but use their divided authority to fend off partisan influences. When necessary, each commissioner could resist political pressures rather than refuse them outright by citing a "militant colleague" who would object and insist on putting all the adverse facts into the public record.[25] As party identification has become less important in the postwar years, protection offered by the commission's leadership structure has diminished. One career executive who worked with commissioners over several administrations described how

> the conflicts, when they occur, generally haven't divided commissioners by party. The minority commissioner might have been intended as a watchdog but this hasn't developed in practice. Not since the days of Arthur Flemming have they viewed themselves as watchdogs to be vigilant against abuses by the party in power. . . . Each administration tends to look for a "safe" minority member. . . . The procedures are pretty collegial. Everyone is a little bit too worried about offending everyone else.

The main tools for carrying out the commission's protective responsibility are now contained in its vast system of rules and regulations. These procedural safeguards have increasingly come to apply not only to "front door" admission to the civil service, but also to the "back door" by which bureaucrats are relieved of duties. Taken as a whole the current procedures add up to a formidable body of protections for those knowledgeable in their use. The procedures, however, are aimed at protecting the individual employee's right to a particular job and not the career service as a system. And this is a natural, since it is a particular position, not the person, that carries the rank. In an operational sense an official who is not appended to a particular job is not a civil servant but a "rated eligible."

Current protections-by-the-book attempt to offer a legal redress of individual wrongs and to establish evidence of personal fault in those charged with wrongdoing. The focus of attention is not on the final quality of a career appointment. Instead, the commission is mainly concerned with whether proper procedures have been followed. Hence everyone

25. Lewis Meriam, *Public Personnel Problems* (Brookings Institution, 1938), pp. 359–61.

in personnel work has a self-interest in becoming preoccupied with procedures. It is not just that protection depends on procedural rectitude, however, but that in the legalistic sense there also has to be an individual victim who complains. This overriding legal casework approach to protecting the civil service is reflected in a number of ways. For example, for special Civil Service Commission investigations to occur, general information and suspicion have not been regarded as sufficient; complainants have had to provide a specific allegation backed by a signed and sworn affidavit. To critics of the commission, this formality often seems an excuse for not vigorously investigating and exposing misdeeds in cases that are politically sensitive, especially to the White House, department heads, and the commissioners themselves. The commission's rationale, on the other hand, has been that by acting only on specific allegations, frivolous charges are discouraged and investigative sources conserved in dealing with the 3,000 inspectable units of the federal government.

The result is often a series of Catch-22 situations, where hard evidence is required to trigger an investigation and where hard evidence is unlikely to develop until there is an investigation. In this system any individual grievance against blatant favoritism is apt to occupy attention while informal, pervasive manipulations of the personnel system are apt to be overlooked, since these almost by definition will not produce clear cases of persons who have been wronged. If the competitive procedures are not followed, commission officials acknowledge that often there is little alternative but to leave well enough alone. This is true, for example, when there is no competition and therefore no "victim" to claim redress, or when the person appointed cannot be shown to have conspired in gaining preferential treatment.[26]

Moreover, the Civil Service commissioners are not in a position to act on or enforce the formal theory that the political department heads are responsible for any abuses of the civil service system that might occur in their agencies. Even though such a head may preside over patronage rings, offer little help to commission investigators and, in the face of information to the contrary, deny there are serious problems, these high political levels are not a place where the commission is likely to develop "hard evidence" to support specific charges.[27] Even if it did, Civil Service commissioners (like other agency heads) are presidential appointees and

26. *Violations and Abuses of Merit Principles*, Hearings, pt. 1, p. 13. Commission requirements for specific allegations are discussed on pp. 75–76, 133.

27. Ibid., pp. 109, 138.

can do little more than refer these matters for such action against top political executives as the President may care to take. Added to all this is the previously described tradition of tolerance for informal manipulation of civil service procedures in both Democratic and Republican administrations.

From 1969 to 1973 all these limitations of the commission combined to render it ineffective in safeguarding the higher civil service from the strategic and systematic attempts at politicization described in an earlier chapter. Waiting for specific evidence and affidavits to be brought to it before investigating general charges, the commission was in no position to prevent abuses from escalating. The commission paid its customary attention to a case-by-case redress of individual grievances and was therefore unlikely to perceive the systematic, if victimless, abuses of the career system as a whole. Issuing their own personal referrals and participating in other manipulations for preferential treatment, Civil Service commissioners in the administrations of both parties had already contributed to the climate of acceptance that could facilitate subsequent Nixon efforts. Atop all of this was a White House bureaucracy that not only failed to support protective efforts but expected the same team loyalty from Civil Service commissioners as from other presidential appointees.

Consequently the Civil Service Commission only belatedly, in 1973, began investigating the first specific allegation supported by affidavits. One employee later credited by the commission with giving a key affidavit said of his role in the case:

> I wasn't even working in the department, but I could see what was going on and could give a couple of names. The commission people were very reluctant to get involved because it wasn't a specific enough case. Hell, I don't see why if the commission is there doing inspections it should take someone like me to start the thing rolling.

Even the commission's corrective efforts at the end of the Nixon administration, however, revealed the weaknesses of its legalistic approach to protecting the general civil service system. Finding the charges of politicizing to be supported, the commission in 1974 made exceptional attempts to dismiss or suspend nineteen employees in three departments who were charged with breaking civil service rules. Since there was no hard evidence against the relevant agency heads in these departments, they went untouched. Historically, the commission's primary disciplinary power has always rested in its authority to direct political agency heads

to take corrective action and to expose to the President and the public
the failure of those who did not. Instead of taking this route in 1974,
the commission tried to take direct disciplinary action against middle-
and lower-level employees. After two years of litigation all nineteen cases
were dismissed or dropped in the administrative law courts as being outside the bounds of the commission's proper authority.[28] Legally, the commission had gone after the wrong people in invoking its authority; politically, it had avoided going after the higher appointing officers who were
politically, if not legally, responsible for what was happening in their organizations. In the end no penalties were imposed on anyone for the many
abuses of the civil service system during the Nixon era.

The overall result of present arrangements is that each of two commonly cited and seemingly contradictory complaints about civil service
protections contain an element of truth. On the one hand are the familiar
grumblings from government managers about rigid civil service procedures for moving and changing personnel under them. Conventional wis-
dom notwithstanding, it clearly is *not* impossible to fire and move civil
servants.[29] But to do so takes time and is not a job for amateurs who lack
the knowledge or determination to use the complicated procedures. On
the other hand lamentations are heard about the vulnerability of merit
principles to political manipulation, a complaint intensified by experiences during the Nixon administration.

These two complaints about inflexibility and manipulation actually
are more complementary than contradictory. Both problems are inherent
in the incentives of the civil service system. Procedural inflexibilities are
derived from the protection of employee rights to particular jobs. Bureaucrats who are so inclined can insist on legalistic, procedural requirements
that can go far to frustrate the political executives' legitimate desires for
change. As one high-ranking civil servant observed of his own case:

> People are too locked into jobs. Look at me, a veteran with thirty years of
> service. It would be very difficult to get rid of me here against my will. With

28. The basic problem with the commission's case was that it used civil service
rule 7.1 (5 U.S.C. 3301), which grants the commission power to instruct appointing
officers in the agency to undertake disciplinary action. For a discussion of these events,
see articles by Robert H. Huddleston in the *Federal Times*, March 1, 1976, p. 12; and
March 8, 1976, p. 12; and *Final Report on Violations and Abuses*, pp. 119–39.

29. The Defense Manpower Commission explored these complaints in some
detail and concluded they were unfounded. See its report, *Defense Manpower* (GPO,
1976), pp. 236–37; and the related staff paper by Howard W. Goheen, "Limitations on Managers Brought about by Restrictions of the Federal Service System (prepared for the Defense Manpower Commission, September 1975; processed).

what I know about the system I could tie them up for years. I could be downright dangerous to people.

Many higher civil servants, however, do not seek to cling to particular jobs at all costs. If the greatest protections apply to those who wish to stay in particular jobs (especially at the middle and lower levels), the greatest vulnerability is associated with those who try to follow the norms of a professional civil servant—who move on when they are not wanted by a political superior and who do not seek to ingratiate themselves or cultivate outside forces of political support. For these higher civil servants no governmentwide personnel system underwrites the risks of mobility or safeguards their career status. There are few places to look for protection except through their reputations and individual networks. But as efforts to politicize the bureaucracy have grown, there may also be less willingness to trust careers to this fate. A former Civil Service Commission employee said that

> the conventional wisdom is that when you get to these high-career levels you get some good communications going with one or two senators or someone else you might have to depend on later. This was less true in former times. Older careerists seemed to feel less need for protection. There was more of a feeling in currency that these guys had some personal worth on their own. They didn't need to have a patron.

The perverse result is a kind of Gresham's law in moving bureaucratic personnel. It is relatively easy for political executives to get rid of an ethical official who is seriously committed to the idea of a civil service career and almost impossible to move a deficient bureaucrat who allies himself with outside political forces and uses the technicalities of the rank-in-job personnel system.

Whatever else might be said about the desirable amount and scope of civil service protections, it seems clear that most of the safeguards against political abuses rest with the bureaucrats' own efforts. Self-defense may take the form of delays or stringing out the red tape of personnel procedures. It can and probably will involve contacts built up through long participation in particular networks. A few will issue formal complaints to the Civil Service Commission. But as one leading "whistle blower" who went to the commission acknowledged, "In theory my informants should have risked income, position, and their career future by coming to the commission too, but it's unrealistic to expect people in the agencies to do that. They're more interested in their programs than the civil service." The important point is that however higher bureaucrats protect themselves, they will do so as individuals, not as leading representatives of "the" civil service.

The various and powerful means of self-protection are insufficient to protect any general concept of public service careers. The reason is that the ways officials protect their individual positions from political abuse are also the ways they can frustrate the legitimate claims of political leaders for bureaucratic responsiveness. Responsible career executives are the one group who are least protected by the prevailing arrangements in Washington.

Bureaucratic Dispositions

By now it should be clear that one of the worst mistakes political leaders can make is to imagine that all bureaucrats are the same. If nothing else, the unsystematic, individualized approaches to career development and protection mean that higher officials have scope for a variety of approaches but few shared models of what a supergrade official is "supposed" to be. After twenty years as one of the highest-ranking bureaucrats and as a Civil Service commissioner, one man summed up the situation by saying that "civil servants don't really have mutual bonds or images. There's nothing in particular in common except that these are people who know all the angles about how government operates."

Yet to say that bureaucrats have little in common as a group does not mean that political executives face a random collection of government personnel. In old and new, controversial and publicly forgotten agencies, a visitor is likely to hear certain themes repeated among higher civil servants. These themes are best thought of as varying dispositions that suggest the different ways civil servants approach their work rather than as exact, representative descriptions of all officials. In this section I first examine higher officials' dispositions toward behavior (how they usually prefer to operate) and, second, their dispositions toward jobs (their focus of attention while operating). But thinking there is any neat typology sufficient to capture the full reality of all the personal differences in officialdom can be as misleading as the failure to draw any distinctions at all among bureaucrats.

Behavior

By definition the term "bureaucratic behavior" seems to denote caution and opposition to change. While plausible, this view overlooks a number of important distinctions in the dispositions among civil servants. Particularly in the higher reaches of Washington's bureaucracy, these dispositions involve more than a commitment to inertial paper shuffling.

In the first place, the tenure of civil servants permits the luxury of gradualism. What appears to be bureaucratic torpor is in many instances the function of a different, albeit lengthy, time scale within government. In the life span of political executives a change of 5 percent a year may count for little, but to the civil servants whose clocks are set for ten or fifteen years in influential positions (with the possibility of training a replacement for the next generation), 5 percent a year can cumulate into comprehensive change. This year's battle for the preferred agenda may be lost or temporized. There will always be next year.

Thus one reason that the stereotype of bureaucratic inertia needs to be qualified is that gradualism does not necessarily imply a distaste for any change. Naturally some civil servants can be found opposing minor changes at any time, just as others (particularly professional specialists and problem-solvers) are always willing to dare greatly. Normally, however, the gradualist inclination is likely to prevail: small changes frequently and large changes rarely. In illustrating this inclination, one official described the attempt of his political superiors to dismantle a government subsidy program.

> The ideas were dead duck when they started. I knew that was the view of the State Department, Treasury staff, and National Security Council staff, and it didn't take a genius to know where Congress would come out. It was no good telling them we aren't going to have any subsidies at all.... So we ended up moving slowly, as we should have done in the first place. You say you don't need so much, you put in a ceiling, you change the formula. You trim your sails a little bit to get started in getting what you want.

Gradualism counsels that what can be done serially or integrated into an already accepted activity is to be preferred as a means of reducing the agonies of change.

Indirection is another and closely related disposition. Given a choice, bureaucrats usually rate diversion and envelopment more highly than direct frontal assault. The virtues of obliqueness are known in every bureaucratic setting, but they gain special emphasis in Washington, where experienced bureaucrats know that opposition can come from almost any direction and combine unexpectedly. Indirection is applied everywhere. In personnel actions "you know you don't take off directly after people unless they have a place to go. Otherwise, the guy is going to stand up and fight you." In creating a program, "unless it's the only way left us, direct confrontation doesn't help and it strains relations." In procuring special equipment, "coming straight out and asking to buy it would only create trouble. I didn't buy it, I acquired it." In planning implementation, "our influence is mostly a question of maneuvering around the political difficulty—how to do this or that without alienating these groups."

Within the higher civil servants' terms of reference, a preference for gradualism and indirection can find strong justification. Such dispositions help avoid the disruption of other continuing operations which—with or without the arrival of a new assistant secretary—must be carried on. There is less threat to interpersonal networks and the sense of security attached to them. It is not simply a question of civil servants resisting any confrontations or change but of preferences for fights that do not lead to too much unnecessary antagonism and uproar—changes that do not extend uncertainty in too many directions at once. When bureaucrats fight among themselves, often over the integrity of organizational boundaries and missions, only rarely is it the pitched contest of the open battlefield. Left to their own devices, bureaucrats battle about stability and change in much the same way gardens encroach on each other, through a slow, twisting struggle where only the most rigorously enduring species will see the light of day. Political executives can therefore expect to hear a familiar refrain from officials: "Most problems in government can be solved only gradually. Hitting them head on and going for broke is usually not very helpful."

In addition to the normal caution of public and private bureaucracies, the Washington system adds a special kind of political carefulness. This does not mean that various bureaucrats cannot be found identified with political patrons, in or outside the executive branch. It does mean that civil servants, especially those who want to remain civil servants, are likely to be extremely cautious about becoming politically identified by accident. To have a patron is one thing, to have one by rumor but not in fact offers all the dangers and none of the security. Hence many civil servants may want good working relationships with appointees, but they also worry about becoming too close to the political executives of the day.

This caution is a natural response to the comingling of longtime agency-focused careerists with rapidly rotating and collectively inexperienced political appointees. "I learned quickly at Health, Education, and Welfare to choose the institution, not the political appointee," one bureaucrat said. "Seven years ago I joined with John Gardner as secretary. Then it was Cohen, Finch, Richardson, and pretty soon here's Weinberger and Mathews."

The situation can become particularly risky when agency officials are called on to use their in-depth knowledge of government operations to help the highly political figures near the President. Since there is no routinely accepted process for using agency bureaucrats to help look at problems from a presidential perspective, a call from the government center can easily provide a glorified way of putting one's civil service career on the line. As one agency official described such incidents:

> In the Johnson years a large number of career people were detailed to the White House. Then toward the end of the administration I kept getting calls to try and place first this one and then that one back here in the agency. Between fitting them back in, and the White House calls, and dealing with those who'd stayed behind, it was a pretty messy situation.

The disposition to maintain independence and avoid inadvertent political identification is expressed in many ways, from behavior in the office to ways of socializing. "If a person wants to remain a high-level civil servant," said one survivor, "he'd better keep an arm's length relationship with political appointees; he's got to give advice that includes things they don't want to hear." Another said, "I don't speak my mind on politics the way I used to before joining government. I'm not going to be worried about political clearances if I move into another job."

An administrative specialist claimed to follow self-denying ordinances "not to do much partying with political people. [Republican] executives would invite me to their poker games and [Democratic] executives had a lot of social affairs in Virginia but I never went. You've got to be careful of appearing to be too involved with any political faction." Most important, experienced civil servants recognize that the more visibly identified they become with particular partisan controversies, the more others will make inferences about their loyalties, often wrongly. Hence there is a strong preference for more secretive activity. "Once you start building up recognition, good or bad, you won't last long, unless maybe you're J. Edgar Hoover."

A retiring supergrade (resented by some because a cabinet secretary consulted him in preference to higher political executives) perhaps put it best in advance to younger civil servants: "If you are a guy whose day isn't complete without having lunch with the boss, who can't work behind the scenes without a lot of fanfare, then the civil service isn't for you."

Disaggregating the notion of bureaucratic inertia yields a fourth disposition among higher civil servants. This is an emphasis on maintaining relationships, and it is in many ways the reciprocal of carefulness in becoming accidentally associated with short-term political ties. The agency career ladders, cross-agency networks, and various pockets of career development provide the familiar associations through which civil servants can expect to have to continue carrying out their activities. One division head spoke approvingly of the lessons learned from his predecessor.

> To the extent the political heads had something they wanted done, he'd work like hell to do it and nine times out of ten he'd succeed. But he would also work in such a way as to make sure what he did didn't screw up his dealings with the other department or congressional subcommittee. Trying to do it by confrontation would just lead to a shutdown of information.

Hence, however they may feel about their political superiors, higher civil servants usually believe they can do better by keeping their relationships going rather than by trying to win every little battle.

In general, networks are maintained and consulted, not out of a desire for fellowship or good communications, but because officials realize there are others in government who can help or hurt their work; in either case, the aim is usually information. Quite apart from any question of bureaucratic sabotage, higher civil servants recognize that a good deal of their effectiveness, and at least potentially their service to political executives, depends on the integrity of longer-term contacts that may conflict with unadulterated personal loyalty to a given political superior. With such relations, an official said, bureaucrats can "call around to find out if other offices rubber-stamped it. . . . We talk freely about the kind of analysis and data." Another remarked that "using a variety of these contacts to double-check information, people in the other offices will realize you've got to be convinced; you don't just take things on their say-so."

But the relationships are used "with a light touch, not like you're an adversary fighting everything." Over time, officials build up credit with others that allows them not only to protect themselves but also to ask tough, direct questions when necessary. As one supergrade official put it, "I can usually get more out of five or six phone calls than a day of meetings. Does a bill make sense? Why hasn't an order been signed? Sometimes I can tell my boss the date and hour a paper has gone into another undersecretary's in-box, so we'll know who's the roadblock."

Obviously, different bureaucrats interfacing with political leaders have different relationships to maintain—some strictly internal to the agency, some more involved with Congress, interest groups, or the press. Whatever these differences, the tendency to preserve relationships means that higher civil servants are inclined to recognize the legitimacy of behavior that is less than lockstep loyalty to political appointees. Higher civil servants generally expect to be able to assure their contacts a fair hearing, even if it is not what the agency head wants to hear. If future relations are not to be prejudiced, officials will not expect to be required to give false or misleading information, to support agreements that will not be kept, or to "source or attribute" information if that could threaten their networks. They recognize that to get some information, some will probably have to be given up; such advance notice and consultation may frustrate political "movers and shakers," but it also avoids the antagonisms created by springing surprises. Bureaucrats generally tolerate a good deal of seemingly useless and desultory communications, yet if they are not to lose their sources of orientation in the confusing Washington environment, they cannot cut out the noise they do not care to hear without losing the residue of information they need to know.

None of this means that government bureaucracies cannot be made responsible to political executives, but it does mean that any efforts to eliminate a civil servant's contacts outside an agency's formal hierarchy are self-defeating. The type of difficulties most apt to develop are apparent in the statement of a GS 17 in one agency where such an effort was made during the Nixon years:

> They did have a right to say I must not use these contacts against them, but they can't keep me from having contacts. First, you can just disobey and make sure the story gets out in a way that keeps it away from you. Then I might get in touch with [a senator favorable to the administration] because Congress is very dependent on information, and he'll come back to the higher-ups saying, "If you want our cooperation, get rid of this order." What's more, if I'm suspicious that I'm being given misinformation to disperse, then I present it in a suspicious way. Other people get the signals.... And, too, you have friends in the agency. [Two political executives] were writing "eyes only" memos to each other about how to cut me off and I had copies on my desk the same day.

Once political-bureaucratic infighting has reached such a point, it is doubtful if any gains in obedience can offset the costs imposed by bureaucrats' efforts to maintain their relationships with others.

Gradualism, indirection, political caution, and a concern to maintain relationships—these suggest some of the common dispositions in higher career officials' behavior that go beyond conventional images of bureaucratic inertia. Such tendencies can find a good deal of justification in an environment of complex and uncertain political leadership on the one hand and long agency tenures and individualistic job protections on the other. These similarities regarding *how* civil servants approach their work are crosscut by differences regarding *what* they focus on in government jobs.

Jobs

Program bureaucrats are the most familiar category of civil servants. Most agencies have responsibility for carrying out government programs that deliver particular goods and services—building roads, making maps, setting standards, and so on. Even the one domestic agency with the least "operating" responsibility, the Department of Justice, finds itself with a large number of program activities, such as running prisons or administering federal funds to local law enforcement projects. The term "operating programs" implies fairly distinct groups of constituents, professionals, and administrative specialists who are all interested in the receipt or delivery of the particular goods and services. One need not draw a caricature of government as being run solely by baronial bureau chiefs in order to recognize that a great many civil service careers are focused on defending and advancing these established program activities as far as possible.

The preoccupations of program advocates are no particular secret within the executive branch or Congress. Speaking of such advocates, one political executive said, "I stopped worrying whether they were Democrats or Republicans. They love their programs, not the parties." Bargainers in Congress recognize that "most of the issues with the bureaucracy aren't party politics: it's the railway people versus the shipping people." A civil servant outside the programs complained: "Those bureau chiefs who say they've seen political appointees come and go and who just run their programs as they want are awful. They are just the ones that get picked out as typical bureaucrats."

The program bureaucrats (and their de facto equivalents who become political appointees) would probably reply that their organization has been given a continuing responsibility to provide a government service. Throughout large parts of government—the Census Bureau, Social Security Administration, Bureau of Standards, Agricultural Extension Service, Coast Guard, units in the National Institutes of Health, and on and on—the service in question has been a long-standing public commitment. These program advocates do not see themselves in a position to be led first one way and then another by different political executives, for their underlying loyalty is to a broad agenda that may be very slightly influenced by political change. Their job is to build and lead an organization to carry out that agenda. As one such powerful official recalled, "Political types who passed through were useful or not useful in helping carry out the mission, but in no case that I can think of were they particularly influential in modifying the agenda . . . or developing the organization to carry out the programs." The head of a major division in another department expressed the basic sense of proprietorship characteristic of the program bureaucrats:

> I keep the assistant secretary and secretary informed, but not so much that they can really get at it. It's not a question of looking for guidance in advance, because I feel like it is my organization. So when we periodically get the political rhetoric about doing something [on a policy issue], I rely on my experience, which is that they [clients] don't like the hard line. By keeping this area to myself I'm able to see to it things are done in this way and not the way the political rhetoric has to be.

A second category is *staff bureaucrats* who gain their rewards from running internal administrative processes rather than operating programs. The services of such budget or personnel officers, legal or management specialists, generally cut across programs, particularly at the higher organizational levels. Unlike program advocates, staff bureaucrats may have few commitments to a particular subject matter or clients. Budgeteers or management specialists may care about the issues but feel "you are paid to match programs against each other, not sell them." One such official reported taking "satisfaction from a sense of direction over the process," adding that "if you get your views down and a hearing, then you're content to let the process go on with whatever decisions are taken."

Because there is usually more political interest in what government does than in how it does it, staff civil servants usually feel less threatened than program advocates by a change in political leadership. But by the same token it becomes easier for others to complain that officials in high-level staff positions have become identified with particular political executives who might be trying to change programs. This political vulnerability is considerable. Effective participation by staff bureaucrats means that they must spend some time "trying to make sure the secretary doesn't get just one perception from the program people." Hence the image of a bureaucracy run by program bureau chiefs does become a caricature if one overlooks the obstacles their advocacy can face from budget officials concentrating on scarce resources, personnel officers allocating job slots, and even management analysts seeking to reduce red tape. In one agency where such a struggle occurred:

> Combating the bureau chiefs' autonomy started with a group composed entirely of civil servants. The bureau heads had every little thing coming through their offices in Washington. They liked it that way because they could work with Congress on an exclusive, one-to-one basis and earn gratitude with what they could do for individual congressmen by dipping into the paperwork as it passed over their desks. Decentralization was a threat to the bureau chiefs and it was a long, hard fight.

A third category fits other higher civil servants—officials who often dismiss administrative processes as "so much paperwork," and yet who are not uncritically committed to the substance of a particular program. For want of a better name, these might be termed *reformers*, and they can be found hybridized from either program or staff backgrounds. Even the most ingrown program divisions usually contain some officials whose experience has tempered their enthusiasm for more of the same. Often their desired changes are only marginal improvements in accepted missions, but sometimes there is more fundamental requestioning of assumptions about a program's operation. One bureaucratic reformer observed:

> You can support a program without becoming a true believer and refusing to recognize what's wrong. I am one who believed in Great Society programs, but I also learned through some hard experience that the categorical system of centralized grants was impossible. Some of us here were supporters of New Federalism before Nixon had a political name for it.

Reformers' services have always been weakly organized, but attempts have been made in the past ten years to bring more institutionalization to the analysts' role by creating offices for analysis and planning in most departments. Such "policy analysis shops" have usually evolved as staff units reporting to the agency head, and they seem to be the most important residue of the planning, programming, and budgeting movement in in the 1960s.[30] Where they exist on something of a continuing basis in the

---

30. For a description of these emerging roles, see Arnold J. Meltsner, *Policy Analysts as Bureaucrats* (University of California Press, 1975).

bureaucracy, such analysts are often the agency head's only institutional resource for thinking about substantive policy without commitments to the constituents, jurisdictions, and self-interests of existing programs. The analysts involved are a mixture of civil servants interlarded with outside specialists. Many are likely to identify themselves as "partisans for more rational decisionmaking" or "part of a professional analytic group laying out and evaluating the options."

Observing program and staff bureaucrats in the department, a reformer expressed shock "at the extent to which people are worried about where they want to come out and finding reasons for what's already decided, instead of analyzing the issues." Promoting the reformer's cause, of course, is easier said than done, and serious difficulties face such bureaucrat-analysts in trying to become effective participants in any agency's decisionmaking process. Probably their most enduring problem is one of attracting political customers to use their analysis while maintaining constructive relations and access with the program offices being analyzed. Well over 1,000 Washington officials, however, are trying to play this difficult role, and their potential usefulness should not go unrecognized in drawing distinctions among career personnel.[31]

After taking account of the enthusiasm of program operators, the process orientation of staffers, and the critical skepticism of analysts, there remains an amorphous fourth disposition among some higher civil servants, whom I have labeled *institutionalists*. More than anything else, institutionalists seem committed to keeping the machinery of government itself in good working order. They are interested in staff processes but also in capacities for implementation within programs. They may push specific reforms but are probably more committed to evaluation itself as an institutional capability. Given the nature of civil service careers, their interests are likely to be focused on a particular department or agency, but that does not preclude a willingness to move elsewhere if necessary to their self-conception as civil servants. For this minority of top generalists, the career service has institutional values of its own to preserve.

Their own words probably describe the institutionalists best. One supergrade who eventually resigned but was called back spoke of the need

31. At the end of the 1960s the estimated number of policy analysts was approaching 1,000, and by all accounts has continued to grow. See Keith E. Marvin and Andrew M. Rouse, "The Status of PPB in Federal Agencies: A Comparative Perspective," in Robert H. Haveman and Julius Margolis, eds., *Public Expenditures and Policy Analysis* (Markham, 1970), p. 453.

"to deal honestly and provide a service to people above. I've got to assume that with that I'll get support and survive as a civil servant. If the boss doesn't like the job I'm doing, I expect him to tell me and I'll move on." Maintaining an independent view up to the point of a political decision is given equal priority with facilitating a faithful agency response after the decision. An official in one of the few presidentially appointed career · posts said that his aim was

> to see to it that things get executed. I've been the only one around a table arguing against a secretary's view, but once I've had a hearing and he decides, then we go and everyone outside that room is going to see me as supportive and emotionally committed to something I had disagreed with as something I had pushed. Most of these are gray areas, but if it's absolutely crucial, I can always resign.

Programs or processes may be changed, but to the institutionalist there remains an important distinction between the legitimate and illegitimate scope of the political executives' power. One career executive summed up this disposition well:

> Everybody has got limited intelligence—even guys at the top. I don't think institutions should be up for grabs for anyone wanting to take them over and remake them in his own little personal image. When a political guy gets in the driver's seat, he should be able to complain that the machine isn't turning the right way. Or adjust it to suit his needs. Some want more comfort, others more speed, and that's okay. But you have to maintain the integrity of the machine itself; you don't let each set of people come in and play around with the mechanism any way they want. If so, pretty soon you'll have a machine that won't work for anybody.

No doubt some of the dispositions discussed in this section can be found in different aspects of any civil servant's work at different times. But probably no high-level bureaucrat can encompass all these tendencies with equal emphasis all the time. Anyone who could do so would go a long way toward meeting the kind of requirements once set by Civil Service Commissioner Theodore Roosevelt for a Texas customs inspector: "Saddling and riding an unbroken mustang, shooting at a gallop, reading cattle brands and classifying livestock, speaking a little Spanish, and proving his courage and endurance by testimonials."[32] The modern bureaucratic counterpart would be able to harness and master particular programs, quickly shoot down poorly analyzed pieces of advocacy, speak to the ongoing needs of administrative processes, spy out the implications

32. Quoted in F. E. Leupp, "Civil Service Reform and Common Sense," *Atlantic Monthly*, February 1914, p. 274.

and precedents for institution-building, and all the while maintain a high reputation in his or her enduring network of government relationships.

Bureaucracies exist and create a division of labor because such Renaissance men on horseback cannot be counted on to put in an appearance, and in few countries is this official diversity more intense than in the United States. American political appointees with major executive responsibilities will not (as in some other developed countries) find one predominant type of elite administrators populating the top of officialdom. Instead, the American bureaucracy as a whole constitutes a richly variegated resource. Insisting on its own fragmented identities and individualistic protections, it is not, however, a fluid resource compatible with any use that transient political executives might care to make of it.

From what has been said so far, it is not difficult to imagine the sort of political workman who will be out of touch with his bureaucratic materials. Such a political executive will demand that major changes be carried through quickly—violating canons of gradualism. He will want things done in a particular way and will be little interested in hearing about less direct alternatives, disregarding the virtues of obliqueness. He will expect subordinate bureaucrats to bend automatically to his aims and to do so as "his" men (regardless of the cost to their political identification and their continuing relations with others). Not recognizing the strengths and weaknesses of his different materials, he will treat bureaucrats as interchangeable elements that are supposed to coalesce into a uniform whole without a self-interest of their own. And as the grand design inevitably crumbles under the strains of the Washington environment, the political noncraftsman will walk away and leave the smoking workshop behind, muttering no doubt that all bureaucrats are the same anyhow.

At least so things might appear from a bureaucrat's perspective. But since a relationship is being examined here, the time has come to try to fit the two sides together. How does a government of political strangers try to cope with the resident experts in bureaucratic power and vice versa? There are no manuals for these assorted marriages of convenience. In the next two chapters I examine some of the strategies commonly tried and the working relationships that are established for better or worse.

CHAPTER FIVE

Working Relations: The Preliminaries

We must take a man as we find him; and if we expect him to serve the public, must interest his passions in doing so. A reliance on pure patriotism has been the source of many of our errors.
— Alexander Hamilton, *Constitutional Debates*, June 22, 1787

IN AN IDEAL WORLD political executives would take office with a clear notion of what is to be done and how to do it. Their mandates would fit into an agreed upon division of responsibilities among White House aides, political appointees in other agencies, and congressmen. As a matter of course, higher civil servants would respond by providing the vital links between political executives at the top and bureaucrats operating below.

Few people would mistake Washington for such an ideal realm. The real world impinges in many ways. Civil servants can no more count on having an experienced political appointee who knows what he wants to do than a political appointee can count on inheriting bureaucrats who will help him do it. Demarcations between civil service and political jobs have become extraordinarily blurred. The political personnel system creates what is basically an accidental collection of individuals with little past commitment to political leadership and few enduring stakes in government's own capabilities and performance. The bureaucratic personnel system produces people with their own specialized interests and few norms as a collective civil service. Many writers have recounted other facts of life in Washington, all serving to show that government power is fractionalized within the executive branch, within Congress, and between the two.[1] This ensures a multitude of pitfalls—any one of which can block action—and a variety of alternative routes for bureaucrats who might dislike directions signposted by political executives of the day. Taken as

1. See, for example, Louis C. Gawthrop, *Bureaucratic Behavior in the Executive Branch* (Free Press, 1969), chaps. 3, 5, 6.

a whole, it is a system that depends on political amateurs for leadership in an operating environment that is distinctly inimical to amateurism.

And yet it is also a fact that despite these givens in Washington, some political executives are able to handle their bureaucratic relations in a more productive, or at least less self-destructive, manner than are others. In this chapter I try to provide some insight into why that should be the case. What can political executives do to help themselves? Why is such self-help usually insufficient? How are working relations begun amid the initial suspicions? Once these preliminaries have been considered, I show in chapter 6 how vigorous political executives try to work their relationships in order to make their relationships work for them in the bureaucracy.

Obviously many reasons contribute to the tendency for some people at the top of government to do better than others, "better" being used here to mean moving government actions in some intended direction. On anybody's list would be a set of reasons having to do with what the individuals themselves are like. Some people can get along with anybody and others enjoy fighting with everybody. Some are interested in public policies and others have personal preoccupations. Another set of reasons relates to the context for action. Sometimes the aims of political executives are compatible with their bureaucratic settings, but in other instances political and bureaucratic officials want different, mutually incompatible things.

This discussion focuses on a third set of reasons why some political executives do better than others. Events also depend on how people choose to act; political appointees can choose how to use their personal attributes and how to respond to given contexts. Some seem able to capitalize further on an already good situation, and others seem able to turn even the most promising circumstances to their disadvantage. How political leaders choose to act—their statecraft—affects what gets done.

In a government of short-term political strangers there is obviously wide scope in how political executives can choose to act. The consequences of these choices are another matter. Many forces inherent in the bureaucratic setting come into play regardless of what the executive might wish to have happen. These internal dynamics of executive administration go far in determining, not how appointees will choose to act, but whether the choices prove prudent or foolish in coping with other people in government. Listening to experienced public executives, one finds no simple set of rules guaranteeing success. But there is some regularity in the scars left by past mistakes. Since political executives are substantially on their own and politically vulnerable in Washington, their first necessity is to help themselves.

Self-Help: The Starting Point

Experts constantly emphasize that public policy issues pose extraordinarily complicated problems of analysis and choice. What the newcomer to Washington learns is that beyond any complexity in the substantive content of policy, there are second, third, and fourth-order enigmas embedded in the political existence of every policy. Who cares about what? Where can different sources of opposition and support be expected? What ties make issues that are technically unrelated to the rational analyst seem highly interdependent in other, more political, minds?

Political appointees learn to help themselves cope with this political complexity in Washington and some inevitably do better than others. Bureaucrats, congressmen, lobbyists, and others who remain behind report that the successful learners "made possible changes that people who have been around here a long time couldn't have done," or that "you may not have agreed but you had to respect the effort." One unsuccessful political executive was dismissed as someone who "was big-dealing it all over town but what did he leave behind? Nothing." Another was remembered as one of the many appointees who "never found his way around, and that minimized the harm that could be done."

Learning

There are several ways political appointees learn to help themselves. Some are fortunate enough to have experienced mentors above them, like the assistant secretary for whom "the secretary and undersecretary were an education. They could tell you how to get along in town, how to deal with the White House and Congress. With them to help you didn't have to reinvent the wheel like a lot of political appointees." Another important source for learning is the appointee's predecessor in the organization. Those who have actually lived through the experiences often provide valuable information that is too delicate or controversial for the official department or transition briefings. Such information can be useful even if, as often happens, it only gives advance warnings about the personalities likely to be encountered—"who's who in the zoo," as one put it. But there are also problems with this approach. Frequently a heavy discount factor for personal bias will have to be applied, and a political appointee may feel he cannot go to his predecessor because the latter was a complete failure. Often, too, on some of the most sensitive matters there will simply be no desire for cooperation between parties or cliques within the same party. "We were spurned by the Johnson people," said a New Frontiersman, "just as we had spurned our predecessors."

Most learning, therefore, occurs through the familiar process of trial and error, sometimes deliberately but more often accidentally. The frequently heard clichés about trial balloons, testing the water, and so on, all refer to ways of taking tentative actions that can be altered relatively easily in the face of subsequent reactions. As experience accumulates, the trials can rely less on actual reactions and more on mental predictions. At this stage academics will be found referring to "the law of anticipated reactions" and practitioners to their sense of "what will fly." Since most political appointees are not Washington veterans, they will have the advantage of fewer preconceptions about what cannot be done. That, after all, is one of the justifications for their existence. But unfamiliarity also means political appointees are generally taught in the harder school of experience and make more accidental uses of trial and error, especially the latter. The story of one assistant secretary, later rated a generally successful appointee even by his opponents, offers an idea of how this learning process works:

> I came in here and made a big mistake right off. I figured I was going to manage like you would in a company. So I initiated a major organizational study. We were going to get consultants, see just what would be the most rational way of running this place, and ram things through. But I didn't understand and when the time came for the final contract award to the firm [a congressional committee chairman] sent orders to kill it. And [the secretary] killed it.

It was a time for reassessment and learning. He went on:

> So I just settled back and said to myself, "This department isn't run the way I've always thought about the separation of powers." I sat back for about six months and just watched. Then I had a better idea of how to go about getting what I wanted. . . . Hell, [the congressman] has better communication in this department than we do. His contacts with the field offices are incredibly good. In many cases, the employees go to him before they come to us, and they know he'll protect them when they do. The kind of thing I wanted to do inside the department could weaken his hold.

Most political executives can expect to test and develop their statecraft by experiencing similar on-the-job training. Such sources of learning (also called the real world) are never in short supply, but they tell little about what it is that political appointees actually learn to do by way of self-help.

Circles of Confidence, Lines of Trust

Much of what political executives do to help themselves can be put under the general rubric of building personal networks. These webs of individual contacts are what allow political executives to move between the ingrown life in their part of the bureaucracy and the larger, confusing world of Washington politics. In good times the information and leverage of these networks allows a public executive to exert a maximum of influence in pushing through what he wants done. In bad times an appointee is at least able to operate with some understanding about who or what is causing him all the pain.

At issue is something more than chumminess, mutual back scratching, or superficial techniques for making friends and influencing people, though all these may be present. What political appointees need and work at building (often unconsciously) are relationships of confidence and trust. "Confidence" is used here to refer to assurances about the nature of the surrounding environment; trust is rarer and only gradually earned. It refers to a deeper, mutual exchange of commitments within a community. Confidence is the kind of security a city-dweller acquires by knowing what the different parts of town are like, what streets to avoid, how anonymous strangers in many different roles can be expected to behave. Trust is the kind of security a villager has by knowing that people he meets are like him and committed to a group-life together.

Building confidence brings predictability, even from strange opponents; with trust comes loyalty, especially from people depending on each other's efforts. The pick-up game described for political executives in chapter 3 becomes less complex and more certain as participants acquire both confidence—the sense of game rules and relations among different teams—and trust—mutual dependability among members of the same team. By extending their circles of confidence political appointees can see better where they fit in. They become able to carry out more effectively the persuasion, reciprocity, and bargaining that are pervasive in Washington. By creating lines of trust, executive leaders gain help automatically as it were through mutual loyalties. How then, do political appointees build trust and confidence and thereby help themselves become credible participants?

WHAT FITS

Sociologists and psychologists are inclined to argue about which is more important—inherited traits or acquired context. In Washington the performance of political executives is best seen as correspondences between, rather than the absolute priority of, either factor. On the one hand is the particular situation a political appointee confronts, and on the other is what he or she brings to it. Obviously both personal resources and situations vary widely, but these variations do not mean that anything goes. They mean that what goes requires very careful attention. Otherwise, mismatches between the expectations of an appointee and the requirements of a situation can make relationships of both confidence and trust impossible.

Examples of the failure to understand what kind of executive actions fit their context abound in Washington. Appointees can find themselves in political appointments that emphasize many different meanings of the term "political." Jobs in agencies with a well-established service or mission—the Social Security Administration, Census Bureau, National Aeronautics and Space Administration, and so on—may be political in the sense of making important decisions on society's behalf but not necessarily partisan in their professional and technical standards of behavior. Without a sensitive and light touch, efforts to increase political responsiveness can easily destroy the effectiveness of any political executive making the attempt. In one such agency a participant told how an attempt was made to increase political control by adding more appointees below the director and by handling congressional requests for information in a less bipartisan way:

> They [some of the new appointees] . . . were high-quality people, but it was too partisan for the professionals in the organization. Some of them resigned in protest and on the Hill congressmen were making noises about the trouble we would have with appropriations if things went on in this way. . . . Eventually, the appointees left and things went back pretty much to what they were before.[2]

By the same token, even one of the most respected, impartial figures

2. For evidence on some of the turmoil surrounding such events, see *Investigation of Possible Politicization of Federal Statistical Programs*, H. Rept. 92-1536, 92 Cong. 2 sess. (1972).

in Washington could find his standing eroded in a position requiring partisan forcefulness:

> They wanted a stalking horse to take some of the heat from Congress on reorganization. . . . I should have gone earlier but I didn't leave with a bad taste. The President even called me personally to say he wanted me someplace in the administration, but they really needed a more political type here to handle this kind of fire.

By trying from the start to understand the relationship between their own objectives and the expectations surrounding their positions, appointees are more likely to avoid unnecessary disappointments in the future. For example, top government executives are often assumed to have concrete policy objectives. Yet anyone talking with such officials will undoubtedly be surprised at how few can identify any clear objective in their work—at least none connected with government policies. During a survey in the Nixon administration, somewhat less than half the presidential appointees (47 percent) could express clear proposals to solve the most important problems (as identified by the respondents themselves) facing the nation in their areas of interest.[3] The objectives of some political executives can most accurately be described as self-promotion, as in the case of the man who "had looked at people in high-level jobs, like Elliot Richardson or Nelson Rockefeller. They had all been assistant secretaries, so I thought it would be good to get in some service now." Other appointees seem to gain their main satisfaction from presiding as a kind of keeper of the keys. As one expressed this attitude, "I was going to retire anyhow." Such political executives become the idler wheels of the executive branch, transmitting but not generating movement in government policy.

There is no need to condemn one or another type; if for some reason it is government quiescence that is desired, then they too may serve who only stand and wait. Rather than trying to live up to any one "best" model of executive leadership, appointees help themselves by trying to match their individual aims and the situation at hand. Just as presidents do themselves a disservice by expecting driving loyalty from cabinet secretaries chosen to repay a political debt or to represent a constituency, so political executives at all levels help or hurt themselves depending on their sensitivity to incompatible positions and missions. Trouble rains equally on the activist operating where there is little scope for more than

3. The comparable proportion for both career and noncareer supergrade officials was about two-thirds. The figures are taken from the American portion of the Comparative Elite Project, directed by Joel D. Aberbach at the University of Michigan.

a holding action and on the passive administrator who finds he must cope with major innovations and confrontations. In one recently created agency a presidential appointee expressed an appropriate sense for "choosing horses for courses":

> [My predecessor's] style was to ride roughshod. . . . Everything was in an uproar, people being kicked around and fired, disenchantment and transfers out—real hard-hat stuff. I, on the other hand, go out of my way to talk with people, bring them along, and show an interest in them. But that is the difference. He was interested in getting x done in y amount of time, taking Hill 101. I'm interested in creating an organization that can function for any leader, although of course any leader can wreck it. He started a program; I'm involved in implementing it. He was trying to complete a mission; I'm trying to create a tool.

LOOKING UP

Political executives are usually linked upward to particular political superiors. Some of these links appear in the formal lines of authority (cabinet secretary to President, undersecretary to cabinet secretary, assistant secretary to undersecretary, etc.) of organization charts. Other appointees are linked informally to the particular patrons influential in their placement. Given the nature of the selection process and the permeability of the executive branch to outside political forces, these loyalties upward are necessarily weak, but political appointees can often be found strengthening their position by working to garner loyalty and support for their work from higher quarters.

It is striking how often the same tendencies can be found among appointees who are trying to help themselves at all different levels, from the cabinet secretary dealing with the President to the second deputy factotum dealing with his assistant secretary. Seeking aid from above involves an exchange of commitments—in this case of who supports whom under what conditions. The support is therefore contingent, but it is a broader and more enduring relationship than the bargains that are struck with outsiders and based on this or that particular issue. Operationally, these understandings between political superiors and subordinates generally concern agreed upon directions of general movement, areas that are delegated and reserved, and amounts and kinds of access between the higher and lower official.

By working at building topside support and interest in their activities, political appointees lose some freedom to maneuver and cloud their identification with the interests of those below them. But amid the uncertainties of Washington what is gained can be even more important. By strengthening their ties upward, appointees can gain additional resources for resisting or persuading others on anything from the narrowest case-work to the broadest policy initiative. A low-ranking appointee in a sensitive area reported:

> He [a White House aide] and others are always wanting the wrong kinds of things from this department: to intervene in court cases, government grants, that sort of thing. You can resist these guys if you've got the backup. If you don't have the backup, you've got to get out. Your power base depends first on your boss or whoever got you the job.

The same need to build support from above applies at the highest level of executive politics. An undersecretary explained the initiation of a major new program:

> Between the secretary and the White House and me we developed an understanding of what I was going to do. . . . Come trouble, I could go to the secretary and say, "Look, we're getting our brains beat out trying to staff this." He could take it to the President and get the commitments. . . . The big advantage was that we could say we had a presidential program. With that commitment you've got clout, you can move fast.

Most appointees who lack or cannot create such ties to higher political levels become not only expendable (almost all political appointees are that) but unnoticeable in the work of government agencies. Faced with opposition or indifference, they cannot draw down on any wider reserves of support created by joint commitments from above. "When our last assistant secretary was kicked out," a high civil servant recalled, "it didn't affect us. He had no ties outside his office. You've got to have a lot of sympathy for these people who don't have heads higher up who are interested in their activities."

STANDING UP

If political executives are usually engaged in building support upward and if power is dispersed across many different layers and organizations, then the scope of random conflict high in the executive branch seems illimitable. In practice, conflict is somewhat constrained or at least channeled by another and equally important dimension of the way political executives use superiors as a means of helping themselves. Experienced appointees not only look up to build support, but they also learn they have to stand up to protect prerogatives. These prerogatives are largely procedural: the right to be heard within one's jurisdiction; to appeal against an intermediating spokesman, to hear directly from a political superior about changes in an understanding.

However commonplace or petty the issues involved may seem, the Washington landscape is strewn with the wasted tenures of those who failed to stand up for their own procedural prerogatives. No amount of technical competence or integrity can help an appointee who does not realize the politics of his position and, as one said, does not "sit tall in the saddle." In essence this means that an appointee needs to have a relationship with his political superior that is as close as any other executive's at the same level and closer than that of any subordinates within the appointee's own part of the organization. The more aggressive frequently try for more than their share of access and communication upward, but at a minimum every political appointee needs a sense of self-protection strong enough to work for a position of parity. A friendly observer described a colleague whose effectiveness was destroyed by refusing to stand up in this way:

> I've had some long conversations with him and he is a sincerely warm and honest guy. He showed his trust in a lot of ways, but that wasn't enough. He was too naive. . . . He didn't believe people would conspire against him in the way they did. He could have stopped it if he'd been strong in time, while he still had the strength. But he didn't put his foot down when he was denied access. . . . He let [a political subordinate] develop those relations without fighting it. Now, [the appointee's successor] wasn't as warm a person, but he stood tough even if it meant a lot of people didn't like him.

Egotism aside, the loss of prerogatives is crucial because it undermines an appointee's chances both of building support upward and of understanding where he fits. Invitations to the important meetings cease, front-office staff more easily bypass the appointee with their own orders, and those inevitable subordinates who are beholden to other patrons for selection feel more secure in trying politically to outbid him. As confidence in his surroundings declines, the unfortunate political executive is likely to be left dependent on those immediate associates who can flatter his unjustified sense of accomplishment.

Particularly in Washington's fragmented executive branch, individuals standing up for their right to appeal to, hear from, and be heard by political superiors provide a valuable if indeliberate collective service. The effort of each helps check unrestrained and precipitous efforts by all other political entrepreneurs to build support. It helps verify the accuracy of signals within the political marketplace of the executive branch. Since most appointees will not wish to use up their resources by appealing every issue, their selective actions can yield important clarifying signals about what they actually regard as most vital to them. A particularly garrulous presidential appointee explained the basic forces at work:

If you aren't willing to confront people who say they're speaking for the President, you aren't going to find out if they're playing straight. . . . But you've also got to be able to judge the issues and leave the brownie issues to the brownies. If the issue is so important and it upsets you the way you are being treated, then you take it up. If you are not willing to take it up, then it's not so important, or else you've got a yellow streak.

With good reason, therefore, access and appeal upward are often referred to by participants as "the safety valve of the whole system," and "the only way of keeping the game honest." According to one assistant secretary: "Many people are free-lancing and you have to call their hand and say, 'OK, if that is what the boss wants, I'm going to have him tell me that.' A lot of the time they are just bluffing." Those called too often in this way will lose their own credibility and capacity to build support.

DUE PROCESS

To political executives on the receiving end of such prerogative protectors, the choices and confrontations can be painful. "Yesterday," said an undersecretary, "I literally had to keep two assistant secretaries from physically assaulting each other, but it's better than things festering." As political superiors, some of the most experienced government executives have realized that they can help themselves, not by hoping to avoid or abolish, but by trying to manage the inevitable confrontations that develop as subordinates try to build support and protect prerogatives. Abdicating to these forces produces only more disorientation and loss of confidence. "The thing I remember most," said a veteran of one such agency, "was the fearfulness and insecurity of the appointees. They were always fighting to protect their turf, always bucking the reins, not willing to cooperate on anything."

Rather than abdicating to such turmoil, other political executives have in effect tried to abolish the conflict generated from lower political layers. An instructive example occurred midway through the Nixon administration when the President eliminated the customary right of cabinet officers to appeal personally to him regarding final decisions on their agencies' budgets.[4] On the whole the experiment can safely be pronounced a failure

4. The White House instructions read as follows:
Roles of officials and units involved in decision-making process: 1. *President*. Presidential decisions on agency budgets will be made in series right after [OMB] Director's Review sessions. . . . The Director, with Ehrlichman/Kissinger and the Deputy Director, will consider Director's Review results and furnish presidential determinations (consulting with the President as needed).
(U.S. Office of Management and Budget, Executive Office of the President, "Review Process and Schedule for the 1972 Budget" [Director's Review material from the Office of Budget Review, OMB Records Section, series 7202 and 60.25 September 18, 1970].)

and for reasons already suggested. Strong officials intent on defending their prerogatives could and did individually insist on personal appeals. Others were not sure if presidential decisions were in fact decisions of the President. Conflicts once reserved for the Oval Office were not ended but merely diverted elsewhere to other—and often more public—arenas. Without an accepted way to terminate arguments by appealing to a political superior, one White House aide said that a situation arose "where either people went behind the President's back or else they created a problem every time they walked in his office." Uncertainty was increased on all sides and confidence and trust among the participants declined.

The basic need to use conflict among subordinates, rather than to merely accept or try to deny it, applies not only to a president's relationships with cabinet members but throughout the political ranks. Approximately at the same time President Nixon was trying to mandate an end to his involvement in the cabinet officers' budget arguments, an undersecretary in a supposedly unmanageable department was learning how to use the self-interest of subordinates in protecting their prerogatives as a means of helping himself. "I already had the secretary's support, but my predecessors didn't have control of a lot of jurisdictions. I had to get squarely in the line of action. Where you can get in real trouble in a department like this is if you are blind-sided and don't get all the views." Part of a workable answer was a practice that has frequently been used at various times and places in the executive branch. The struggle of individual subordinates for access to and support from above was transformed into a more general understanding about due process; in this case the undersecretary achieved such understanding by using an executive secretariat that

> keeps the pressure up and we make sure all the views are aired. Everybody involved knows there's been a fair hearing before a decision is reached. With that people can be brought along better. They understand the basis of decisions and they know they've had a chance to give it their best shot.

Due process produces no perfect answer or harmony; it usually requires more—not less—executive leadership, since exposing the choice process also exposes the choosers. It can produce unnecessary delay when subordinates already concede loyalty in the form of fairly passive obedience. In the words of one such presidential loyalist:

> There's no limit to the depth of feeling for the man. . . . Chances are he's right or he'd be in your job and you'd be boss. . . . You are there to do what the President wants. You don't, like Jerry terHorst, resign just because you're left out of the loop. For our class of appointees the feeling was that

"You, Mr. President, and your top three or four advisers will make the decisions. We will be the people who implement them."

The point is, of course, that it is difficult to see any means, short of ideological litmus tests, that could hope to provide such unquestioning loyalty among most political executives under most circumstances in Washington. What experienced political appointees learn is that some trust is still possible—if not in having bosses always come up with the right answers, at least in the process by which the answers are found. By creating an atmosphere of fair hearings in which those involved have a chance to defend their stakes and build support, political executives help themselves. They do so by trying to ensure that the inevitable arguments will be limited to the content of choices rather than spilling over to include the way decisions were reached.

LOOKING OUT

To a greater or lesser extent most public and private executives seem to become accustomed to looking up to build support and protect prerogatives and looking down to manage their subordinates' conflicts. New political executives in Washington, however, are frequently surprised by how vigorously these efforts have to be counterbalanced by building relations beyond the superiors and subordinates of their own organization. Given a second chance many would agree with a recent resignee who said he "should have moved more quickly to establish contacts, working more with the Hill, interest group factions, people [in other executive agencies]."

Experience leads political executives to seek outside relations because of the essential uncontrollability of their environment. Their opportunities for coercing bureaucratic subordinates are few, and for those coerced the alternative sources of support from Congress, lobbies, press, and the executive branch are many. Rarely can political executives hope to fulfill the textbooks' requirements and to exercise power commensurate with their responsibility. Instead, they try to gain influence consistent with their immediate needs.

These needs obviously vary. For some appointees the outside relationships come easily, partly as a result of the selection process, partly because support based in private-interest groups or congressional committees is likely to be more stable than that offered by the transient teams of political executives. As long as a political appointee is content to fit into the pattern of existing understandings with interest groups or other patrons, he may expect to survive contentedly, even defiantly. For example, an undersecretary complained of one assistant secretary: "If I try to get him out of town his friends will be kicking us on every one of our bills and appropriations. Even if I could win I'd use up so much strength I probably couldn't get any new guy I want confirmed. It's best to try and confine the damage he can do."

The price of such security for the agent of outside patrons is a narrowly focused sphere of influence and abdication of political leadership, as the term is used in this book. Other political executives interested in a broader constituency, wider issues, or more adaptable allies, will often seek to bypass an official who is known to be locked into outside relationships. Thus his chances of building support upward are severely limited. Moreover, what is outside support to one participant can be sabotage to another, and higher political executives are not helpless in trying to combat it.[5]

Political executives less committed to specific outside supporters travel in more poorly charted waters, and for that reason they must work even harder to find the external navigation points and shoals. Methods differ among participants, but the need is much the same everywhere. One veteran executive in Washington said:

> I call it establishing a political wheelbase. You do it mostly just by working with people and getting to know them. You learn the subject matter areas of concern to them—where and how a man goes about doing business. . . . If he is a rivers and harbors guy, he'll be tied into certain groups and not others. An environmental type may be the reverse.

Inexperienced political appointees lack such networks and thus the insights afforded by them, as an outside management expert emphasized: "The subject matter doesn't give me trouble, it's been my inexperience. I mean, how to get things to happen inside government. This means, above all, who are the people to know, how are they likely to react, where can you look for allies?"

Methods for building such outside relations are legion. One vignette suffices to suggest something of the range of ways political executives go about helping themselves through outside support. During separate and lengthy interviews, a presidential appointee and his successor described the withering political fire directed against their agency. The counter-

5. Since this subject is usually thought to implicate bureaucrats more than short-term political appointees. I discuss in chapter 6 the ways political leaders can try to cope with the so-called iron triangle between subordinate officials, interest groups, and congressional committees.

measures they took are an encyclopedia of ways in which prudent political executives help themselves by "looking out":

—Where to go, who to see—you're looking for whoever has a stake in your issue.

—The General Accounting Office is a good ally. We've got one of their men in working on a particular set of plans. The Office of Management and Budget, as far as we can tell, we don't need in this area, so they don't get in on the planning stages.

—You know you have to massage the egos of the White House. I didn't know many there but held some dinners to make sure I knew and had a line on the people [several presidential aides] most directly concerned.

We're captured by the industry if that means trying to know the industry, the people and their problems. Not just bitchy problems like "give us more money," but what makes the industry tick. You can't get the information you need by sitting behind this desk. We do our own analysis of where we want to go, but the industry people know we listen to them seriously.

—You've got to realize from the beginning how important congressional staffers are. The dumber the congressman the more important it is to cultivate the staff.

—The unions can get to the President too. You've got to watch your behind and show them what's in it for them—namely, job security.

—When they wanted to abolish [a certain program] we went public by giving it a new component of women and blacks. Wait for the reaction if they try to dump it now. . . . Much of the industry has always been tied to [agency X], but the budget of [X] was being cut to hell and [Y] was rigidly enforcing the antipollution laws. So that part of the industry had no place to go. We, too, were looking for friends, so here was a new source of support for us.

—We figured if we could entice more people [in one part of the program], it would help [the other part] that was under attack.

—I knew there was no way we could do this while [a congressional subcommittee chairman] was in charge of things up there, so we waited until he got sick.

What emerges in these and similar experiences of political executives is something more than opportunism and random strategies for looking out. Without being too schematized, a kind of scale can be said to apply between the optimum influence political appointees might like and the minimum information they require in order to feel some assurance about their operating environment. "Trust," as it has been used here, is usually not expected to play a leading part unless the appointee wishes to lock his primary loyalties into one of these outside groups. Instead, most leading executives in Washington, regardless of type (self-promoters, agency empire builders, presidential loyalists, or whatever), can be found trying to move somewhere along a four-point scale of confidence.

1. At best they would like to establish networks with outsiders who recognize the mutual advantages that can flow from a particular course of action or inaction. With that, bargains and understandings can be struck on the issues at hand. The influence of both participants is increased. Obviously the more enduring and less issue-specific the exchange becomes, the more confidence shades into trust.

2. As second best a political appointee often tries to convince outsiders that his analysis and aims are essentially correct and justified. Even if active support is for some reason impossible, passive acquiescence can be of some help.

3. Desirable as either support or agreement are, both are elusive and often transient. The third point along the scale of confidence is therefore less dispensable. Experienced appointees try to build outside relationships so that they will at least be recognized as legitimate participants whose views should be listened to seriously.

4. The last point along the scale may suggest only the most minimal amount of influence with outside veto groups, but as the starting point for all other contributions to confidence, it is the most essential. Political appointees learn that in the uncertain Washington environment, the most dangerous form of power is unknown power. Allies, agreement—even legitimacy—may be lacking, but not knowing the location of political forces can mean that one is not even a participant in the right game. Since to be hit by opposition is less dangerous than not to know what hit you, prudent political executives work hard at finding intruders into their circles of confidence.

Perhaps the best way of appreciating the process at work is to listen to an appointee describe how he and an adversary tried to move along the scale of confidence—from identifying unknown power toward building mutual advantage:

> We were trying to make [the adversary's department] share some of our costs and he would have no part of it. He resisted every entreaty from every official here and from everybody in his own agency up to but not including the secretary. Because we had once worked together I could call [the secretary] personally, and only after the secretary's direct order did this guy come along. He wouldn't have had his reputation for survival if he'd just been obstructionist and not known when to accommodate.
>
> But here was his real trick. After all this happened, he started calling around to find out who had done it to him. He realized that someplace there was unknown power, something hidden that could get at him and he didn't know about it. Eventually he tracked me down and simply asked me

out to lunch. He didn't say, "You son-of-a-bitch, why did you do this to
me?" What he said was, "Look, Joe, any time you want something over
here, you just come straight to me." That was his ability—not just to find
out who had hidden power, but he had the sensitivity to try and make that
person part of his own network.

In Review

There is no neat, mutually consistent list or *Robert's Rules of Order*
for guiding political executives. If there were, it would reflect much more
of a common culture than exists at the top of the U.S. executive establishment. Instead, general tendencies reflect typical responses to fairly
common problems. A few of the most prominent tendencies have been
sketched in this section. Taken together, even these generalizations do
not constitute one set of consistent rules, each of which can be pursued
to the maximum. Fitting too well to expectations can destroy any independent sense of prerogatives; appointees too dedicated to establishing
an outside political wheelbase can threaten their chances for building
loyalty from above, and so on.

Yet the ways political appointees characteristically try to help themselves are more than a self-canceling set of homilies for political administration. By reenforcing their lines of trust and extending their circles of
confidence, political executives can build resources for becoming more
credible, effective participants. Their information base broadens to help
them understand the context of why something is happening or not happening. The trade-offs explored in chapter 2 between bureaucratizing and
politicizing become less intense as political appointees learn to see where
they fit in and feel able to operate with more and more confidence about
the true nature of surrounding threats. Their advice appreciates in value
because they have a better idea of what will and will not follow from it.
Advance warnings can be exchanged, bargains struck, pitfalls avoided, and
the chances of success improved, though never to a certainty.

Self-Help Is Not Enough

Political executives have to learn, however, that it is not enough to help
themselves. Those few important characteristics that appointees share—
impatience, short-term tenures, inexperience as a group—are at war with
what they most need—a patient fashioning of relationships of trust and

confidence. The latter require time and experience, both of which are in short supply in the political layers.

Through sufficient trial and error a political appointee can learn, for example, that the temporary difficulty he sees ahead is actually part of a recurring feud between organizations. Far better, however, that those with the memory of troubles should forewarn the new traveler. Many circumstances will combine to show a political executive the constraints he faces, but learning his opportunities is likely to be more difficult and time-consuming. Hence political appointees need positive help as well as warnings. Support from above and outside may be entirely reliable, and yet if an appointee must always use appeals to superiors as a means of controlling those below, he quickly loses his usefulness to his superiors. Moreover, he actually becomes vulnerable to subordinates who, by forcing constant appeals, can cause the appointee to quickly use up the goodwill of those above him. And in the end, no matter how many purges he conducts in frustration, there will always be someone further down the line in the bureaucracy who is not "his man" and who is thus in a position to frustrate the transient appointee.

In short, self-help is usually not enough. Political executives also need to look downward for the kind of assistance that civil services were invented to provide—knowledgeable continuity to warn and propose, and institutionalized responsiveness to help carry out executive decisions. The closer one looks at the power and services of high career officials, the larger loom the reasons why political appointees acting alone usually cannot do enough to help themselves become executive leaders.

Power

The basis of the top bureaucrats' power vis-à-vis political executives lies primarily in the services they can provide or withhold. Straightforward as this statement seems, it is a crucial point that is frequently overlooked in the self-centered atmosphere of many top political offices. New political appointees are often preoccupied with the civil servants' negative power: their ties to congressional committees and interest groups and their opportunities to leak information to the press and subvert political leadership through noncompliance. Bureaucratic sabotage does occur (and should at times be expected), but political executives are not without means of defense, including help from other civil servants. Nor should the important problem of bureaucratic compliance be downplayed; every

large organization encounters difficulty in ensuring a reliable correspondence between what leaders want and what subordinates actually do.[6] But
this general problem of noncompliance among subordinates faces civil
servants in high positions as much as it does political appointees. It may
actually trouble top bureaucrats more, since many political officeholders
leave before there is very much time to worry about faithful implementation.

The fact is that for the mixed collection of senior civil servants who
interact with political executives, power does not typically derive from
refusing to do what their superiors want. Absolutely passive compliance
to political superiors—the "yes, boss" approach—can be the easiest means
of obstructing political leadership if bureaucrats are so inclined. It was
expressed figuratively by an official who had seen the technique used off
and on for many years. "If [a certain political executive] wants to order
hemlock, they'll let him have it. If he wants a new air conditioner, they'll
do it and not tell him it will cause the ceiling to collapse; he'll just come
in one day and see the building half torn down and when people start
complaining, there will be his order—in writing."

Compared with the saboteur's negative acts, the top bureaucrats'
power derived from withholding positive help is enormous. Unlike the
"legislative veto" (in which executive actions take effect unless disap-
proved by Congress), the "bureaucratic veto" is a pervasive constant of
government, for without higher civil service support almost nothing
sought by political executives is likely to take effect. It is a power that
can consist simply of waiting to be asked for solutions by appointees who
do not know they have problems. One supergrade official illustrated what
is at stake by comparing his former and present political superior:

> With [the former superior] we worked hard, but this guy is just here to
> further his career, not do a job. . . . We aren't trying to scuttle him, but
> what happens is you just perform your job at a merely acceptable level. You
> don't go out of your way to make him some shining light. You don't find
> out things for him or volunteer information. No one's coming in early and
> staying late like before.

Because most political appointees require considerable help in government, higher civil servants normally need do little by way of harmful
actions in order to prevail. All that is usually necessary is for officials to

6. For complementary discussions of the obstacles to compliance in foreign and
domestic policy, see Morton J. Halperin, *Bureaucratic Politics and Foreign Policy*
(Brookings Institution, 1974); and Herbert Kaufman, *Administrative Feedback*
(Brookings Institution, 1973).

fail to come forward with their services. "That," as one undersecretary declared, "is their ultimate truth."

Services

What is the nature of these services? And why could not even more subordinate political appointees be used to supply them? Obviously any exact answer will vary with the agency or program in question and with the relative mix of personnel types available (program advocates, analysts, and so on). Bureaucratic services potentially available to political executives are broadly similar, however. Trying to discuss several "typical" agencies would be difficult, but a montage of overlapping experiences, some elements of which are observable in almost any agency in any recent administration, is possible.

ORIENTATION

The services of top bureaucrats begin with helping to orient new political executives to a particular agency. First, of course, will be the formal briefing books and meetings to describe the organization and resources of the agency; current key issues and their status; and possibly external relations with other departments, Congress, and interest groups. But some bureaucrats can also provide the vital kinds of personal information that appointees need. They may talk about "the cast of characters," "the strengths and weaknesses in our organization," "how we're viewed at OMB and on the Hill," "the ties a lot of our officials have to the interest groups," "who to see in the lobby groups and the Hill, as well as what they're like," and "some of the entrenched fights that have been going on."

To those coming in from the outside this flow of gossip can help provide important contextual knowledge about the particular organization and its subgovernment. Especially since the classic theory of party government loyalty is unlikely to have much relevance among political executives, the careerists' knowledge of interest groups and bureaucratic politics merits serious attention. One official said: "I remember that the secretary consulted industry people, asking them who to put in charge in order to shake up the department and get rid of people from the other party. The industry guys came back opposing changes. They know it's program and interest group politics, not party politics."

A political executive always steps into a moving current of activity, dealing for at least the first year with a predecessor's budget. Past decisions have already begun to affect him; future decisions are already moving toward him. Civil servants are in a good position to describe the background of what has previously been set in motion—the inherited controversies and bargains that outsiders will probably hold the new appointee responsible for. Some officials will bring forward supposedly new initiatives that appear to have exhaustive justification; other civil servants will be able to point out that this is an agenda regularly presented to incoming appointees that they pursue at their peril. Orienting advice is also needed on what things are urgent or on what decisions can be delayed and thus possibly be made more subject to the executive's control. Unless subordinate political appointees have spent a good part of their working lives in or near the particular government agency, they probably will be unable to provide their superiors with very much of the valuable information that top bureaucrats acquire as a by-product of their careers.

TECHNICALITIES

Any substantive actions a political executive may wish to take are embedded in extraordinarily complex rules about administrative processes, such as rules on personnel, budget, procurement, reorganization, regulation drafting, and so on. Few appointees have the expertise or time to cope with these intricate mazes, and yet such seemingly technical difficulties can provoke some of the greatest delays, frustrations, and unexpected consequences for political leaders.

A monopoly of knowledge about these technicalities constitutes both the source of many bureaucrats' power and also the positive services they can supply. Depending on how much help bureaucrats give, administrative processes and red tape will become a way of facilitating the political executives' aims or just another means of ensnarlment. An assistant secretary described his own experience during efforts to start a program for minorities:

> The bureaucrats I worked with were competent and hardworking, but damn if they couldn't give reasons why any particular thing couldn't be done— quote the law, previous secretaries' decisions, Civil Service and General Services Administration regulations, executive orders out of the past. . . . Later I found out they knew there were ways to do things, but they weren't volunteering that information.

As time passes, such a political executive may recognize how to get help in overcoming the supposedly technical problems, but by then time may also have run out on the transient leader. The assistant secretary continued:

> Eventually, I just ordered [a reluctant office head] to implement it. Then there was a long delay and I kept asking for it, but the excuse was there were all kinds of technical problems. Then when he brought it back it didn't seem like the draft regulations really represented my decision. Some other bureaucrats I took it to said I was right: he was trying to finesse me, so together we rewrote the regulations. But by then it was too late, and I left them in a folder for my successor.

INTELLIGENCE

As political executives continue in office their appreciation for the complexity of government is apt to grow. The pluralistic political environment in Washington means that frequently it can be extremely difficult to separate the real from the symbolic positions of other actors whose reactions need to be taken into account.

Experienced bureaucrats are in unique positions to provide intelligence of all kinds for imputing the intentions and attitudes of these government and nongovernment power centers. Where is opposition likely to occur and where can one most fruitfully shop for allies? Who will listen sympathetically, even in groups supposed to be uniformly opposed? As problems develop, what contacts elsewhere can be counted on to give a reliable reading of the situation? What new allegiances have been emerging in recent years and what old ones seem to be disintegrating to provide new opportunities? "Some civil servants could pick up the phone and get what I had bounced around for three days trying to find out," an assistant secretary reported. Another pictured his officials as "moving around the department as my eyes and ears and protecting my backside." In a highly unpredictable environment, the civil servants' own networks help them anticipate what will be considered in a favorable light elsewhere and what signs suggest that a serious explosion is in the making. An assistant secretary described how his career people

> could find out more of what is happening and the mood in the industry or with labor and the mayors than almost anybody else. From this you get a feel for the trends. This was the way we found out last month before their convention that [a lobbying association] was going to call for the resignation of the secretary. We hurried up and got the secretary out there looking active.

As information flows in, so it also flows out. The leaks of specific information (which worry many appointees) are often less important than the information that civil servants are constantly asked for or volunteer concerning the characteristics and intentions of their political superiors. These readings do much to affect an appointee's standing and reputation in the various networks. Dispensers of bureaucratic intelligence therefore vitally affect how far any political appointee will be able to help himself by building lines of trust and circles of confidence with others in the executive branch, Congress, interest groups, and elsewhere. Some sense of the importance of these bureaucratic signals can be gained from a familiar occurrence—exchanges of information between well-placed bureaucrats and the press:

> Jack Anderson's number two man called to tell me about the story they were going to break on some alleged improprieties in my boss's background. He said, "Bob, we've known each other for years and our advice to you is to stay out of this one." When I started arguing, he said, "There's no point. We've got him cold, so let's talk business. Do you think this guy is any good?" And I said what I thought: "It depends on who you're comparing him with. His predecessor was an eagle scout who spoke his mind and played everything absolutely straight. He is like an Armenian rug dealer. He'll negotiate the best price he can, but once you agree on a price it's a genuine Persian rug you'll get. He is a good man who won't sell out to the interests." So Anderson's guy said, "Okay, if that's the case we'll use the information but instead of making it the lead story, just tack it on at the end."
>
> Well, when it came out that way last week, my boss was naturally pretty upset. He wanted me to go out and defend him, but I said that it wasn't my job to defend him personally. We worked it that he would prepare a statement and I would see that it got to the right people. Of course, I also suggested to the news people that if they weren't too tough on him they could have somebody at [his new agency] that could be a good source for them later.

As sources and dispensers of information higher civil servants are not sufficient, but they are necessary if political appointees are not to be overwhelmed by the confusing noises and dangerous signals in executive politics.

RESISTANCE

The price of using the civil servants' networks and sources of intelligence is rebuttal and disagreement from officials who feel they have some knowledge to share, even if it is not what a political appointee cares to hear. Paradoxically, civil servants can provide some of their most valuable service by resisting what political appointees want. The positive nature of bureaucratic resistance (as opposed to obstruction) was summed up by a GS 18 who said, "I'm supposed to fight for what should be done until there's a decision—not let things go wrong and then say 'I told you so.'"

Such resistance provides important warnings about objections likely to be raised later by congressmen, interest groups, or local governments—even if there is no question of civil servants conspiring with these groups. It also provides signals about the persuasive efforts still needed among lower bureaucratic units if any change is to continue beyond a particular political executive's tenure. Moreover, because higher civil servants have to remain behind to justify what is being done, they are likely to worry about consistency, both retrospectively and prospectively. By looking backward, bureaucrats can use their objections at times to remind political executives of their own policies, which are often only general themes easily lost from view during the daily press of decisionmaking. Looking forward, officials are likely to caution against the precedents being created by today's expediency for what will come across their desks tomorrow. In all these instances civil servants usually have less incentive to compete for a political executive's favor than do political subordinates under the same executive. A number of career officials probably feel it is part of their obligation to "pipe up with objections, even though something is rolling down the political runway, the stands are up, bands playing, and all the fans cheering like crazy." In such cases the career tenure of civil servants is important, if only because the first reaction of the fans will often be to turn on the skeptic, not answer the objections.

Bureaucratic resistance in the form of circumspection can serve political executives in seemingly small matters. A clumsy personnel action, the use of special funds in a way different from that set out in legislation, an action readily misinterpreted by the press—this small change of government life is recognized by experienced bureaucrats as being what opponents can seize on to prejudice a political executive's reputation and influence. In one agency an executive complained that "responsive" bureaucrats "left my ass in one of the biggest slings in town by letting me redecorate the offices." In another the secretary, who desired an executive dining room, did well to succumb to bureaucratic arguments that he "shouldn't get in a position of having to waste time defending this sort of thing before the appropriations subcommittee." In a third agency an assistant secretary looked back and appreciated the bureaucrats' delays "in processing the papers for some of these dubious personnel actions the

White House wanted. It kept me out of a lot of trouble that some of my peers got into."

Policy, even presidential policy, rarely seems to involve a group of political executives walking in, thumping the table, and giving the administration's marching orders into an indefinite future. More often there is a continuing dialogue in which bureaucrats are important participants helping extract the mutual understandings that eventually become known as policies. Over the years reputedly "great" civil servants have recognized the overall changes in the political and social climate that create opportunities for major policy innovations. Such opportunities, however, are rare, and more often the gradualist, indirect disposition will prevail. Although higher civil servants are unlikely to offer ideas for dramatic radical departures (such freshness of thought is presumably one reason for having outside political executives and advisers), proposals for more meliorative, piecemeal improvements are among the civil servants' valuable potential services. In part this is because of their special technical expertise and in part because of their continuing involvement in the operations that reveal specific weaknesses in need of correction. Analysis by outside consultants may help, but political executives often find, as one assistant secretary reported, that "it's the people who have been here in the agency, worked in it, and have an itch for change who can tell you about its real problems." The value of such advice is heightened because of the bureaucratic capacity to convey information about what happened the last time particular things were tried.

Bureaucrats' services to political executives need not involve policy proposals. Tactical proposals help too, since to be warned about a pitfall is only half as helpful as being shown a way around it. What diversionary fight or what differences in timing can leave potential opponents distracted? What seemingly minor changes might open up new opportunities to garner support? Are there generally accepted ways of bending regulations that will accomplish the purpose without arousing opposition or loss of confidence? An experienced assistant secretary emphasized these kinds of services in describing his preference for dealing with "old-time bureaucrats":

You could find nice, friendly, wonderfully cooperative political appointees. Call up one of these guys and he says: "Who wants it; will it do us any good?" You tell him and he says, "Okay, sure we can do this, fine, right

away." And you say, "Wait a minute; I called you because we have a problem with it." He then simply bucks it somewhere else; weeks spill by and
eventually you might end up doing it for him. Call up some of the old
bureaucrats around and tell one of them what you need and he'll say,
"Look, you shouldn't go this route; here's what happens when that is
tried."

Well, what can be done? "Maybe we can do it this way," he says, "but
then we'll have to do this and that." You then bargain back and forth, he
puts a guy on it and so do you, and pretty soon something is actually happening.

EXECUTION

Political dependence on officialdom seems self-evident when it comes
to carrying out government policies. Whether the policies involve writing
more "bureaucratic" regulations or encouraging more free market competition, some official somewhere will usually have to do or stop doing something if the policies are to take effect. Within the extremely complex
process of implementation (the bulk of which falls outside the scope of
this study), higher civil servants interacting with political executives play
a particularly important part.

Since policies are often bundles of mutual understandings rather than
clearly spelled-out directives, senior bureaucrats are in a strategic position
to interpret the policy themes accurately or inaccurately to officials further
down, who in turn are expected to relate their choices on specific issues to
the overall intentions. One supergrade explained how interaction with
political appointees could be a key factor in gaining a sense of what has
gone into a decision and, hence, in guiding those below:

> I don't want to run my hands over every little scar from the last battle, but
> we do need to know the general way something was decided. I'll be dealing
> in the same area again, and knowing that something was decided on its
> merits gives an indication of what policy is meant to be. If it was decided
> on tactical, or personal, or party grounds, that's okay, but then I know that
> the next time someone asks it's all up for grabs.

Since the career ladders of subordinate bureaucrats often depend on
higher officials in the agency, the latter are also listened to carefully for
the signals they provide about their general reactions to both the political
executive and his specific aims. "I have a hundred people under me,"
said one official. "Where there isn't a good working relationship with the
assistant secretary, even without my saying anything, it filters down; they
don't work so hard."

At the same time, civil servants experienced in the slippage between thought and action in government realize better than political appointees the need to work at implementation. As one GS 16 said, "You cannot expect things to happen simply because the word goes out from on high." An undersecretary elaborated the point by citing the experience of a neighboring agency, where a program reorganization supported by both the President and the secretary was eventually forgotten:

> There was a kind of naive view that presidential messages and secretarial proclamations were self-fulfilling. There wasn't any follow-through, no constant pressure, and so nothing happened. They thought it was disloyalty when in fact it was mainly the inability of a complex machine to perceive what's expected of it.

If top bureaucrats can be found to help appointees push for follow-through, the value of the service performed can be immense. Acting alone, a political executive is a temporary force, and this well-known fact can tinge the responsiveness of the entire organization. On the other hand, a senior bureaucrat supporting a political executive is probably known as a persisting and tenacious figure. Few of those lower down in the agency can count on outliving his or her displeasure.

In Review

The preceding list of bureaucratic services amounts to a formidable array of help potentially available to public executives. Yet once again—this time from the bureaucrat's perspective—the incentives characterizing the present system of executive politics are at war with what is needed to help political leadership. The further higher civil servants go in providing their services to a political executive, the riskier their situation becomes. One of the greatest risks is that of political identification and later reprisals by succeeding appointees. Since political appointees are responsible for but not particularly interested in the career system of higher civil servants, a helpful bureaucrat can find his career development as a civil servant thwarted (although there may of course be an offer of employment in the private sector). Moreover, since political executives frequently have trouble organizing themselves, there is also the danger of creating a confrontation with one or more of the many uncoordinated political appointees elsewhere in the executive branch who might take exception to the help being offered. Not least is the risk of upsetting the bureaucrats' own more enduring networks and the security they bring to the fragile structure of the higher civil service.

There is no need to paint an idealized picture of the officials themselves. By no means are all higher civil servants interested in offering information, criticism, proposals, and follow-through in a timely fashion that would help political executives. Neither are all obstructionists proficient only at showing why any particular thing cannot be done. And that is precisely the point: bureaucrats are not all anything. Rather, these people in government are a highly variegated resource. Like most other resources, they can be squandered or conserved, left fallow or used. Whether and how they are used depends heavily on the actions of particular political executives.

Hence some expectations associated with the use of higher civil servants in the United States will be less productive than others. Political executives, including presidents, who expect outstanding feats of ecumenicalism in dealing with interagency problems are usually disappointed, particularly if the issue requires civil servants to deal outside their customarily narrow networks. Executives sometimes assume that they will readily meld organization personnel into one team of loyal players who pay little attention to the downside risks of cooperation; such executives do not understand the nature of bureaucratic careers, dispositions, and protections in Washington. A political appointee who plans to get along without the bureaucracy's help, or to acquire it automatically, or to cease worrying about it as long as civil servants are simply doing what they are told does not recognize the substance of the bureaucracy's power and its capacity to withhold needed services.

Whom Do You Trust?

The real test of a political executive's statecraft is his ability to institute the changes he wants without losing the bureaucratic services he requires. It is a question of needing positive services and not just passive obedience from top bureaucrats; of understanding that while political and career roles differ, there nevertheless must be a commitment to mutual performance by members of the same team. Thus working relationships between political executives and higher civil servants have to move beyond mere confidence about the surroundings to at least some minimum level of trust. In democratic theory this relationship should exist automatically between political leaders with a legitimate popular mandate and bureaucrats committed to norms of civil service responsiveness; in practice it must be worked at strenuously and carefully since the natural starting point for political-bureaucratic relations in Washington is one of pervasive suspicion.

Suspicion in Perspective

Reflecting the attitudes of the American public at large, political executives typically arrive in office expecting to deal with "Washington bureaucrats," not people. Those from executive positions in private business are deeply imbued with notions of gaining management control. This, combined with suspicions of government activity in general and Democratic social programs in particular, seems to predispose Republican appointees to be particularly distrustful of career officials. But executives from both parties can be expected to exhibit the suspicions of transients against their complex and uncertain surroundings. One supergrade summed up thirty years of experience by saying that "the normal thing in all political appointees is to begin by being down on the bureaucrats. Distrust is the one thing in common for all administrations and among appointees within the same administration."

Signals indicating a lack of trust are readily apparent. Frequently a political executive says so directly, either within his agency or in the ubiquitous speeches outside Washington condemning "the bureaucracy," i.e., the same collection of officials who will do much to make his tenure a success or failure. "He let it be known all over that he thought everyone around here was out to bag him," said a high civil servant about one appointee. "I had to assume that he regarded me as one of the chief bag men." Other political appointees suggest their blanket suspicion by supposed reassurances to officials, as one did who called in all the career people and told them: "I'm assuming there is no problem and that you are going to do your job, but if I find out later that I was wrong, then heads will roll." Implicitly, of course, everyone was also being told that he was on trial, and an already cautious mind-set grew more so.

Actions mean more than words in signaling suspicion, as in the agency where all operations were halted pending review by the head office, or in another agency where extensive new clearance requirements in the head office demonstrated an indiscriminate distrust of agency officials and their work. Everyday working relations may be arranged so that contacts with higher civil servants are channeled through the personal aides of a political executive, or orders are communicated but not the reasons for them. A kind of insecurity and suspicion is also conveyed by appointees who seek to begin by emphasizing their symbols of control—"redecorating their offices, moving the furniture, and playing with the organization charts."

The suspicions do not stem simply from public stereotypes or political ill will. In a number of cases the newcomer's distrust may have some justification. For example, a survey found that the attitudes of Nixon political appointees were significantly more conservative and opposed to extensions of government social services than were those of career officials, particularly officials in the social service agencies. But it must be remembered that the term "bureaucrat" embraces a variety of people and attitudes. The same survey showed that by the same standards at least one-fifth of career supergrades could be classified as being to the right of center, compared with 31 percent of political appointees in 1970.[7] No doubt Republican appointees did have fewer potential allies in the particular program units they were seeking to cut, but this only pointed up the need for greater skill and selectivity in dealing with careerists. Instead, a number of political purges were conducted. By failing to discriminate in their initial distrust, Nixon appointees became ingrown and cut off from almost all bureaucratic services that were available in other parts of the same agency. The new leaders soon led themselves into administratively stupid courses of action, resulting in an eventual explosion of public spending that was the direct opposite of what the appointees had intended.[8] The basic point is that indiscriminate suspicion, like indiscriminate trust, forecloses the political executive's chance to learn which particular suspicions are justified or where trust may best be placed.

Although political executives, rather than career officials, are nominal heads of the civil service system, they are initially in a poor position to assess and judge their bureaucratic subordinates. This is particularly true if the appointees are inexperienced in Washington, as is often the case. There is always a wealth of unsubstantiated rumors. Personal knowledge

7. Joel D. Aberbach and Bert A. Rockman, "Clashing Beliefs within the Executive Branch," *American Political Science Review*, vol. 70 (June 1976), table 3, p. 461. Other attitude surveys show the career bureaucracy to be somewhat more liberal and Democratic on some redistributive questions but far from monolithic in these views; on many policy issues their views are quite similar to those of Republican politicians and party officials. See Allen H. Barton, "Consensus and Conflict among American Leaders," *Public Opinion Quarterly*, vol. 38 (Winter 1974–75), table 2, p. 513.

8. Martha Derthick, *Uncontrollable Spending for Social Services Grants* (Brookings Institution, 1975), pp. 113–14.

may be extensive within the subgovernments of bureaucrats, interest groups, and congressional committees, but across the broader areas of government where top political executives operate, interpersonal networks are fragile and incomplete. One appointee provided an insightful comparison between his small-town newspaper background and the Washington environment of strangers:

> Back home you had to be more careful and accurate with what you said. Half the town heard it and you could actually run into the person you wrote about. He might punch you in the nose. Here you can't be sure who saw what and if you say something carelessly that affects someone, it probably won't reflect on your personal relations. . . . Of course, you too might get a knife in the back some night without knowing who or why.

The techniques available for gaining preliminary information about the bureaucracy are necessarily crude. Political clearance of career positions is one informal procedure that is commonly used, but this can be an extremely misleading source of information about people in government. In some cases the transitional arrangements with an outgoing appointee may help give a new executive a working knowledge of officials and their performance. The most pervasive method of suspicion-testing, however, occurs through personal word of mouth among people in and at the fringes of the agency. Always, it seems, there is somebody who knows somebody else in Washington (although they are all unlikely to know each other as a group). Obtaining readings on people from friends and friends of friends is part of the way of life.

Where there is a measure of professional political continuity among government executives—even of different parties—these soundings may be well-based. One official described how it worked in his case:

> Secretary of Labor Jim Mitchell brought me up from the ranks in the Eisenhower administration. Then when the Kennedy administration came in, Secretary Goldberg had been a labor lawyer and knew his predecessors and people in the department pretty well. . . . Then Wirtz was undersecretary to Goldberg, so I knew him well when he became secretary. When Nixon came in, Secretary Shultz had been a consultant to the department, so not only did I know him but Wirtz gave Shultz a good reading on me.

Without such linkages among trusted old hands (ties that seem less and less common in the Washington community), word-of-mouth signals can easily become haphazard and dangerous. During their customary courtesy calls to congressional offices before Senate confirmation hearings, presidential appointees are frequently told about bureaucrats they should distrust in their agency. Such comments are as likely to be self-serv-

ing as informative, and similar distortions can be picked up from lobbyists resentful of bureaucrats who have resisted pressure. And sometimes—
as one career personnel director said—other bureaucrats "try to get ahead
with a new guy by peddling tales to him about who to watch out for." On
all these counts the newcomer who rushes into personnel actions can
quickly become entangled in longstanding bureaucratic or congressional
feuds about which he knows nothing.

Even if political executives have no personal ill will against the bureaucracy, they can be badly misled if they fail to test the rumors that
constantly circulate in the political layers. Two high officials, an assistant
secretary and one of his career division chiefs, described their perceptions
of a common experience. Here is how the division chief saw it:

> He [the assistant secretary] had very little respect for the government bu-
> reaucracy when he first came in, and within twenty minutes of our first
> meeting we were fighting. But after that meeting he called around people
> in the government and industry and got mostly good reports on me. It's
> your reputation that matters. Later when he left, he recommended me to
> his successor.

The assistant secretary in question described the kind of soft information
with which inexperienced political appointees frequently deal and the
need for careful checking:

> He [the civil servant] was due for removal because he was a Democrat. Even
> worse, people were calling him a Kennedy Democrat. So I called over to
> [another political appointee] and asked where he got this information
> about the guy, and he said it came from a newspaperman. I asked him if he
> had checked it out, and he never had. Here they were ruining a guy without
> even an afterthought. When I checked him out with people who really
> knew, I found that getting rid of him would be one of the biggest mistakes
> I could have made.

Thus preliminary efforts to establish working relations in government
can easily become colored by the readings picked up by political appointees—strangers to government whose need for accurate intelligence
about subordinate personnel is often matched by their ignorance about
the character and self-interests of those proffering the information.

Since political executives are in charge of higher career personnel
actions but are in a poor position to make careful assessments, even the
most conscientious careerists are vulnerable to reactions based on little
more than the fact that different sets of political appointees do not happen to know each other or do not know enough to acquire reliable information about people in government. One young GS 17 expressed a common problem among high-ranking civil servants: "Notions of political

identification and who is unreliable often grow without good verification. The question is how do you break through the suspicion without becoming somebody's man?"

As explained in chapter 4, part of the answer is that higher civil servants try to safeguard their reputations and move cautiously in order to prevent indeliberate political identification. Often, however, they also try to counteract the initial, indiscriminate suspicion held by political appointees. Officials report, for example, that new appointees sometimes ask directly "Who should be contacted to find out about you?" One prudent careerist reported picking people that "like and don't like me so that when the guy goes around he will see that I tried to play straight with him." By now it is almost a meaningless cliché in Washington when some bureaucrats declare to a new boss that they are there to do whatever he or she wants. Civil servants with something to offer political leaders are more likely to feel that such ceremonies suggest "you're just a cipher. If you say anything it should be that you're there to do the best job you can, that you'll speak your mind when you disagree." Generally, in fact, high officials seem to feel that it is best not to say anything by way of reassurance. One veteran supergrade made the point with colorful precision: "It's like if your wife suspects you of running around with another woman. If you start arguing to try to prove your innocence, you're done for. The best thing you can do is take your wife up to the bedroom and prove it by performance."

Since not all top bureaucrats are interested in offering help, sensitivity to the signals of those who are becomes that much more important for new political executives. The specific acts range widely, but the basic technique is for officials to try to show they can produce something of value. For example, five high-ranking careerists described the signs they use in their different departments:

—I try to set it up so that I've got someplace else to go when a new assistant secretary comes in. This shows in advance that I'm being serious when I let it be known that he can replace me if he wants to.

—He's got to see you as a human being, not just a block on the chart. You've got to get in early, even if it's just helping with the little annoyances like where a piece of paper is supposed to go, how to get an aide appointed through the maze of regulations. You tell him just to give you a buzz when anything comes up.

—You create trust by showing from the beginning you can meet deadlines and even if the decision goes against you, you're willing to carry it through.

—If you're going to deal with the suspicion people come in with, you've got to not only be responsive but appear responsive. Don't be one of these guys who the first time he hears something figures out twenty-eight reasons it can't be done. See what you can work out. Now a lot of new people are coming in with the idea of zero-base budgeting, but you don't start off by telling them it can't work. We try honestly until the guy sees the folly. But I'm not going to create a credibility gap personally with him and render myself ineffective over discussion of a concept.

—I try to counteract all the mistrust by servicing them to death, cutting corners as I can and hurrying up things they want. When you become more familiar with the man then you can take a harder line and play less at servicing them so much. Usually the first thing they're interested in is office space and creature comforts.

Whatever the particular technique, experienced civil servants recognize that demonstrating they have something to deliver far outweighs any effort to argue against the distrust of new executives.

Trust, within Limits

After the first year or two most political appointees do seem to learn to qualify their preliminary distrust of the bureaucracy. Many actually leave Washington regretting the bulk of their early suspicions. The following statement from a relatively long-time cabinet officer can stand for many of its kind:

Sitting around the table year after year, you could see changes in cabinet secretaries. To some it happened more quickly than others. They'd come in flailing out in all directions—going to get control. [A secretary of the interior] fired his entire planning staff. [The secretary of agriculture] came out early with press releases condemning the bureaucracy and how he was going to get after them. . . . [The secretary of the treasury] was particularly antagonistic. You found in every case that at the end of their terms these men were giving credit to civil servants, appointing many to very high jobs. [The secretary of agriculture] ended with a luncheon where he even apologized in public. He admitted he hadn't known anything at all about the department when those news releases were written by one of his aides. Mind you, some bureaucrats in the department were playing partisan politics and making trouble, but he apologized for condemning the whole group because of these few.

Behind such reports lies more than a preference for harmony over hard feelings and more than an indicator that political executives inevitably become pawns of their agencies. The cabinet official continued by drawing a lesson of critical relevance:

If you're too strong-minded, you can create a lot of mistrust and trouble for yourself. On the other hand, you can also let your people run you. It's a question of balance. New people would come in and until they were on top of their jobs they couldn't do many things they wanted. They didn't know why, but they couldn't. They couldn't get things done until they had learned to get the trust of people in the department.

Indiscriminate suspicion may indeed prevent political executives from obtaining the bureaucratic help they need. But why should public appointees make an effort not only to reserve their suspicions but to actively establish relations of positive trust in the bureaucracy? Three reasons stand out from the preceding discussions.

In the first place some minimum level of trust is necessary for the everyday, personalized interactions of executive politics. Since officials in government are also people in government, beliefs about political leaders in general can readily contaminate specific issues in a way that might seem illogical for abstract, rational models of decisionmaking. Discourse, much less leadership, is impossible if every action has to be accompanied by reassurances that the general intentions are honorable. Attempts by the second Nixon administration to institute a government-wide system of management by objectives provided a good—if extreme —example.[9] This management technique, which seems to have been not only without ulterior motives but largely ignored by the Nixon White House, sought to systematize methods for keeping track of progress toward meeting agreed upon agency goals. Whatever the pros and cons of the idea, by the end of 1973 the executives in charge realized that they had to institutionalize the process by gaining bureaucratic support and involvement but that they had little chance of doing so except in isolated circumstances. According to one of the management experts: "There was no way you could make department people take this seriously on its merits. By then they could only see it as a way of seeding CREP [the 1972 Committee to Reelect the President] people throughout government and putting a Plumbers Unit under every bed."

The second reason why some degree of political-bureaucratic trust is essential has to do with political appointees in executive agencies being in a political twilight zone. However adept a public executive may be, there are—as one said—"times of crunch when, if things aren't going to turn very ugly for you, people in your agency just have to accept that you're acting in good faith." Such times may occur, for example, when all the

9. The experiment with management by objectives is analyzed in Richard Rose, *Managing Presidential Objectives* (Free Press, 1976).

normal ploys have been exhausted and personnel or budget cuts are still required if the appointee is to appear as a "good soldier" for the new administration. Or circumstances may force a decision that subordinate officials cannot be informed about in advance or given reasons for. Without an established positive balance of trust, public executives are unlikely to be able to borrow on their abstract authority as political appointees to gain bureaucratic compliance. Trust facilitates forbearance.

The final imperative for trust stems from the bureaucratic caution that has been built up by long association with a series of transient political executives. Many of these appointees will have expected much and offered little in return except recriminations against the bureaucracy when things did not go as smoothly as they had expected. Without a sense of mutual trust and teamwork with at least some experienced career officials, political executives will find that services offered by the bureaucracy—the orientations, warnings, positive advice, and so on—are too tentative and too passive to be of very much value.

Political executives do not need to trust everyone in the bureaucracy, but they need to trust some. Equally important, they themselves need to be trusted to at least some degree. "If the permanent people see me as untrustworthy, I'm cut off at the legs," an undersecretary said. Thus an executive who has cultivated bureaucratic trust is like a man with a good credit rating. People dealing with him feel less vulnerable and will not ask him to prove himself each time he wants something. He will have to pay less to borrow on the resources of others. They will forbear with him longer before any repayment need occur. All of this is particularly important for would-be government leaders, given their own limited political resources and brief tenures.

Morality aside, trust and good repute are good politics for public executives. What is at stake was best summarized by two experienced appointees from quite different agencies. The first, a departing undersecretary, described how he tried to warn his replacement in a small staff agency that has few program responsibilities and little outside interest group pressures:

> I tried to tell him that if he made everyone around here think they were on trial pending his approval, it just wasn't going to work. Everybody will play cautious too. They'll sit on their haunches taking orders and not volunteering information for fear of being stepped on. It's not so much what the career man will do to you, but what he doesn't tell you that you ought to know. I told him, "Some day you're going to have a big problem and wake up shaking your head and it's going to come off."

The second, an assistant secretary, recounted a similar experience in a huge program-oriented agency under pressure from vociferous clienteles and interest groups:

> If you don't get some of the bureaucrats on your side, you're going to get the hell kicked out of you. You don't get straight answers. A paper the secretary is supposed to have by 10 A.M. just doesn't turn up, or they don't tell you something that occurred at a meeting and you find yourself lambasted at another meeting the next afternoon. Then in testifying on the Hill it's not just the factual basis for answers but their ability through staff contacts to anticipate what a senator is interested in and then help you get prepared on that. . . . And when you're tempted to cut corners dealing with Congress a good bureaucrat will show you how much trouble that creates in the long run. If you've got good relations with the career people, their contacts are going to help you. If relations aren't good, they can cut your throat with their contacts.

In sum, holding Washington's higher civil servants at arm's length begets arm's length treatment in return. As a last-ditch strategy casting aside lines of bureaucratic trust may be required, but as an original premise it also casts aside the bureaucracy's services. It is a strategy that promises few rewards and much pain to political leadership.

The tempering of initial suspicions and the acknowledgment of some trust are preliminary but necessary conditions for establishing the working relationships of political administration. Most appointees seriously involved in government work do come to recognize their need for assistance from below, and those who do not are probably beyond help. The more difficult issue is why bureaucrats should feel they need the political strangers. Here the answers are more obscure. If it is a need based only on fear of political reprisal and punishment, then bureaucratic passiveness can usually suffice to outlive the threat. Faced with this situation, political executives who have survived the preliminary refinements of trust and suspicion usually try to cope by using a fairly limited but important set of strategic resources. In the next chapter I identify these resources and describe how they are used.

CHAPTER SIX

Working Relations: The Main Event

The majority will be governed by their interests.
—George Mason, *Constitutional Debates*, August 29, 1787

ONCE POLITICAL EXECUTIVES have learned to qualify their initial distrust and have established preliminary working relations in the Washington bureaucracy, they are ready to move on to the main event: using these relationships and networks in a strategic way. Political appointees are not and should not be in a position to gain absolute power over their agencies, but they can strengthen their hands for political leadership.

Experts writing about private organizations have described two different orientations toward management control. Under so-called Theory X it is assumed that an average subordinate avoids work if he can, loathes responsibility, covets security, and must be directed and threatened with punishment in order to put forth sufficient effort to achieve managerial goals. Theory Y emphasizes a worker's need for identity and personal growth through work, rewards rather than punishment as a means of motivation, and the cooperation toward objectives that can be gained by commitments to mutually agreed upon goals rather than by strict supervision from above.[1]

1. The arguments are reviewed and set out in much greater detail in Douglas McGregor, *The Professional Manager* (McGraw-Hill, 1967); Frederick Herzberg, *Work and the Nature of Man* (Cleveland: World Publishers, 1966); and William K. Graham and Karlene H. Roberts, eds., *Comparative Studies in Organizational Behavior* (Holt, Rinehart and Winston, 1972). One of the few relevant studies of civil servants is Fremont James Lyden, "Motivation and Civil Service Employees," *Public Administration Review*, vol. 30 (May-June 1970). For a discussion of the generally lower level of commitment in government executives, see Bruce Buchanan, "Government Managers, Business Executives, and Disorganizational Commitment," *Public Administration Review*, vol. 34 (July-August 1974), pp. 339–47.

What matters is not so much the academic models of "nice guy" or "tough guy" management but that public executives constantly come to Washington acting as if they subscribe to one or the other of these views. Consider again the social service agencies mentioned in the last chapter, where political and career executives held strongly opposing views. After several years on the job two of Nixon's leading appointees in these agencies pondered their different routes to ineffectiveness. Here is how one, a self-acknowledged muscleman, looked back on his approach to subordinates:

> In the short run it probably helped me to be known as a monster. It established me as a force to be reckoned with. A lot of people were afraid to join battle with me. But in the long run it hurt a lot because it put people on the defensive. You'll get some reaction if people think you're mean enough or are going to be around a while or have enough powerful allies, but it can't last long enough to have much impact. You're not likely to know when you're getting real cooperation and when they're just acting out of fear. If I had to do it again, I'd spend more time getting to know the people under me and their programs. I'd keep asking why do we do it this way, why that? It is not really effective trying to browbeat people and win every little battle.

The other political executive (in the same agency) avoided all the mistakes of his tough colleague, but reflected on the futility of his wholly compassionate approach:

> I made the decisions but they [bureaucratic subordinates] just continued to argue. The delays went on until I left office. . . . The biggest problems were the procedures and paper work and special pleading by office heads under me. I was overburdened because I couldn't count on delegating it and have things turn out the way I wanted . . . I think they figured I would be an easy mark. . . . I made the same mistake the secretary did. He was too nice to knock heads and let people know he meant what he said. [A successor] came in and got things going. He let people know he expected orders to be followed in a timely fashion and when they weren't, heads got knocked, people transferred; there were early retirements.

Lessons can be drawn from these and similar experiences, but frequently only the bureaucrats are around long enough to do so and to learn from such failures. According to a high bureaucrat who watched both appointees:

> They did all the wrong things. I don't think they ever understood that governing is about making a lot of different forces coalesce. The feudal bureaus, interest groups, congressional politics—these are all things to be used. There are pretty firm limits on your control and how far you can persuade people to change, but there is some room for progress by pulling these things together. . . . The smarter guys choose a manageable number

of things they care about and promote key people already here who can help still the rebels. They try and bring around those opposing them. It can take three to four years and will never work if you start off by telling bureaucrats they're crap. . . .

You don't let people buck you and run behind your back. If you catch them at it, you can isolate them and get rid of them. . . . But you also don't get far by coming in and setting up separate people, programs, and ideas to the exclusion of existing ones. If it's going to stick, what you want has got to be associated with what's going to be here after you're gone. An appointee has got to make other people feel a part of the credit line.

Of course this bureaucrat is only one of the many people involved in executive politics who are constantly judging and ranking each other in numerous different ways. Yet in Washington anecdotes of this kind (many of which are naturally self-serving), there is a core of agreement about what has constituted the statecraft of effective political executives.

The basic theme of this chapter is that experience reveals the shortcomings of both Theory X and Theory Y and suggests the value of a third approach to working relations between political executives and ranking bureaucrats. It is what might be termed "conditionally cooperative behavior." Any premise of compassionate cooperation and participatory management overlooks the bureaucracy's divided loyalties, its needs for self-protection, and its multiple sources of resistance. Unconditionally negative approaches fail to recognize the enduring character of bureaucratic power and a political leader's need to elicit the bureaucracy's help in governing.

Conditional cooperation emerges between these extremes. It implies a kind of cooperation that is conditional on the mutual performance of the political appointees and the civil servants. It emphasizes the need of executives and bureaucrats to work at relationships that depend on the contingencies of one another's actions, not on preconceived ideas of strict supervision or harmonious goodwill. Conditional cooperation rejects any final choice between suspicion and trust, between trying to force obedience and passively hoping for compliance. By making their reactions conditional on the performance of subordinates, political appointees create latitude for choice—possibilities for various types of exchanges with different bureaucrats. The basis for the executives' leadership becomes strategic rather than "take it or leave it."

As opposed to a set formula that assures success, conditional cooperation is a strategy that suggests a variety of resources and methods for trading services. It increases the likelihood that some political executives will do better than others in getting what they need from Washington's bureaucracies. Superficially, conditional cooperation might seem to be simply a matter of exchanging favors with the bureaucracy on a quid pro quo basis. The reality of executive leadership is more subtle. It involves bringing others to appreciate not so much what they have gotten as what they might get. Would-be executive leaders, remember, are like poor credit risks in a well-established credit market; they have had little chance to acquire a favorable standing or reputation in the eyes of other participants who are used to dealing with each other. The new political strangers have to work at building credit in the bureaucracy precisely because they have not had—and will only briefly enjoy—a chance to put anyone in their debt. Even so, memories are short and debts are often not repaid in Washington. The real basis of conditional cooperation lies in making bureaucrats creditors rather than debtors to the political executives; that is, giving them a stake in his future performance. Any past exchange of favors between appointees and careerists is far less influential than the general hope of grasping future returns. It is the grasping rather than the gratitude that drives executive politics.

Using Strategic Resources

Strategic resources are important because they provide the possibility of exchanges with the bureaucracy that can create commitments to mutual performance. In theory, of course, it is conceivable that trust could be based on unconditional cooperation—a kind of gift relationship in which political and bureaucratic leaders expect little in return from each other. In practice, exchange is a way of life cultivated by those in the ambiguous executive roles of Washington. Political appointees cannot expect to stand—much less move—on the basis of their formal authority as appointed political leaders; neither can high careerists expect to be automatically accepted as carriers of the internal norms of civil service responsiveness. Even the institutionalist bureaucrat, the clearest example of a "model" civil servant, expects that his cooperation will be repaid with some degree of political respect for the integrity of government institutions. A distinguished academic "in-and-outer" colorfully described the public executives' strategic situation:

> I spent the first days up with [the secretary], and it was marvelous all the plans we were making—the executive suites, limousines, and all that. Then

I went down into the catacombs and there were all these gray men, you know—GS 15s, 16s, and I understood what they were saying to me. "Here we are. You may try to run around us. You may even run over us and pick a few of our boys off, but we'll stay and you won't. Now, what's in it for us, sonny boy." And they were right, there was nothing in it for them. The next time I got a presidential appointment, I made sure there was something I could do for them and they could do for me. We sat down together and did business.

Strategic resources in Washington are means by which executives and bureaucrats try to show "what's in it" for each other. These resources can be grouped into a few serviceable categories: goals and opportunities, procedures for building support, and ways of using people. But to many observers the most immediately obvious resource is an executive's political power. Paradoxically, a closer examination shows that political power may be one of the clearest but also one of the most limited assets for purposes of political leadership in the bureaucracy.

Political Clout

Appointees with political clout—those who are willing and able to use the means of self-help described in chapter 5—not only extend their circles of confidence for dealing with outsiders but also create resources for dealing with civil servants inside. One such resource is a political executive's potential *access* to higher political levels. Career officials recognize that political contacts can mean the difference between the views of their agency being heard versus being merely tolerated or even ignored in the secretary's office or the White House. A careerist recalled longingly:

> Our last assistant secretary had terrific relations with [the secretary and two high appointees in the White House and the OMB]. He could call up, tell them our problems, and get them to listen and see if they could help. It improved our odds. Not everything, but an awful lot in Washington is done on the strength of these one-to-one relationships. Now we can't even get in the ball game.

Information carried back from higher political levels also aids top civil servants if their political executives convey it. It helps to know, for example, "whether it's just an ad hoc decision or something implying a policy," or "what's of interest and worrying the political people; maybe it's just some prior notice the President is giving a speech on a certain subject." Without such information higher civil servants know less in advance and worry more. "You spend your time on papers that no one really cares about . . . you have no idea of how the other political people are likely to react. . . . You don't know whether it really is a topside decision by the President or secretary or a call by some young political aide three times removed."

Thus the more adept a political appointee becomes in building his circles of confidence and in protecting his prerogatives, the more the value of his *advocacy* appreciates in the eyes of the bureaucrats below. In every department in every recent administration, one of the chief ways political executives gained support in the bureaucracy was by being, or at least appearing to be, their agency's vigorous spokesman. "Fighting your counterparts in other departments creates confidence and support beneath you," one acknowledged. In reference to a strong advocate in his department, a civil servant said: "He was well regarded on the Hill and dealt from strength with [the interest group]. A lot of White House people were afraid of him. You could get more of what was wanted approved and through Congress." Less politically effective executives may be personally admired by civil servants but have little to offer in return for bureaucratic support. As one such cabinet secretary was described by a bureau chief: "He had charisma, a really fine and open man who a lot of civil servants around here liked. But he never got a grip on the department. He didn't really fight for what was needed and if he made a decision it was because he got maneuvered into it by the staff." Experienced bureaucrats recognize that such appointees leave their agencies and programs vulnerable to more politically aggressive competitors elsewhere. In this sense, career officials will typically prefer a strong if unpleasant advocate to an amiable weakling.

A politically effective appointee is involved in speaking out, making claims, attacking other people. Openly exercising political muscle in this way involves a high degree of public *risk-taking*, which civil servants themselves are likely to shun. The very fact that a political executive not only is expendable but certain to be expended can paradoxically provide a strategic resource of sorts. Since any large bureaucracy is rarely of one piece, some civil servants consider a new face that is willing and able to expose itself politically to be an opportunity for support that had better be used while it is available. After serving under a string of cabinet secretaries, a bureaucrat observed:

> One thing I've eventually learned is that new people coming in can often get things done that others around a long time can't. People in the bureaucracy are telling them it's impossible, but they don't know that something can't be done and they do it. Like some Republicans have come in with no

real obligations to the unions after an election, and that can be a big advantage. On the other hand, sometimes the unions will take things from a guy
they regard as "one of them" that they'd never take from anybody else. It
cuts both ways, and when you get a new guy who's tough and knowledgeable, you better make hay while the sun shines.

Thus a political appointee who shows himself able to take political risks
can evoke responses that belie the stereotype of bureaucrats waiting to
outlast political appointees.

Generally all these resources—political access, information, advocacy,
and risk-taking—are by-products of any appointee's efforts to build
credibility amid the maze of strangers in the government community.
Political executives who can help themselves (like those already advantaged politically by the selection process) gain compound interest in
dealing with the bureaucracy. For other executives, nothing fails like
failure; political weakness in dealing with outsiders exacerbates all their
problems of coping with bureaucratic insiders. To those who have, more
is given, and those with scant political support are likely to have even
that taken away by government infighting.

The resources derived from political clout, however, are also severely
limited for would-be political leaders in government agencies. Risk-taking,
advocacy, and so on, all point outward and are only very indirectly related
to changing the behavior of officialdom itself. If political executives do
not already agree with, or are unwilling to adopt, the bulk of the careerists'
own agenda, then other resources for dealing with the bureaucracy are
required. A politically powerful undersecretary explained: "We got along
very well in the department because we wanted to and helped the bureaucrats do what they wanted to do." But the need for political leadership
often goes further than bureaucratic advocacy. The same undersecretary's deputy recalled:

> We got a lot of loyalty and backup from the civil servants in return for his
> confidence in them. But the result too was that we got sucked in a number
> of times—I mean accepting and defending their advice that something
> couldn't be done. Then when the heat got turned on in Congress or the
> press, you found out you could do these things after all. . . . What we didn't
> get was a lot of critical, innovative thought, because going along with the
> careerists in the accepted ways wasn't the way to get that. You also have to
> double-check, push bureaucrats, get mad sometimes.

The paradoxical fact is that the political clout of the appointees can help
bureaucrats get more of what they want, but it offers little assurance that
appointees can get what they want from the bureaucracy, especially if this
implies changes in policy. If mere appeals to outside political power could

compel changes among officials inside, the executives' lives would be easy; indeed their leadership would be unnecessary in the executive branch. But life is not so simple. As government leaders, the executives' problem is to gain the changes they want while acquiring the services they need from the bureaucracy. For that, they have to unite managerial brainwork and sensitivity to whatever political muscle they may have.

Goals and Opportunities

The pressure of time and circumstances forces political executives to confront many choices they would rather overlook. It also forces them to overlook many things they might like to consider.

In a general sense this need to focus attention is a constraint on leadership, yet in a strategic sense it can also be an asset. Experienced political executives have found that the process of goal-setting can be an important source of strength in dealing with the bureaucracy.

The underlying logic seems obvious, but it is often lost from view in the press of events and crises. A political executive who does not know what he wants to accomplish is in no position to assess the bureaucracy's performance in helping him do it. Likewise, an executive whose aims bear little relation to the chances for accomplishment is in an equally weak position to stimulate help from officials below. By trying to select goals in relation to available opportunities, political appointees create a strategic resource for leadership in the bureaucracy.

The operational word is selectivity. By the time they are leaving office, political appointees commonly regret the waste involved both in trying to do everything at once and in trying to do anything that is unrelated to the available chances for success. Here is how appointees from three different departments described what they had learned.

An assistant secretary:

"We didn't figure out what could and could not be moved in the department, with OMB, with the appropriations committee. . . . We bloodied our noses on things that couldn't really be changed.

An undersecretary:

Deciding what you can win is important because then you don't use resources needlessly. For example, here are six decision memoranda on decentralization. I had no idea there'd be such a strong congressional backlash. Next time I wouldn't try and get some general authority through. I'd decentralize only a small bit of programs at first. It's a matter of what you can and cannot win and how you can or cannot win.

An assistant secretary, after eighteen months on the job, describing a standard situation:

> There's a budget cycle, a personnel cycle, a planning cycle—for what it's worth—and lots of other smaller recurrences in the department's business. It can take a year for these to unfold so you understand about them and see it is a matter of which cycles you leave for civil servants to keep running and which you try and make work for you. Doing it again, I'd spend less time trying to deal with 60 percent of everything and drop to 30 percent on some things and 90 percent on others I care about.

Obviously such comments have much in common with the bureaucratic dispositions mentioned earlier—gradualism, indirection, and so on. This does not necessarily mean that appointees have been captured by the bureaucracy, but it does suggest an accommodation to the need for fitting ends and means in the exercise of leadership. Such discrimination can be found alike in appointees who seek to expand or cut government programs and in those who see their aims as stemming from their own agenda or (as in the cases quoted above) from overall White House desires.

How do political appointees try to link choices on goals with available opportunities and thereby strengthen the incentives for bureaucratic cooperation? Specific circumstances obviously vary, but they have some common features.

PREEMPTIVE STRIKES

The early days in office—particularly with a new administration—constitute a particularly rich set of opportunities for any objectives aimed at major change. "After the first year the magic is gone, the weaknesses start to show, and you get bogged down with criticisms about what's gone wrong since you came in," one appointee remarked. A top appointee in another administration related how

> setting out major policy lines quickly means you're at an advantage because things are still loose and flexible in government. Later, people get more locked into positions; it's easier to get out-maneuvered. If people under you are confused in the first year about what's wanted and control is lost, then it is hard ever to get it back.

The advantages to be gained from scheduling major changes early, however, are extraordinarily difficult to realize in Washington. Most appointees cannot expect to enter office at the very beginning of a new administration. Even if they do, the incoming presidential party will rarely arrive with an operational plan for what it wants to accomplish in specific agencies. Moreover, the advantages of prompt action fit poorly with the needs of new political appointees to learn about their jobs and establish a network of relationships in the nation's capital. The exception to the normal situation was cited by one executive who had reorganized his agency, cut the work force by one-fifth, and won legislation to substantially redirect the major objectives of its programs:

> The only reason we could do it was because we knew what we wanted and moved between February and May, right after the inauguration and my confirmation. People in other agencies weren't quite sure what was happening and anybody getting upset didn't know where to go. Later in the year, without the honeymoon feeling and confusion, I'd have been stymied.

AREAS OF RELATIVE INDIFFERENCE

As political executives learn more about the particular views that seem to be locked into congressional committees, interest groups, and subordinate officials, they often seek advantages by choosing to act in areas of relative disinterest to other participants. They try, as one appointee said, "to charge down the corridors of indifference." Thus in many agencies the temporary executives generally find that they create less antagonism by concentrating on overall administration and organization rather than on detailed program delivery, on money grants rather than people services, on planning rather than implementation, and on squeezing rather than eliminating a program.

These strategic choices obviously reinforce inertia and marginal change in government. Such incentives can mean that many political appointees find it in their interest to deal with the easiest, not necessarily the most important, issues. But even (indeed especially) those appointees who recognize their leadership responsibility to cope with important controversial issues learn the value of selecting proximate goals that at least do not arouse a maximum of opposition initially. An executive trying to deal with programs in the Department of Agriculture described the details of a common situation:

> This is not what you'd call a common sense environment. You can't just go after things. With the Agricultural Extension Service, state and local governments pay the majority of their salaries. The state directors of FHA [Farmers Home Administration] are appointed by state political groups. The county office heads of ASCS [Agricultural Soil and Conservation Service] are appointed by elected county committees, but it handles farm programs at the core of this department's operations. We can't end the pilot school milk program, even though we now have the school lunch

program, because of the school lunch lobby, equipment manufacturers, milk lobby, and our own Nutrition Service. Each program also has a certain congressman's stamp on it. Eliminate it and it is an affront to him, the clients, and the bureaucrats delivering it to them. There are just a lot of people around who can tell you to go to hell when you go after program delivery. We decided to leave this alone and not get into how they sit down with clients.

MANAGEMENT MISSIONS

Even if political executives are unable to take advantage of early opportunities or areas of indifference, they can acquire advantages in dealing with the bureaucracy on the basis of objectives that are what some science administrators call "project-like." Such goals identify a given point to be reached with a particular set of resources and within a particular time. Expectations between political appointees and civil servants become more firmly based; the mutual performance that each expects of the other becomes clearer. Everyone, as one official said, "knows the mission. You have a schedule, costs, and a group of interlocking activities that have to be performed in order to get from here to there."

Some potential executives fear the disadvantages of such engineering analogies in government (among other problems, outsiders can more easily assess the executives' own performance); others feel they make the job easier. "You've got a better idea of where you stand, who's producing it, how to motivate officials to pull together," one said. The space program of the National Aeronautics and Space Administration (NASA) is the example most frequently given, but other executives may point to a major building program, a new accounting system, a given reduction rate in subsidies, and similar "missions."

A number of efforts have been and are being made to systematize the treatment of objectives in the executive branch, and no doubt further improvements can be made. Indeed the ability to provide clear, measurable objectives is often taken as the sine qua non of rational programs and political leadership in government. There is no need to review the ample literature on attempts to analyze (the planning, programming, and budgeting system), monitor (management by objectives) and reevaluate (the current program evaluation movement) agency objectives. Here it is enough to emphasize that as a practical matter the ability of most political executives to use project-type objectives in their working relationships with the bureaucracy are often severely limited. Businessmen experienced in government usually cite the lack of measurability compared with the

situation in private enterprise. "In the private sector you know the name
of the game—to get a percentage return, a certain productivity increase.
Here there're no profit guidelines. Dollars aren't the measure of your
performance." One explained that in government since "dollars aren't
the bottom line, you get proxies for performance, input measure related
to doing the work, providing a service, not producing an output." Knowing when a business has increased its market penetration from 40 percent
to 42 percent is not like knowing when people have decent housing or
proper health care.

Even beyond the problem of measurability, however, there are other
powerful constraints on the political executives' use of mission-like objectives. One of these limitations is that what can be measured is often unrelated to the effectiveness that is judged and rewarded. "If I sweated fat
out of my organization and increased productivity by 5 percent," said an
executive, "I'd be a big man in my company. Here I could do that and be
out of step with the secretary or a senator and get zinged every time. Or
I may be a boob and with a politically favored program still get my funds
increased in a way unrelated to how I'm doing as a manager."

Another inherent limitation is that since an executive's mission in
Washington usually depends on contributing actions by a number of
semi-independent outside participants, it can become extremely difficult
to judge who is responsible for poor performance when objectives are
missed. "At NASA we were lucky because there weren't six other agencies
. . . involved in trying to put a man on the moon. If our people blew it,
they couldn't pass the buck as easily as they can in most places." Political
appointees will probably have to accept the legitimacy of much of the
outside participation in their missions, even if this blurs accountability.

Still another constraint on mission-like political objectives lies in the
temporary executives' difficulty in learning enough about their organizations to assess the normal gamesmanship familiar in all organizational
objective-setting. As one management analyst in government observed:
"Objectives set unrealistically low just make people look good when they
surpass the goals. Set very high they may just frustrate people into finding
ways around them. The only way to get a sense of realism is to have
good substantive knowledge and experience with the programs themselves." As noted, not many political appointees can be counted on for
that kind of in-depth bureaucratic knowledge.

A final and most important constraint on the public executives' use
of objectives is that political leadership commonly involves changing

goals, not just hitting targets. An assistant secretary in one of the few agencies where measurable objectives were established by congressional statute acknowledged: "I was there just to get the program in place and running. There wasn't the time or opportunity to look back to ask if these are still the goals we should want to accomplish. It'll have to be someone else's job to worry about redirecting the agenda." Redirection may come from a new "man with a mission," but it is more likely to evolve slowly as new men cope with the circumstances. Goals are changed, not simply because political leaders renege on promises, but also because people who are affected complain about the old goals; or because some objectives (particularly in social programs that are oversold) cannot be achieved or achievement does not have the desired effect; or because people and organizations interested in self-preservation realize that having only one finite aim can be a terminal occupation—in short because of the normal course of self-interested interaction called politics.

CLIMATIC PRESSURES

Since discrete missions normally are difficult to use as a management tool, political executives improve their ability to deal with their organizations by treating goals, not as givens, but as part of an ongoing political process. "Climate" is a term frequently used to describe a variety of factors involved in adapting goals to prevailing circumstances. Sometimes a scandal may provide the impetus: "Billie Sol Estes was the best thing that ever happened to our plans for creating a post of inspector general [in the Agriculture Department]." Less drastic outside criticism can also help.

> Our secretary used to complain that the GAO [General Accounting Office] should get off his back. I was there when [the secretary of defense] told him he ought to get smart and do like he did: take advantage of every GAO report to get changes he wanted. With these reports he'd go to people in the interest groups and bureaucracy saying, "Look, these guys are breathing down our necks. Here's what we have to do." Sometimes he even did what GAO recommended.

Frequently less tangible "ideas in good currency" surround the bureaucracy and provide some of the best opportunities for realistic goal selection. Political executives who link their aims to ideas in good currency can gain a broader base to deal with even the most entrenched bureaucracy. One experienced official watched a succession of appointees gradually change a government agency that had once been considered to be in an impregnable alliance with its powerful clientele:

You can't really trace it to any one administration or appointee, but over time the bureau's budget was squeezed, some things taken away, nothing new added. A series of people coming in reflected the feeling in the air that there were broader policy issues that mattered more than the particular prerogatives of this bureau.

The continuity to accomplish such long-haul change exists in points of view rather than in particular people. This gradualism, of course, may not provide very much gratification for political executives interested in big payoffs within their relatively short terms of office.

Hence, as a strategic resource, the selective intermixture of goals and opportunities is important. It helps a political executive specify how his exercise of political clout on the bureaucracy's behalf is conditional on the bureaucrats' performance. It sensitizes executives to the fact that working relations with the bureaucracy depend not only on winning fights but also on selecting, transferring, bypassing, and often running away from some fights in favor of others. Yet there are also considerable limitations. Political appointees in Washington may not be able to act early or to find areas of indifference. Neither can they count on acquiring clear missions against which to measure and climatic opportunities with which to spur bureaucratic performance. And as the next section shows, however well an appointee manages to point people in a particular direction, he will discover that his job in the bureaucracy is one of selling, not pointing.

Building Support

Since few political executives have the clear missions or massive public and political backing with which to generate spontaneous cooperation, they must usually work at procedures for building support in the bureaucracy. Changing words, plans, and pieces of paper is easy. Changing behavior, especially while not losing the constructive services of officials, is much more difficult.

Efforts to build support may embrace a specific policy objective or something as vague as improvising goals through the everyday interactions of government. Whatever an executive's aims, the inertia he faces in any agency is generally a compound of at least four elements. First are the Opponents, who see vital interests harmed by change and who are unalterably opposed to the efforts of political executives. Second are what might be called "Reluctants," people who may be opposed to change but who are not immune to persuasion that there are some hitherto unrecognized advantages: they will at least listen. Third, are the Critics—civil servants who feel they have views to contribute and are willing to be supportive as long as what they have to say is seriously considered. Finally, the Forgotten are those whose failure to support political executives stems from their failure to hear what is wanted or to hear correctly.

These four bureaucratic types can no doubt be found in any organization, but they are particularly important in the public agencies of the U.S. executive branch, where a gulf of mistrust and many differences can separate the temporary leaders from those who spend their lives in government. Inexperienced appointees often visualize only the Opponents and respond with indiscriminate suspicions and withdrawal from the bureaucracy. Political executives more accustomed to the Washington environment make more efforts to cultivate the different sources of potential support, lest their reactions to Opponents prejudice possibilities of help from the others. Here I describe these efforts in terms of communications to deal with the Forgotten, fair hearings for the Critics, and consultation for the Reluctants. Outright Opponents fit more naturally into the discussion of bureaucratic sabotage at the end of the chapter.

COMMUNICATION

Veteran bureaucrats usually cite failures of communication as the greatest weakness in the political appointees' relations with the bureaucracy. A typical comment: "Being so suspicious, political people are hard to talk to. They and bureaucrats aren't able to get their views through to each other. What you really need is better communications." Standing in isolation, this view is difficult to assess because the same official later noted that "when you do give out information it can leak all over the place, cutting off confidence and strengthening the opposition." Political information is a strategic resource that should not be dissipated. Like the warnings, orientations, and so on that bureaucrats can offer to new executives, information held by appointees is not a free good. Hence selectivity is obviously as important for communication—in the sense of passing strategically important information—as in goal-setting.

Communication in the sense of "getting the word out," however, is another matter. It seems difficult to have too much of this kind of communication. Executives cannot tap into potential bureaucratic support if large groups of people do not know what is wanted or, even worse, if they are only vaguely aware that an appointee exists. In the musical chairs at the top, political appointees typically begin communicating by at least trying to establish a personal "presence" in their agency, although how they do so varies with personal style. Some like to "press the flesh," to make the rounds of everybody in every office. Others are more comfortable with large meetings, and still others do better to avoid personal contact if it only betrays an insincere gesture.[2] Of course, a mere presence is unlikely to change anything, but it is a beginning.

In a larger sense, political executives often fail to recognize that they are always communicating—by example, by innuendo, even by a refusal to talk with people. The real need in building support is to communicate what is intended, for both intended and unintended signals are picked up in the bureaucracy.[3] For example:

—The agency was supposed to be preparing a tight budget, and here he was big-dealing it by flying all around the country with a huge staff contingent.

—We read [the appointee's] address to [an outside conference] pledging to meet the needs of these people. Then when we loosened up the program and it grew, word came down complaining that things were out of control. Everyone here was dumbstruck. It showed his ignorance about what he himself was doing.

As noted earlier, even an apparent refusal to communicate provides its own signals to civil servants. "Suddenly, you're not asked things or talked to, just told what must be done. You are supposed to be just a tool—not a professional."

Particularly in the Washington environment, communication cannot consist of simply saying something once in the bureaucracy. Persistence and follow-through lie at the heart of efforts to convey accurate messages. In part this is because the immense federal organizations find it difficult to transmit any messages through their many layers. Moreover, the executives' statements often produce little detailed guidance and leave much room for competing interpretations. There is another, less obvious reason

2. New department heads are especially prone to ritualistic mass handshaking sessions. As one bureaucrat said: "Everyone had to be lined up, one by one, to get the glad hand. It was like an internee camp. Besides, he was so dumb that he did it when everyone wanted to go to lunch."

3. Such indirect influence from the top is illustrated in Robert Sullivan, "The Role of the Presidency in Shaping Lower Level Policy-Making Processes," *Polity*, vol. 3 (Winter 1970), pp. 202–21. Similarly, the history of corruption investigations in Washington is replete with officials' claim that their actions were not intended to influence pending cases or decisions, even though others caught the significance of small signals, including a raised eyebrow. See Bernard Schwartz, *The Professor and the Commission* (Knopf, 1959), p. 234.

why follow-through is probably the most important aspect of the political appointees' communication. The complex Washington environment makes it extremely difficult to separate the players' real moves from symbolic ones. Those on the receiving end of messages from political executives are accustomed to applying a heavy discount factor to mere proclamations. A supergrade explained that "over the years you see that a lot of the instructions aren't intended to be carried out. It takes extra effort to make it clear to people down the line that something is meant, not just another statement for the record or some speechwriter's inspiration."

Hence for political executives to say something once is a statement of intention; to show others what is meant and that it cannot be forgotten becomes a strategic resource. These extra efforts may take the form of reporting procedures, instructions committed to writing, informal reminders, complex management information systems, and a host of other techniques. But again, none of these techniques are substitutes for personalized networks and discussions. For purposes of communication follow-through, these networks need to include people at the operating levels of the bureaucracy. After describing the sophisticated reporting requirements he had helped create, an agency manager concluded by recognizing that "all these statistics and reports do is throw up some signals that things aren't happening at the point of impact. Our best techniques give only the signals, not the story. That's why you need personal contacts down there." There is therefore little point in advising political executives to concentrate on broad policy decisions rather than waste time on details. General decisions or guidelines may communicate little to subordinates without specific interventions and "casework" to demonstrate what is wanted in particular types of circumstances. But it is a waste of time and a source of confusion to impart details that are irrelevant to the executives' major purposes.

Follow-through often requires more persistence than appointees have time or inclination for, but there are few surrogates for the extra effort at communication required from political executives. Higher civil servants may help, but as pointed out in chapter 4, few generalist career officials have the responsibilities and stature that would permit them to oversee any broad-scale follow-through for a department or policy. "Try that," said one civil servant who did, "and you have political appointees jumping up against you all over the place saying that that isn't the way they understand administration policy."

DUE PROCESS AGAIN

Efforts to get the word out imply the reciprocal: listening to those who feel they have something to say. Political executives who are unwilling to provide a fair hearing to people in the bureaucracy generally find they have forced two otherwise distinct groups into the same camp. Working relations deteriorate not only with diehard bureaucratic Opponents but also with Critics who did not feel they had to win as long as they could gain access for their views.

Particularly for those labeled here as analysts, institutionalists, and staffers, the complexity of many policy issues can reasonably justify a range of decisions by political appointees. For these bureaucrats a specific outcome may be less important than the kind of due process noted for relations among political appointees themselves. As one career supergrade said:

> The options aren't all that different regardless of which party is in power. Most of the [policy decisions] are in gray areas and could go either way. You're not facing a lot of moments of truth as long as you have a chance to have a serious input. What many career people do care about is that their sorting out of the alternatives comes into play, that however they [political executives] decide, there is evidence they've paid attention and at least had to wrestle with the issues worrying us.

Political appointees denied due process (at least those interested in self-help) can be counted on to raise a ruckus with each other; bureaucrats usually shop quietly among the many alternative listening posts in Washington and find other ways of getting their views heard. At any given time the consequences can be observed in a number of agencies. A GS 16 described a familiar set of choices and his own decision on what he regarded as an important issue:

> I think a lot of people feel they aren't being taken into account and are just expected to rationalize decisions from on high. It's when you are denied a voice that life becomes tough. You've got to decide if you can live with this and yourself or if you want to try and outlast it, or move. Or do what I'm doing now—find an ally elsewhere with more power than you to help make the case.

In another large agency a prominent bureaucrat described the slide into demoralization:

> The feeling has grown in both the Johnson and Nixon administrations that the bosses didn't really want to hear what the career people had to say. You're not part of anything, just stuck out in an office somewhere, doing God knows what, that has an impact who knows where. I've seen the dis-

content filter through the whole structure. Productivity is falling, leaks are increasing, people are playing safer than ever before.

Obviously, listening to the bureaucrats' views on every issue may be unduly costly and time-consuming for a political executive. The value of working to establish a reputation as a leader who listens is cumulative, not immediate. Such a reputation is a strategic resource because it contributes to the trust that will undoubtedly be needed as specific pressures require forbearance from those below. Moreover, whatever the substantive value of the information communicated from lower-level officials (and it may be considerable), fair hearings can create a competition among perspectives that strengthens an executive's hand.

CONSULTATION

With the Reluctants in the bureaucracy, political executives face the choice of seeking out or avoiding more active consultation. Such consultation may involve anything from the initial selection of goals to discussions about implementation. A great deal has been written about the pros and cons of so-called participatory, or democratic, management. The argument in brief is that "significant changes in human behavior can be brought about rapidly only if the persons who are expected to change participate in deciding what the change shall be and how it shall be made."[4] A number of case studies of public agencies suggest that the degree of participatory management is unrelated to effectiveness in accomplishing the intended goals of reorganization but does improve the employees' support and reduce resistance to change.[5]

These studies, however, also suggest a more important point: that the arguments for or against active consultation with subordinates are highly dependent on the particular situation and context. For purposes of political leadership in the bureaucracy, participatory management (trying to create a sense that "we are all in it together") seems largely irrelevant if it is followed simply as a maxim or proverb of good management. Only in an abstract sense are political appointees and civil servants in anything together, other than their agency. Consultation becomes relevant as a

4. Herbert A. Simon, "Recent Advances in Organization Theory," in Stephen K. Bailey and others, *Research Frontiers in Politics and Government* (Brookings Institution, 1955), pp. 28–29. For a more recent review of this subject, see Philip Sadler, "Leadership Style, Confidence in Management and Job Satisfaction," *Journal of Applied Behavioral Science*, vol. 6 (January-March 1970), pp. 3–19.

5. Frederick C. Mosher, *Government Reorganizations: Cases and Commentary* (Bobbs-Merrill, 1967). See especially pp. 526 ff.

strategic resource when it is offered or withheld so as to serve the purpose
of executive leadership. When and for what do experienced political executives feel a need to consult in detail with those bureaucrats who, far
from being helpful, may actually resist the exercise of political leadership
in "their" agency?

The answers from many different agencies and administrations seem
clear. In-depth consultation (which is *not* the same thing as indiscriminate information-passing) makes sense when bureaucratic resistance may
be susceptible to persuasion, either through intensified argument or by involving Reluctants in processes that lead toward largely unavoidable conclusions.[6] Consultation for what? To find what might be called the points
of mutual self-interest. Since there is never enough agreement to go
around, political executives generally do better by trying to search for
these possible points of shared advantage rather than by assuming from
the outset that initial resistance is immutable. Even if complete agreement between political and bureaucratic executives is impossible, consultation may reveal a partial overlap of interests that suffices for the
purposes at hand. "You're looking for places where you can support him
so he can support you," as one official put it. A former strong man in the
Nixon administration learned to respect bureaucratic power in the agencies "because they could push as hard as I could push them." He concluded: "You can't mandate change there. It's a question of sitting down
with people and showing how things can be of use to them."

Mutual advantage produces institutionalized change. As the desires of
a political executive become connected with the interests of at least some
of the officials who will remain behind, the chances of an enduring impact
grow. Here, for instance, is how one fifteen-year veteran in the bureaucracy compared the results of the tenure of two assistant secretaries:

> The government is used to absorbing tigers. Thomas was bright and tough,
> but if you asked him what actually got done, what around here actually
> operates differently since he came and left, he couldn't point to any-
> thing. . . . It was all put in on top and like a big spring, things went back to
> normal when the topside pressure left. . . . Williams, I think, got people
> believing it was their own ideas. You still see some of the changes he got
> through because people [in various bureaus] were working out and adapting
> the system so it became their own way of doing business. To get rid of this

6. An official known for his wide-ranging use of interoffice consultations said:
"This does not mean you bring the bureau chief into the secretary or undersecretary's
office and lay out all the sensitive information that he can then use against you with
[the interest groups] and Congress."

after he left you'd have to change operating procedures and nobody likes to do that.

The particular bargaining tactics used to arrive at a sense of mutual advantage are far too numerous to discuss here. They range from the creation of formal task forces and joint decision documents, to quid pro quo side payments, to indirect leverage through third-party pressures. Again, some of the essential flavor can be conveyed by a compendium of experiences, in this case from a political appointee who cited methods used to produce a variety of changes over the course of seven years.

When we wanted a reporting system on things of interest to minorities, the statistics section said there weren't any data. I had them publish the table headings with empty columns. That got egg on their face, and they figured they'd better get some data on minority services before they were published again. . . .

Quietly we started letting it be known about how the delays were hurting a lot of people in the agency. People started getting upset and asking how improvements could be made. "Well," we said, "here are some ideas that might work. . . ." The task forces helped show who was interested and where the pockets of resistance were. There's always somebody over in the weeds, and fifteen people sitting around a table can help bring that out and gang up on him a little bit. . . .

We involved at least one person from each program division. The important thing was that with them working together, when it came out, you'd have some allies among the program people. . . . You could appeal to them by saying, "Look, why are you using all this manpower for things that aren't really connected to your bureau's objectives? With this plan you can use some of the cuts and reallocate them to things you really care about. . . ." Eventually they had to come up with suggestions themselves. The subsidies clearly were not working, and you could show that continuing in the same way meant at some point down the road we couldn't afford it; people would be hurt and there'd be a big hue and cry. Middle-level people fought like hell, but ultimately the division heads couldn't argue against the logic of the situation. . . .

You know when you write the procedures you're the big gun in that field and anyone trying to change them is a threat to the foundation of your authority. The real back of the opposition was broken when we won over the dean of the budget officers, who'd built his power by letting the agencies go their own way on these things. Finally, through persuasion and a lot of argument, he was won over, and I remember as clear as day the meeting where he publicly capitulated. He said that if he'd known years ago what he now knew he'd have tried to put this through then.

As with other strategic resources, there are severe constraints on the political appointees' ability to consult and bargain toward mutual advantages with reluctant bureaucratic supporters. These processes require time, which temporary executives can often ill afford. Not everyone in large bureaucracies can be brought into discussions, and so a good deal of in-depth knowledge of the organization is likely to be required to identify at least proximate sources of resistance. Another obvious but often forgotten constraint is that any executive proposal needs to make substantive sense. There is little point in trying to persuade tenured officials with a case for change that does not have the merits to stand up against strenuous argument from those affected; often this requires more substantive knowledge than political appointees can muster. A related difficulty is that active consultation downward can strain a political executive's relations with his own political superiors, particularly if they are unwilling to tolerate compromises inherent in the give and take of any serious consultation. Without some leeway in what could constitute an acceptable outcome, consultation becomes perceived as a cynical attempt at cooptation and destroys rather than builds trust.

The various procedures described above for building support do not require that political executives avoid major fights with the bureaucracy, or accept whatever bureaucrats say, or cower behind the lowest common denominator of joint decisions. They do mean that some delicacy is required if appointees are to move among the natives in the bureaucratic villages without being captured. Experienced political executives do not necessarily make efforts to build support in the bureaucracy so that they can avoid the confrontations required by political leadership. They do it so that the fights, when they do come, are not one against all and to the death.

Many things—including personality, partisan politics, and intolerant political superiors—cause some political appointees to shun such delicacy in governing people. But the price of weak communications, restricted access for lower officials, and disregard for the self-interests of subordinates is the alienation of potential support in the bureaucracy. Many of the temporary executives in Washington choose to pay this price, and thus their initial suspicions about bureaucratic inertia and sabotage become self-fulfilling. What they cannot prudently do is to pretend that their actions exact no cost at all. The following comment by a Nixon appointee, who was surprised by the lack of bureaucratic cooperation he received, is an object lesson in the lack of statecraft:

> We began by going after the big issues and pretty much ignored the bureaucrats and opposition in Congress. The idea was to create some major points to rally Republican troops for the years ahead. . . . After a number

of defeats in the first years it was decided to drop the legislative route and work through rules and regulations in the executive branch. The bureaucrats were very uncooperative toward this administrative strategy.

In this case the imprudence consisted, not of seeking partisan advantages, but of thinking that any "administrative strategy" could easily be built on bureaucratic relations that had already been cast aside in previous years.

Using People

So far strategic resources have been discussed in terms of political power, the selection of goals and opportunities, and methods of building internal bureaucratic support. People are also a resource that needs to be used for executive leadership. Political appointees often are unable to manage simply by motivating and bargaining with incumbent bureaucrats; in many cases changes in personnel are required in order to build a team that is in agreement about what needs to be done.

The idea of using people comes easily in Washington—too easily. Political executives naturally feel a need to have people around them who can be trusted from the outset and need not be won over. Given their own limited knowledge of people in government, inexperienced appointees are unlikely to believe they can count on this loyalty from below. More to the point, the civil service system—far from offering a basis for reassurance— often exacerbates doubts that good working relationships with career personnel can be expected. The labyrinthine civil service procedures and job-specific protections, the informal personnel practices and blurry intermixture of political and career jobs, the past attempts at politicizing the bureaucracy, the organizationally ingrown civil service careers, the standoffishness of civil servants who recognize the political vulnerability and career dangers that come in working closely with political appointees—all these offer public executives ample reason to doubt the people in government they inherit. Even if new executives harbor no ill will toward the Washington bureaucracy, they have to question whether this is a civil service system they can count on for help in exercising their legitimate leadership functions.

Thus the personnel system they walk into encourages the inclination of new appointees to think that their primary strategic resource and means of control lies in filling all key jobs with an outside retinue of personal loyalists. Unfortunately those who have watched the migrations of political appointees over the years generally seem to agree on one thing: importing a large number of outside lieutenants is usually an ineffective strategy for high political executives.

By now the reasons should be clear. The new subordinates can multiply all the difficulties of the executive's inexperience by bringing with them their own problems of self-help, short tenures, mistrust, needs for orientation, and so on. Not only do their personal loyalties fail to substitute for the institutional services the executive needs, but their intermediation can further separate the executive from bureaucratic services and vitiate opportunities for building support through communication, access, and consultation. Moreover, the proliferation and general bureaucratization of political appointees readily generates a false sense of security, a feeling that enduring changes in the behavior of government officials, and thus policies, are somehow being created just because more appointees are talking to each other.

One of the more aggressive assistant secretaries in recent years acknowledged his early admiration for "Machiavelli's advice: when you capture a town, bump off the top ten people, put in your own guys, and the rest of the population will settle down." Later he thought differently. "But you've got to realize this is a lousy communication system you're setting up. . . . There's nothing wrong with being tough, but doing it again I'd be more sensitive. I was having to work fourteen hours a day just to keep the place running myself until I got a good career deputy who knew how to get things done." The deputy described how this executive "had intimidated people so much that some were withholding bad news from him and others were beginning to play around with the statistics just to get results that would please him. . . . All the schedule C types had become a filter between him and the bureaucracy, calling their own shots and creating resentment. They were costing him more than he gained."

In the end a strategy of governing through outside placements also fails because it is normally an organizational impossibility. Without a massive reversion to spoils politics in government hiring, no top political executive can begin to place enough personal loyalists in all the important positions of his organization, i.e., in positions down to the level where discretionary guidance over the work of others shades into substantial routinization. "In this agency," said a top administrator, "we have six political slots; if you tripled that you'd still have less than two dozen of your guys in an organization of 62,000, and how long will it take for those 18 to figure out what's going on?"

Again, the more productive route lies in selectivity. Experienced political executives everywhere try to build strategy resources by selectively managing the various types of career personnel. In practice this means taking personnel actions to acquire officials already in the bureaucracy who show they can be of help, and if necessary bringing in outsiders to replace the unsuitable. Every cabinet secretary will want (though by no means will always get) his own lieutenants in top executive positions at the undersecretary and assistant secretary level. But below those levels (as noted in chapter 2) the distinctions between civil servants and political appointees blur rapidly. It is here that political executives can gain a strategic advantage by using people in the bureaucracy.

The consensus of informed opinion on this point is impressive, among both bureaucrats and appointees and in Republican and Democratic administrations alike. Asked what advice they would give to new political appointees, most high civil servants would probably echo the one who said that "a smart guy should spend a while finding out who's productive, build on the ones who will help you do things, move them, use them to get other good people, and ride them as far as you can." Political executives with service in a variety of agencies report their experience in similar terms. For example, a Democratic assistant secretary with an expanding program said: "You can't motivate everybody. Some of these divisions are disaster areas with their leaks, but if you look, there are competent people around. I moved a regional director in to work in my office, replaced him with another good man I had watched. Then I took [a GS 15], consolidated some functions under him, and raised his status." In an agency where cutbacks were the executive's aim, a Republican undersecretary learned: "You didn't need to bring in a lot of new people because there was already an undercurrent of some who wanted changes; they could be found, encouraged, and promoted so you had a hard corps of bureaucrats in key positions to ride herd on things."

The reason there is such consensus about using careerists goes back to all the bureaucratic services described in the preceding chapter. They were summarized best by the self-styled Machiavellian assistant secretary quoted earlier:

> I could have, and almost did, run around [an office director], and he could have beaten my brains out. But that isn't the point. The point is that no one understanding his function should want to run around him. I'm supposed to be smart enough to know what a guy like that is worth and realize that I should use him. [He] was a great civil servant, not because he did what you told him to, but because he would tell you how to solve

problems, what you could and couldn't do and why. With him I could get the changes through in one year instead of it dragging on until I'm out of the picture.

To use bureaucratic personnel as a resource does not necessarily imply a political appointee's acceptance of the status quo. Sometimes political executives can create more flexible, innovative arrangements of officials and become less dependent on the established bureaucratic routines. The practical needs of decisionmaking, not management theory, lead experienced political executives to use bureaucrats in crosscutting and self-monitoring ways. These arrangements take many different forms. Career personnel may be used in policy analysis shops to foster competing analyses with program units; in an executive secretariat to make sure that views are canvassed, work processed, and decisions followed up; in mobile evaluation teams to report on activities further down the line. The reckless appointee may set everybody on edge by creating "my special strike force to go into the program divisions and report back only to me." The cooler agency head may get further with "a low-key special operations group that lives with the program people, gets in on things every step of the way, and plays it straight, letting those people know when and why they are reporting disagreements to me." By making these and other flexible uses of career people, government executives can provide a constructive service to both themselves and the bureaucracy. Such efforts show that if government officialdom is ingrown and cannot see new ways of doing things—as is often the case—there is an alternative to letting the career service go to seed and pushing political appointees ever lower in the bureaucracy.

If they are to use bureaucratic officials, even the toughest political executives need sufficient sensitivity to discriminate among the different capabilities of civil servants and match them to the appropriate jobs. Noticing that a civil servant is weak in one area, new appointees frequently overlook the needed help that could be given in other areas. "I almost made a mistake and dumped Williams because he couldn't negotiate with the other agencies," one said, "but he was superb in running the procedures. Starting a program, it's a two-fisted guy you want to bridge the torrent, but to keep things running smoothly you look for a diplomat who can still the tempest."

If political executives do not isolate themselves, they have ample opportunity to make these deeper assessments and go beyond the initial hearsay and apprehensions about Washington bureaucrats. These executives will watch meetings, responses to circulating papers, and special assignments. They will see that some "make serious efforts and are actively interested in finding ways of doing things" while others offer only "rote responses, reasons for not doing anything." An experienced political executive also looks for evidence of officials who avoid withholding information that puts him at a disadvantage. Some officials rarely create attention because they are anticipating and heading off problems; others may gain prominence by solving problems that are often of their own making, and still others may only look good because they leave the problems for someone else to solve. All of this requires more than superficial observation by political appointees interested in using civil service personnel actions as a strategic resource.

The real difficulty for executives in Washington does not lie in making these assessments but in finding the *constructive* flexibility in the civil service personnel system to do something about them. Contrary to popular beliefs, firing civil servants is not impossible, but it often requires experienced personnel experts to help work through the complicated procedures. There are such officials. As one said: "If you come up through the system you get to know procedures political appointees can't begin to cope with. I've fired civil servants who are incompetent or undercutting the leadership. The section in the book on firing is twice as long as the one on hiring, and it's dog-eared in my book." But what experienced officials will know and will usually encourage political executives to realize is that outright firings are extremely costly, not in dollars but in strategic resources.

> Sometimes appointees seem to want to test you and ask "How do I fire a federal employee?" I tell him to give me the names and I'll have the employees out of the job in a month or two. But think of the implications, and you'll see there's a better, more indirect way of getting rid of a person you don't want on that job.

Given the career system outlined in chapter 4, it is far easier and therefore much more common to use the indirect means available: quiet talks, early retirements, and exchanges (such as a favorable send-off in return for a graceful exit). Or as a former Civil Service commissioner said, "There are smart ways and dumb ways of getting rid of civil servants, ways that increase or decrease tension." Personnel advisers also recognize that the more hostile and unresponsive the civil servant, the more difficult removal becomes because of the likelihood of his using outside political connections. The general practice is to try to move unwanted officials to less troublesome positions. One career executive gave an accurate assessment of the options for anyone managing government personnel:

What are you going to do with the guy who isn't doing you any good? You can make it known he isn't wanted, but some people don't get that signal. A confrontation can simply disrupt things and tie you up in procedures. You can try and make his job disappear [through a reorganization and reduction in force], but that's likely to backfire because he probably has got seniority and can bump young people below him who are better than he is. A transfer out of town is possible, but then he can use the grievance procedure that this is an adverse action. The normal thing is to move him to where he can do the least harm.

The difficulty for the public in these strategic moves is obvious: the other areas of the public's business used as dumping grounds are likely to suffer and the payroll costs and inefficiency of government employment are likely to grow.

But the problem of utilizing bureaucrats an executive does want, and of doing so without prostituting the concept of a career civil service, is a more important one than the oft-publicized inability to get rid of civil servants. The agency career ladders, the officials' vulnerability to political reprisals, the haphazard arrangements for broader executive development in the public service—these and more barriers obstruct efforts to utilize career personnel in a way that is both flexible for political managers and constructive for the civil service system. Good working relationships with political appointees are more apt to prejudice than to aid the bureaucrats' status and advancement as career public servants. Constructively using and moving permanent officials is a "hard sell" because bureaucrats recognize that, as one said, their "power base and career is a function of a particular job, or bosses, or relations and support from outside groups."

None of this means that experienced political executives fail to use career personnel as a strategic resource in support of their leadership. Quite the contrary. It is often precisely because institutional means are lacking that top government political executives can commonly go very far in using careerists. The point is that political appointees generally are not interested in the implications of their personnel actions for the civil servants' careers, much less for the civil service as an enduring system. In fact there is every incentive for an appointee to "milk" civil servants for his own short-term advantages.

The selective efforts of political executives to use various bureaucrats readily shade into the development of personalized and politicized corteges. Rather than import a mass of outside loyalists or simply manage the capabilities of existing personnel, political appointees frequently nurture their own bureaucratic families of protégés. An assistant secretary described this common approach as follows:

> People you yourself hire are going to be more supportive than anyone else. They can be career guys, but they should be your guys and have primary loyalty to you. For example, Roberts is an excellent career man. I expected little but gave him some things to do and he performed wonderfully after plodding along in [the bureau] for eight years. I got him a promotion from a GS 14 to a 15 and took him with me to [a different agency] and made him a project director. Now he's an office head. That's the kind of person you have to attract and hold with you.

An undersecretary described how inexperienced people in the White House

> were stupidly checking into the party registration of career people. You can sense who in the agency is with you, working late, referring with approval to what you say. These are the guys who you move up rapidly, a GS 15 to a 16 and maybe an 18 in later years. These career guys tie their job prospects to the political appointee above them and so can succeed or fail spectacularly.

The costs of the tendency for career personnel management to merge into the development of personalized and politicized bureaucratic protégés are not felt directly by political appointees, who typically move on to their own private careers. The price is paid by public officials who, although ambitious to move into challenging jobs, wish to retain some identity as career civil servants. Individual careerists can find they have indeed been used—"working your butt off for the guy and ending up as some executive assistant to a political appointee with no career development to show for it." A longtime participant in government described how those associated with a particular political executive can be "exposed, used up, and then become the holdovers and obstructionists for the next appointee to jump on." Of course, some careerists in this system will simply decide for very good reasons to cease being civil servants and to take political appointments. Others will have little choice. As one bright supergrade said: "Since he [the undersecretary] left government and [the assistant secretary] moved to HUD [Housing and Urban Development], I've got no clients for my work."

In a larger sense the real costs of the appointees' haphazard creation of bureaucratic families lie in the denigration of the concept of a career civil service. A well-known political executive went to the heart of the matter in describing the personal cortege that had moved with him between government agencies and the Executive Office of the President:

> In my experience these supergrade types in government compare favorably

with almost any group I've seen in the private sector. A guy in his mid-thirties and a GS 15 has got to have a lot of political savvy and good moves. I've carried five of them with me in every job. They're my personal supporters and I look after them. . . . Civil servants identifying with people pose a real problem for the bureaucracy, but it doesn't bother me. It helps me as a political appointee because I can really deal with them. The whole civil service thing is so automated, promotions come automatically, grade-step increases, and pay changes. The only way for these guys to break through this automated system is through personal identification. What should happen if it were operating right is that the system should be throwing upwards and promoting the good, bright guys, not depending on personal identifications with patrons.

There is no need to idealize bureaucrats as "the" public service. Civil service systems are created to institutionalize a limited but important set of values in government. Among these are not simply nonpartisanship and obedience but also (and especially at higher levels) a continuous capacity to offer honest advice and uphold the integrity of government operations. Perhaps an obscure GS 15 said it best: "As the distinction blurs between an institutional career role and personalized loyalty, people start hedging. They hedge their best independent judgments, either so as not to be put into jeopardy of political identification or because once jeopardized they're trying to ingratiate themselves." Using career people as a strategic resource may help particular appointees, but it is no real help in establishing the civil service as an instrument of reliable government performance.

Mutual Support and Its Limits

My argument here and in the preceding chapter has been that political executives can usually do better by evoking conditional cooperation rather than by invoking their authority. There are no magical management systems or organizational changes for "getting control of the bureaucracy." Reorganization plans or techniques like management by objectives and zero-base budgeting are all executive proclamations that presume rather than create changes in subordinates' behavior. Instituting new management techniques and making them part of the bureaucracy's standard operating procedure lie at the end of statecraft, not at the beginning.

In the preceding discussion I have also emphasized selectivity and calculation in dealing with the political resources, opportunities, people, and procedures for building support. This suggests that while would-be political leaders in the executive branch *can* be agents for changing what government is doing, convulsive root and branch changes fall outside the range of everyday statecraft. If political policy calls for revamping most of the major assumptions behind what an agency is doing, there is little point in a political executive appearing on that scene in the guise of a selective strategist who uses a variety of resources for encouraging bureaucrats to terminate their way of life. An entirely new organization will in all likelihood be required. Also needed will be a genuine, widely perceived sense of crisis—an economic disaster, an unambiguous foreign threat, an acknowledged need to "war" on some domestic problem—in order to galvanize the many disparate competitors for attention and agreement in Washington. Without that general sense of alarm, trying to shake up the bureaucracy by appealing to the people for support simply misses the point.

A desire to capitalize on such opportunities for Big Change can therefore create one of the limits on mutual support between political leaders and bureaucrats. Fortunately for the stability of government institutions, such overwhelming crises seem relatively rare and are short-lived when they do occur. Moreover, once the bright new organization has been created, the familiar imperatives for statecraft reappear with time. These facts, along with the dispersed veto power and shortage of agreement that permeates most of everyday life in Washington, mean that no political executive need apologize for working at relationships that are usually based on conditional cooperation with the bureaucracy.

Occasions for Big Change suggest a situation in which the political leaders' demand for performance is more than the bureaucracy can supply. Limits are also set on mutual support when bureaucrats demand more performance than political appointees can supply. Civil servants have their own expectations about what is due from political leaders in their agency. The tenure of officials who wish to remain civil servants but who also allow themselves to be used by political executives is conditional on the executives' own behavior. Appointees need to reduce the risk of added exposure and insecurity for such officials. When trouble develops— something upsets a political superior, the Office of Management and Budget attacks the agency's goals, a congressional committee takes offense—a political appointee who attempts to shift blame to subordinates quickly experiences an evanescence of bureaucrats, protégés or otherwise. As one observed, "The self-preservation instinct blossoms." Careerists involved in executive hearings and consultations expect to be serious participants dealing with issues of substantive importance, not "hacks rationalizing some piece of political propaganda." Officials helping a political executive will expect as their due some clear guidance in advance rather than to have to hope for support later. Since all strategic resources are limited, conditional cooperation breaks down when—for whatever reason —bureaucrats expect more in exchange for their cooperation than political executives are able or willing to provide.

Hence demands from either side can outrun the supply of mutual performance. But conditional cooperation involves more than bureaucrats and executives in their agencies. There are third, fourth, indeed nth parties implicated in the exchanges of executive politics and they too set limits on the degree of cooperation between the appointee and the bureaucrats. A political executive's primary constraint rests in his links to other appointees and political figures. An oft-quoted opinion of a former secretary of state is that "the real organization of government" at higher levels "is how confidence flows down from the President."[7] A similar but broader principle of confidence is at work throughout and across the levels of government. Depending on the political executives' specific allegiances and accidents of selection, their ability to deal with the civil servants below them is limited by their need for live political connections up to political superiors and out to the many sources of external power.

From this perspective it becomes clear why there is much more to the politics of executive branch leadership than simple-minded assertions about a natural animosity between presidents who long to control their administrations and parochial cabinet officers who love to be captured as departmental advocates. The fact is that requirements for statecraft in the agencies do not fit well with political prudence as seen from behind the White House gates. A president marshaling his power stakes expects to advance when there is credit to be had and withdraw as losses grow. When unpopular actions have to be taken in a government agency, his political appointees there should be hustling into the trenches of front-line support, not picking and choosing their advantages. After all, does not the President's generalship consist of using the strength of others and conserving his own?[8] Bureaucratic politics contemplates quiet, behind-

7. Dean Rusk, quoted in Morton H. Halperin, *Bureaucratic Politics and Foreign Policy* (Brookings Institution, 1974), p. 219.
8. A new appointee in the Executive Office of the President provided a good example involving the transfer of a bureau from one department to another:
    We wanted the secretary to recommend its removal from his agency. Then the White House could accept the recommendation but still not have the President's neck on the line

the-scenes workmanship, strategic reversals, caution, contentment with results for which everyone can share some of the credit. Presidential politics mobilizes its vital resources with the public by taking all the credit for dramatic, readily intelligible actions: big cuts, major new programs, flashy changes. Why, when the President has staked his reputation on getting something done in government, are his political executives reaching for the rapier instead of the bludgeon?

Executives in the agencies may argue that their achievements with the bureaucracy reflect favorably on the President, but to those in the White House reflected glory may not be enough. Why not? Because a political executive's selection of goals and areas of indifference may not be what the President wants or would want if he could know what goes on throughout government; because to build support in the bureaucracy invites more delay and compromise; and because the people an executive uses may become his people but not necessarily presidential supporters. In these and many other ways an unconstrained use of his strategic resources may help a political executive with the bureaucracy but leave him vulnerable to the President's "true" supporters in the White House. Yet the more detached, broadly presidential view an executive takes of his agency, the more difficult it becomes to acquire support from its officials below and clients outside.

Hence the tensions of political leadership in its presidential and executive department guises are inherent. Being unavoidable, they suggest their own lesson: prudence for any president interested in the problem of controlling the bureaucracy consists of trying to use the inevitable tensions with his executives constructively, not of trying to eliminate or drive these tensions underground with simplistic notions of cabinet government and unified executive teamwork.

Third-party relationships also limit the performance that civil servants can supply to executives as well as vice versa. Since these outside ties and allegiances are a favorite theme of academic observers and insider news stories, bureaucratic sabotage deserves a closer look. Again, depending on how political executives choose to act, the circumstances are not quite as hopeless for political leadership as they might seem.

---

if it fell through. But here was the secretary coming out with all kinds of negative statements—a real case of disloyalty some people thought. Finally, when the White House staff did some checking, it turned out he would go along with the decision and wanted to be overruled. From his point of view, the problem was that if the transfer failed, that bureau would really have it in for him. Even if it succeeded and he hadn't publicly fought it, everyone else in the department was going to wonder if he was a guy who would support his department's interests.

Sabotage

Bureaucratic subversion can be thought of as the final limitation on mutual support in the U.S. executive branch. It is one thing new political appointees generally do expect. The intractable bureaucratic Opponents have been left until last in this discussion in order to emphasize the other more normal working relationships in political administration. In the preceding discussion I tried to characterize the thousands of constructive interactions that occur without dramatic intrigues or relentless infighting. These are the everyday dealings among people in government that become all the more noteworthy the less noticeably they operate.

Not all bureaucratic resistance, however, is simply "the friction that habit . . . offers to readjustment."[9] Political executives who try to exercise leadership within government may encounter intense opposition that they can neither avoid nor reconcile. At such times some agency officials may try to undermine the efforts of political executives. Any number of reasons—some deplorable, some commendable—lie behind such bureaucratic opposition. Executive politics involves people, and certain individuals simply dislike each other and resort to personal vendettas. Many, however, sincerely believe in their bureau's purpose and feel they must protect its jurisdiction, programs, and budget at all costs. Others feel they have an obligation to "blow the whistle" as best they can when confronted with evidence of what they regard as improper conduct. In all these cases the result is likely to strike a political executive as bureaucratic subversion. To the officials, it is a question of higher loyalty, whether to one's self-interests, organization, or conscience.

The structure of most bureaucratic sabotage has been characterized as an "iron triangle" uniting a particular government bureau, its relevant interest group, and congressional supporters. The aims may be as narrow as individual profiteering and empire-building. Or they may be as magnanimous as "public interest" lobbies, reformist bureaucrats, and congressional crusaders all claiming somewhat incongruously to represent the unrepresented. There are alliances with fully developed shapes (e.g., the congressional sponsors of a program, the bureaucrats executing it, and its private clients or suppliers) and those made up of only a few diverse lines (e.g., a civil servant looking forward to post-retirement prospects

9. V. O. Key, Jr., "Politics and Administration," in Leonard D. White, ed., *The Future of Government in the United States* (University of Chicago Press, 1942), p. 154.

with a particular lobby association or a congressman unconcerned about a bureaucrat's policy aims but aware that his specific favors can help win reelection). Some bureaucratic entrepreneurs initiate their own outside contacts; others have been pushed into becoming involved in outside alliances by former political appointees.

The common features of these subgovernments are enduring mutual interests across the executive and legislative branches and between the public and private sectors. However high-minded the ultimate purpose, the immediate aim of each alliance is to become "self-sustaining in control of power in its own sphere."[10] The longer an agency's tradition of independence, the greater the political controversy surrounding its subject matter, and the more it is allied with outside groups, the more a new appointee can expect sub rosa opposition to develop to any proposed changes. If political leadership in the executive branch is to be more than the accidental sum of these alliances and if political representation is to be less arbitrary than the demands of any group that claims to speak for the unrepresented, then some conflict seems inevitable between higher political leaders and the subgovernments operating within their sphere.

Often sabotage is unrecognizable because of the virtually invisible ways civil servants can act in bad faith toward political executives. In addition to the bureaucracy's power of withholding needed information and services, there are other means. Like a long-married couple, bureaucrats and those in their networks can often communicate with a minimum of words: "If congressional staffs I trust call up and ask me, I might tell them. But I can also tell them I don't agree with the secretary by offering just technical information and not associating myself with the policy."

An official who does not want to risk direct dealings with Congress can encourage a private interest group to go to the agency's important appropriations and legislative committees, as one political executive discovered: "When we tried to downgrade the . . . bureau, its head was opposed, and he had a friend in a lobby group. After they got together rumblings started from the appropriations committee. I asked [the committee chairman] if he had a problem with this reorganization, and he said, 'No, you have the problem because if you touch that bureau I'll cut your job out of the budget.'" An experienced bureaucrat may not be able to make the decision, but he can try to arrange things to create the reaction he wants. "A colleague of mine," said a supergrade, "keeps a file on field offices that can be abolished and their political sensitivity. Depending on who's

10. Douglass Cater, *Power in Washington* (Vintage, 1964), p. 17.

pressing for cuts, he'll pull out those that are politically the worst for
that particular configuration." The everyday relationships between people with specialized interests can shade effortlessly into subversion: "You
know what it's like," said a bureau chief. "You've known each other and
will have a drink complaining about what's happening and work up some
little strategy of your own to do something about it." Or bureaucrats can
work to get their way simply by not trying to know what is happening.
One assistant secretary reported how his career subordinates agreed there
might be mismanagement in the regional offices, "but they also said they
didn't know what these offices were doing and so there wasn't enough
information to justify doing what I wanted." Ignorance may not be bliss,
but it can be security.

Political appointees can sometimes encounter much more vigorous
forms of sabotage. These range from minor needling to massive retalia-
tion. Since information is a prime strategic resource in Washington, the
passing of unauthorized messages outside channels often approaches an
art form. There are routine leaks to build credit and keep channels open
for when they might be needed, positive leaks to promote something,
negative leaks to discredit a person or policy, and counterleaks. There is
even the daring reverse leak, an unauthorized release of information apparently for one reason but actually accomplishing the opposite.[11]

There is no lack of examples in every administration. A political executive may discover that an agency subordinate "has gone to Congress and
actually written the rider to the legislation that nullified the changes we
wanted." A saboteur confided that "no one ever found it was [a division
chief] who prepared the list showing which lobbyist was to contact which
senator with what kind of argument." Still another official reported he
had "seen appointees kept waiting in the outer office while their subordinate bureau officials were in private meetings with the congressional staff
members." But waiting lines lack finesse. The telephone can be used with
more delicacy, particularly after office hours: "The night before the
hearings [a bureaucrat] fed the questions to the committee staff and
then the agency witnesses spent the next two days having to reveal the

11. One recent example involved a presidential assistant rather than a bureaucrat.
While jockeying with another staff member, the assistant leaked a disclosure of his
own impending removal from the West Wing. The opponent, who obviously stood
the most to gain from the story, was naturally asked to confirm or deny the report.
Since he was not yet strong enough to accomplish such a removal, the opponent had
to deny responsibility for the leak and its accuracy, thereby inadvertently strengthening
the position of the presidential assistant who first leaked the story.

information or duck the questions and catch hell." A young staff civil servant described how his superior operated:

I used to sit in [the bureau chief's] office after 6 P.M. when all the important business got done. He'd call up a senator and say, "Tom, you know this program that you and I got through a while back? Well, there's no crisis, but here are some things I'd like to talk to you about." He'd hang up and get on the phone to [a House committee chairman] and say, "I've been talking with Tom about this issue, and I'd like to bring you in on it." Hell, you'd find [the bureau chief] had bills almost drafted before anybody else in the executive branch had ever heard about them.

Encountering such situations, a public executive becomes acutely aware that experience as a private manager provides scant guidance. As one corporate executive with a six-figure salary said, "The end-runs and preselling were incredible. To find an equivalent you'd have to imagine some of your division managers going to the executive board or a major stockholder behind your back." Learning to deal with sabotage is a function of an executive's political leadership, not his private management expertise.

How do political executives try to deal with bureaucratic sabotage? By now it should be apparent that there is a considerable difference between an executive coping with sabotage when it occurs and operating from the outset as if his main problem in government is disobedient and incompetent bureaucrats. The former circumstance is being discussed here, and once again differences in statecraft help explain why some political appointees are better able to cope than others. One approach is simply to ignore bureaucratic sabotage. Since the damage that may be done can easily cripple an executive's aims, diminish his reputation, and threaten his circles of confidence, those adopting this strategy can be presumed to have abdicated any attempt at political leadership in the Washington bureaucracy.

A second approach, especially favored by forceful managers, is to try to root out the leakers and prevent any recurrence. But political executives usually discover that this straightforward approach has considerable disadvantages. For one thing, it is extremely time-consuming and difficult to actually investigate acts of subversion and pin down blame. For another thing, there are few effective sanctions to prevent recurrences. Moreover, a search for the guilty party can easily displace more positive efforts and leadership initiatives an executive needs to make in dealing with the bureaucracy. Even if it were possible, trying to censor bureaucratic contacts would probably restrict the informal help these outside relationships provide, as well as the harm they do. And in the end any serious sabotage will probably be buttressed by some mandate from Congress; punishing the saboteurs can be seen as an assault on legislative prerogatives and thus invite even sterner retribution. It is circumstances such as these that led an experienced undersecretary to conclude:

> Of course you can't be a patsy, but by and large you've got to recognize that leaks and end-runs are going to happen. You can spend all your time at trying to find out who's doing it, and if you do, then what? [One of my colleagues] actually tried to stop some of his bureaucrats from accepting phone calls from the press. They did stop accepting the calls, but they sure as hell returned them quickly. In this town there are going to be people running behind your back, and there's not much you can do to stop it.

However, while academics write about the iron triangle as if it were an immutable force, prudent political executives recognize that although they cannot stop bureaucratic sabotage, neither are they helpless against it. They can use personnel sanctions where misconduct can be clearly proven. But far more important, they can work to counteract sabotage with their own efforts—strengthening their outside contacts, extending their own lines of information and competitive analysis, finding new points of countertension. In general, experienced political executives try to use all their means of self-help and working relations so as to reshape the iron triangles into more plastic polygons.

To deal with sabotage, wise political appointees try to render it more obvious:

> I make it clear that all the information and papers are supposed to move through me. It increases your work load tremendously, and maybe you don't understand everything you see, but everyone knows I'm supposed to be in on things and that they are accepting risks by acting otherwise.

They try to counteract unwanted messages with their own accounts to the press and others. The more the agency's boat is leaking, "the more you go out and work the pumps. You can't plug all the leaks, but you can make sure to get your side of the story out."

Political executives also make use of timing to deal with sabotage:

> I put in a one-year fudge factor for an important change. That's because I know people are going to be doing end-runs to Congress. This year lets congressmen blow off steam, and for another thing it shows me where the sensitive spots are so I can get busy trying to work out some compromises —you know, things that can serve the congressmen's interest as well as mine.

Substantial results can be achieved by bringing new forces into play, dealing not with just one alliance but creating tests of strengths among the triangles:

> It's like when officials were getting together with the unions and state administrators to get at some committee chairman. I hustled out to line up governors and show the congressmen that state administrators weren't speaking for all of state government.

Washington offers more opportunities to search for allies than is suggested by any simple image of political executives on one side and bureaucratic Opponents on the other. Political appointees may be "backdoored" by other appointees, higher bureaucrats by lower bureaucrats. Fights may be extended to involve some appointees and bureaucrats versus others. As the leader of one faction put it, "Often a guy preselling things on the Hill is hurting people elsewhere, making it tougher for them to get money and approval and straining their relations. I use this fact to get allies."

A political executive who works hard at outside contacts will discover what subversives may learn too late: that many groups are fickle allies of the bureaucracy. This has seemed especially true as Congress has increased its own bureaucracy of uncoordinated staffs. A veteran bureaucrat described the risks run by would-be saboteurs:

> Everybody you might talk to weighs the value of the issue to them against the value of keeping you alive for the next time. I've seen [a congressman] ruin many a good civil servant by getting a relationship going with him and then dropping him to score points off the agency brass. Now, too, there are more Hill staffers running around telling appointees, "Hey, these guys from your department said this and that. How about it?" Then the appointee will go back to the agency and raise hell for the bureaucrat.

Thus the political executives' own positive efforts are the necessary— if not always a sufficient—condition for combating sabotage. Since some bureaucratic subversion is an ever-present possibility and since punishment is difficult, the government executives' real choice is to build and use their political relationships or forfeit most other strategic resources for leadership. Speaking from their different perspectives, an assistant secretary from one agency and a highly placed bureaucrat from another described the fundamental point at stake. The assistant secretary:

> [The cabinet secretary] tried to put a lid on relations with Congress to keep bureaucrats from going over there and let him know when there were contacts. But it was no use. We've got a lot of big, highly visible grant programs and congressmen love them. What I have to do is go up to the Hill and counteract these contacts from our program people. It often works. I tell the congressman that I know guys under me think differently, but

this is what I think for these reasons. It's got to make sense to him. I work on the senator. I know his staff guy is having contact with my agency, and I tell him quite frankly he'd better see the senator again because I've worked it out with him. This way, congressional staff have to take into account my judgment as well as the bureaucrat who's been running to him from my organization. Nobody wants to get caught out on a limb.

The bureaucrat:

People under me can deal with another agency or the Hill and sell me out. OK, maybe in the first year you're too green to know how to do much, but if you're still being sold out in the second year, then it's your fault. I can render any subversives ineffective with my personal contacts. I've watched secretaries and assistant secretaries for years, and it is true for them too. Right now [X] is one of our effective assistant secretaries, and you can see how he does it with personal talks to lay it out for the congressman or senator. That legislator is more likely to respond. Then it's not just the congressional staffer and some supergrade over here, but the congressman responding to the personal input from an appointee. A strong congressman isn't going to do everything his administrative assistant tells him. Now [X] is in on the action.

There are no guarantees that any political executive's efforts will be sufficient to cope with sub rosa opposition from the bureaucracy. Some triangles can indeed seem cast in iron. Even the most skillful political executive can discover, as one did, that "it's a frustrating system and one of the things you do about it is get frustrated. I've tried everything I know, even inviting some of these people around to drink my scotch and still everything drips with venom."

A few appointees may have the temperament to seek solace by looking further into the future:

I know the administrators allied with the congressional committees are going to beat us, but this fight is worth it. This won't pass, but it will begin changing the debate and start a course of action for later years. That's not as idealistic as it sounds. Look at any major act and you'll see it started years earlier with failures before it could build up to passage.

With or without such a long-term perspective, effective appointees learn that their frustrations will only be compounded if they take the sell-outs and batterings in congressional hearings personally. Sabotage is usually a function of substantial disagreements and enduring interests, not of reactions to the executive himself. Those who are used to fighting in Washington recognize that what seems to be personal animosity may not even be based on the point at issue but may instead be a way of publicly denouncing what the executive and his political superiors stand for. As one appointee dealing with Congress put it:

I couldn't understand at first how department officials testifying could sit there all morning getting the hell beat out of them and talk like buddies with the congressman afterwards. But when people around town are trying to stick it out to you, the "you" is probably your program, or the President, or constituents who are watching, or something else that's bothering them. If it is really a personal vendetta and a committee chairman is shaking his finger at the real you, you aren't going to be around long.

A less stoic executive who takes the political infighting personally will probably overreact and frustrate his own efforts to build contacts, to understand, and if possible, to undercut the opposition.

In a political executive's life the leaks, the end runs, and all the rest are not necessarily an uncontrollable pathology. Those encountering subversion from below do well to ask themselves why it is occurring. Many, when they do, find that there are resources of communication or consultation that have gone unused, signals of who cares how intensely about what that have been missed, and weaknesses in the merits of the case that have not been answered. Equally important, a political executive who seeks to cut off the bureaucracy's outside relations also cuts himself off from the most effective higher civil servants, i.e., those who recognize the need to maintain established relations across Washington's divided power centers and are able to use them well.

In a larger sense there are advantages for the government system that would make it very costly if political executives could stifle all bureaucratic opponents. As an assistant secretary recognized, eliminating "creative" sabotage would crush initiative, always in short supply in any organization.

We've got a guy who is a real salesman lining up OMB, the professional suppliers, selling his ideas up on the Hill. He knows why our decision is going to eventually go against him and we know that he's preselling his pet project. I tell him about the need for more discipline, but I'm not going to tear his head off. Try and stamp it out and you'll lose good, bright people. The agency won't get good ideas if you crush the guys running around advocating them.

Moreover, a leakproof bureaucracy would in fact be another name for a government able to control its preferred leaks and thus the press and other outside critics. Important safety valves in the U.S. government and for democracy would be lost. One official acknowledged this in the following way:

When you tell one appointee that what he wants to do is illegal, that's the end of it; another guy will keep working at it. . . . The secretary's office has been after us to stop leaks about one of the appointees who apparently lied during his confirmation hearing. I talked it over with some people here and we came to the same conclusion. We've got no good reason to stop these leaks.

There is no political or legal filter that can be counted on to stop only the subversion based on the bureaucrats' parochial self-interests and program prejudices but let through their constructive contributions to a wider policy debate and alarms about attempts to cover up wrongdoing. Part of the price for exercising leadership in a democratically open system is that, as one appointee said, "you can get clobbered from any side." Political executives who get clobbered and who are unwilling to counteract bureaucratic subversion with a frank, hard-hitting exposition of their own case have difficulties in Washington and may arouse suspicion about their intentions. They should.

Conclusions

As demand exceeds the supply of mutual performance between appointees and bureaucrats, tempers rise in the government marketplace. Although the alienation of executive leadership from operations can catch up with a private company by forcing it into bankruptcy, barring revolution, the government's business always continues in some form. Exchanges of conditional cooperation between political executives and higher civil servants simply break down or are never created in the first place. So what difference does it all make?

The failure to establish constructive working relationships usually produces obscure and indirect effects. This is not only because politicians and government agencies try to hide deficiencies in their operations, but also because of the nature of government activity. Since it is usually difficult to know how or when a policy emerges, it is doubly difficult to identify the effect of only one linkage—that between political executives and bureaucrats—among the many involved in public policymaking. So great are the contingencies among people, institutions, and outside events that it is better to think of probabilities than to expect straightforward one-for-one effects.

When exchanges between political appointees and civil servants break down, there is often more hedging in the recommendations flowing up to the political levels, even though few may be able to identify the consequence of a recommendation or warning not given. Frequently signals sent down to middle- and lower-level officials become more garbled, although again it is difficult to trace the consequences of a higher civil servant's failure to implement and follow through. Presidents and political executives usually seem adept at calling on a variety of political forces to help sell the idea for some kind of action; where the civil service matters to politicians is not so much in marshaling these forces as in helping to work out a program that makes administrative sense and getting something down once it has been politically sold.

It may, for example, take some years to show the self-defeating consequences of decisions that are taken without the participation of professional specialists in the bureaucracy. Political executives can find themselves taking more time to become oriented, operating with less understanding of a policy, and failing to mobilize the varieties of bureaucrats. Where changes remain unconsolidated in political administration, zigs and zags in grand policy at the top echelons can be mere switchbacks in the bureaucracy's slow progress toward its own inertial goals.

Whatever the difficulties of tracing a given policy effect, there is no mistaking the lessons learned by many participants. As noted at the beginning of this chapter, perceptive appointees from both the Theory X and Theory Y schools of management eventually see that the political executive's real job lies between the extremes of giving orders and of taking cooperation for granted.[12] They learn that political leadership in the Washington bureaucracy is not a task for martinets or presiding officers. For those both tough and sensitive enough, it is a job of managing a pluralistic, changing consensus with limited strategic resources.

There is no need to overdramatize the difficulties that occur. People in government can manage without conditional cooperation at the political-bureaucratic interface. When political appointees have little sense of direction or statecraft, the failure to establish a constructive working relationship with higher civil servants may be inconsequential, except that the bureaucracy is left freer to pursue its own agenda. Experienced bureaucrats become quite expert at helping themselves in the Washington scramble. Similarly, some political managers may feel no great loss if

12. It is revealing that the opening quotations in this chapter, taken from office-holders in a domestic department, compare almost exactly with the lessons drawn by a leading political executive in an organization as different as the State Department. See the extensive quotations and discussion in Donald P. Warwick, A *Theory of Public Bureaucracy* (Harvard University Press, 1975), p. 209.

the careerists with whom they fail to build working relations have few analytic or administrative capabilities to offer or withhold; they become adept at creating their own personal teams in place of career civil servants. Appointees and bureaucrats can and do try to compensate for each other's inadequacies.

Yet as each side maximizes its own convenience in this way, the overall quality of American democratic institutions is likely to decline. It is no consolation that appointees and top bureaucrats can compensate for having little that is worth exchanging with each other. If officialdom and professional specialists can get along very well despite an absence of political leadership above them, that should not reassure citizens who expect government bureaucracies to be guided by publicly accountable and removable political representatives. Likewise, political executives may manage without the institutionalized knowledge, continuity, and impartiality that government civil services are created to supply. That, too, is little consolation since the real strength of government machinery in a democracy is its ability to serve effectively, not just one particular set of political leaders, but any succession of leaders with a legitimate popular mandate. If democratic government did not require bureaucrats and political leaders to need each other, it might not matter so much when in practice they discover they do not.

CHAPTER SEVEN

Doing Better: Policies for Governing Policymakers

... what are the ingredients which constitute this [executive] energy? How far can they be combined with those other ingredients which constitute safety in the republican sense?
—Alexander Hamilton, *The Federalist*, no. 70

POLITICAL FIGURES who hope to lead Washington's bureaucracies face the fundamental problem of trying to generate the changes they want without losing the bureaucratic services they need. They have to learn not only how to help themselves but also how to acquire help from the powerful and valuable subordinates in their own organizations. Mere control of personnel—having "my guy" on the job—will not necessarily produce control of programs or improve government performance. One reason is that an appointed political loyalist may not know what to do, or how to do it, or when to stop doing it and check back for new guidance. A second and even more important reason is that real political control (rather than just the temporary appearance of it) depends on access to continuous capabilities in government—civil "services" that are provided not so much out of personal loyalty as out of institutionalized responsiveness. While people in government are always using each other, political appointees and top career officials should have to do so because they require each other's distinctive services.

Such, at least, have been the arguments about statecraft in the preceding two chapters. In this final chapter, I examine the needs and possibilities for improvement. Are there changes that could help establish more constructive relations between political leadership and bureaucratic power? After four decades of ineffectual reform does it even make sense to reraise tired old questions about restructuring the federal personnel system?

The Case for Reform

I began this study by asserting that the search for political leadership in a bureaucracy of responsible career officials has become extraordinarily difficult in Washington. Subsequent chapters have uncovered many reasons for making that assertion. The need for better working relations between political and bureaucratic executives is greater now than ever before. Even if nothing else had happened in government—no bureaucratizing of political leadership or politicizing of the bureaucracy, no constant fumbling with the political personnel system or periodic attacks on the civil service—even if the "fulfillment of tendency" that reformers talked about in the 1930s had succeeded instead of being lost in a blur of formal and informal personnel improvisations, there would *still* be a case for reform. It lies in the progressively more challenging nature of federal government policies. Political administrators have to cope with a proliferation of government activities and organizations. They need to work together across agency lines on policy problems that have become increasingly interdependent. The momentum growing from an ever-larger base of government programs tests any political leader's capacity to come to grips with the executive branch establishment. And as healthy as it may be for democracy, the increasing permeability of national policymaking promises to strain the abilities of any prospective government manager. Facing this operating environment, political executives who merely do as well as their predecessors in dealing with the bureaucracy are likely to fall consistently behind the pace of events.

But the problems of creating constructive working relations go beyond any challenges arising from the nature of government activity. The deficiencies extend to the inherent structure of executive politics. It would be easy to choose up sides between appointees on the one hand who complain about bureaucratic inertia and parochialism and career bureaucrats on the other hand who disparage the lack of effective political leadership. In fact, there is a large element of truth in both views. Political and civil service executives alike are weak links in ensuring responsible control and performance in the government bureaucracy. Here I need only summarize the reasons for condemning deficiencies on both sides.

Political Deficiencies

Despite what is often written about the overwhelming power of government bureaucracies, "iron triangles," and so on, the prospects for political appointees who seek to lead the bureaucracy are not predetermined. Much depends on an appointee's own choices and actions. But in the Washington setting an extraordinarily high order of statecraft is also required to redirect the actions of government agencies and establish the political accountability of top executives. Consider the requirements for leadership by political executives:

—Enduring bases of political support are needed if appointees are to carve out their niches in the freewheeling environment at the top of government. Where such support does not already exist, substantial efforts must be made to build political lines of confidence. Otherwise new executives will lose prerogatives to tougher appointees. They will become less involved in what is going on between their subordinates and outsiders. Most incentives for bureaucratic cooperation will disappear.

—Coordination and an exchange of loyalties among political executives are essential. Otherwise, lower officials at best become confused about what the important decisions are and who makes them. At worst, one uncoordinated appointee undercuts another and gives bureaucratic opponents ample opportunity to subvert leadership by shopping for someone to obey. Coordination, however, must stop well short of regimentation. Absolute loyalty eliminates room for maneuvering and ultimately destroys the effectiveness of political executives who must both serve the interests of their departments and be the President's men.

—Sensitivity is needed, not only in dealing with the substance of government policies, but even more with regard to the contextual nuances of people and programs. This sense of "what fits" enables an appointee to build support among the various sources of help in the bureaucracy, to give or to withhold trust selectively, to push or to yield with some knowledgeable sense of the risks and consequences.

—Time is indispensable because it allows all the other qualities to come into play. Time on the job brings an opportunity not only to learn about the substance of programs and how to operate in the Washington networks but also to use what has been learned. Policy priorities are not immune to change, but they are most likely to respond to leaders who are around long enough to build support, to institutionalize changes in the bureaucracy, and to string together the narrow margins available at any one time into a strand of policy development.

—In the end there is no substitute for commitment on the part of political executives. Theirs is an operating environment requiring a high level of tolerance for continual frustration and personal attack. Although tenacity and patience will not guarantee success, they may convince the immense bureaucracies and other enduring power centers that a temporary political executive really means what he is saying.

Political support, coordination, sensitivity, endurance, commitment— these seem to be the most important requisites for political executives who hope to have a serious chance of exercising leadership in the Washington bureaucracy. But consider now the many contradictory conditions that generally prevail at the top echelons of government:

—The bases of political support are usually highly equivocal. An executive in Washington operates in a political twilight zone, without his own mandate from the electorate and little capacity to gain general public attention for what he is doing. The White House will not readily allow him to borrow on the President's reputation and prestige, and when it does, the executive can find his acceptance and maneuverability in his own organization severely constrained. Of course, support can easily be garnered by adopting a position of pure advocacy for the agency and its interests, but this often divides loyalties further between an executive and the White House and narrows his possibilities for any real leadership.
—The selection process is a haphazard one. Appointees frequently take office for reasons unrelated to the particular needs of their official positions or the aims of the administration. Uncoordinated presidential advisers are apt to dissipate their efforts on the short-term tactics of particularly "hot" patronage cases and lose sight of the President's strategic need for strong executive leadership teams throughout the government. When a mistake has been made in a political appointment it is usually easier for the White House to deflect blame from itself by complaining about an unresponsive bureaucracy than to evaluate an executive's performance and correct any errors by making another appointment.
—The relevant experience of political executives is normally inferior to that of their official subordinates. Instead of sensitivity to the nuances of people and programs, there is likely to be an indiscriminate suspicion of existing personnel and uncertainty about the operating environment. Communication among layers of political appointees readily substitutes for communication downward to the operating levels. Under these conditions the incentive is often to avoid the risks of political leadership or to take them without a knowledgeable calculation of the costs.
—Teamwork among political executives is at a premium. Appointees

generally are unfamiliar with each other as a group and are poorly equipped to exchange loyalties or to coordinate themselves so as to avoid crossed signals and jurisdictional disputes. When political teams do manage to coalesce in the agencies, they often fade with the coming and going of particular personalities.

—Tenure is not only short but known to be short by everyone from whom an executive has to seek cooperation. Bureaucrats become used to compensating for repeated vacancies at the top. The political figures themselves have every incentive to concentrate on fleeting crises and to overlook the need for institutional follow-through and the important incremental changes that are always under way. Their experience, usually gained through a solitary stint of government service, is thus eventually lost rather than accumulated, as it would be through periodic spells of in-and-out invigoration.

—Commitment to the task of political leadership is often strongly qualified by the executives' ties to their essentially nonpolitical careers. Under pressure from Congress, interest groups, or the press, a political executive can find it more comfortable to temporize his leadership role or to leave government altogether. His primary career is unlikely to be affected by any enduring stake in the effectiveness of the administration or its programs.

In sum, a significant distance lies between the extremely demanding qualities needed for political leadership in the bureaucracy and the weak political materials in Washington with which to accomplish it. This mismatch often prompts experienced appointees and civil servants alike to observe that the problems ascribed to unresponsive bureaucracies are commonly due to the inadequacies of political leadership. Possibly some governments, like some musical instruments, might respond well to amateurs, but unfortunately the U.S. executive branch is a place for violinists, not kazoo players. Often it seems that political executives are not so much drowned out by forceful bureaucrats as that they themselves fail to perform. Individual cases of virtuosity do occur, but as a group, the executive players are likely to have little concern for their joint performance unless the President assumes the role of conductor. Only the President has a self-interest in seeing to it that political executives work together to help his administration and its aims. Hence if there are to be significant improvements in the selection and competence of political executives, we will have to look mainly to the presidency for reform.

And if these hard-pressed executives are to get the services they desperately need from the bureaucracy, we will have to think again about our civil service system.

Civil Service Deficiencies

Since political appointees cannot get by on self-help alone, one of the greatest contributions to political leadership would be a well-organized, higher career service distributed across the executive branch. In fact, no reasonable alternatives exist, for in a day-to-day sense only bureaucrats can control the bureaucracy. There are simply too many complicated details and possibilities of delay, too many appeal routes and varieties of subordinate jobs for temporary appointees ever to gain comprehensive operational control. Creating an outside source of detailed management control merely produces a counterbureaucracy (much like the political appointment layers or the recent proliferation of congressional staff). The result is not a system in which the permanent officials can be counted on to check and control each other but another bureaucracy that is out of control.

Potentially at least, the civil service concept offers a way of mitigating these problems. Particularly at the higher levels, where a mixture of policy and administration is inevitable and where political sensitivity is a necessity, career officials are supposed to have a dual nature as both bureaucrats and civil servants. If bureaucracy and its self-interested organizational focus are facts of life, the concept of a civil service is normative, an idea of enduring capabilities that should exist in government under any political leadership and regardless of any personal, organizational, or program loyalties. The civil service system was primarily designed to offer service to others, not to serve the security of its own members. As far as political leaders are concerned, that service was to have two aspects: positive aid to help politically accountable executives apply their energies and talents and negative checks to safeguard the integrity of government institutions and processes against partisan or private abuse. Once again the evidence shows a considerable gap between what is required by the idea of a higher civil service and the tendencies of existing arrangements in Washington:

—That part of the civil service devoted to a professional career system would require a clear designation and the availability of challenging positions to focus career ambitions. Career public servants would be assured that they could rise to these high-level positions on the nonpartisan basis of their ability to perform such jobs. In practice higher career positions blur rapidly into political appointments. The procedures of the career personnel system are subject to considerable manipulation by bureaucrats and appointees alike. The more a young, first-rate civil servant succeeds in gaining promotion, the more he or she is likely to become vulnerable to arbitrary personnel actions based on informal practices and personal or political ties.

—Protections would apply to the general governmentwide system of higher civil service careers in the sense that ranking officials could be moved without threatening their standing as civil servants or opening the vacancies to outside political pressure. Instead, protection at present arises mainly out of a proprietary interest in a particular job and individualized networks of support among outside constituencies. Political executives who do move officials are likely to threaten the latter's compartmentalized career prospects and signal that the positions in question have been politicized. An official who in good conscience feels he should move receives little institutionalized help and must count on his own personal networks in pursuing any broader development of his career in the public service.

—A civil servant would be expected to offer his best independent judgment to a succession of different partisan leaders. Officials would be able to work closely and loyally with political executives without threatening their government careers or longer-term loyalties to the institutions of government. In practice the idea that the higher career service should be a resource for political leadership is still alien to Washington. Constructive working relations with political appointees easily shade into identification with particular political patrons. Pervasive suspicion of the civil servant's role creates strong incentives for officials either to withdraw from offering help or to reassure political figures by cutting corners and ingratiating themselves.

—Managers of a professional civil service would be responsible for using assignments to develop their subordinates' career prospects; they would have a self-interest in protecting and promoting the civil service as a high-caliber career system. Under current arrangements the temporary political appointees in charge of career personnel have little immediate incentive to maintain the integrity of the civil service as an institution, nor are they apt to be held accountable for the career development of their subordinates who will remain behind in government. Appointees are more likely to start with very poor information about personnel and go on to adopt a less institutional, more personally politicized approach to using people in government. Career bureaucrats who control lower-level operations and promotions in the civil service have a vested interest in using personnel actions to maintain the well-being of their particular bureaus, not in developing a broad-gauged civil service. Thus the choice typically presented to ambitious and competent career officials is either to become part of an appointee's personal retinue or to advance by working their way up narrow career ladders at the bureau level.

—In a genuine civilian career service some central organization would have governmentwide responsibility for personnel policy. Problems of civil service policy (and not individual personnel actions) would be an important part of the President's overall perspective and management responsibilities in the executive branch. Yet insofar as there is now any central concern for career personnel systems throughout the executive branch, it is the function of the semi-independent Civil Service Commission, itself a large and self-interested bureaucracy committed to procedural regulations. Its role is muddled with the responsibilities of the Office of Management and Budget for improving management and advising the President on executive development functions that are invariably subordinated to OMB's primary concern for budget activities. Over the years any direct staff assistance to the President on career personnel policy has depended on the varying use of a special assistant here and there or on particular Civil Service Commission chairmen who happen to enjoy personal access to the President.

Inherent Failure

Thus stepping back from the personalities and controversies of any particular administration reveals a number of serious and enduring defects. The overall picture is one with a large number of supposed political controllers over the bureaucracy—transient, structurally divided, largely unknown to each other, and backed by a welter of individual patrons and supporters. Held vaguely responsible for the actions of the government's huge organizations, these national political executives are too plentiful and have too many diverse interests to coordinate themselves. But without a massive return to spoils politics, they are also too few and too temporary to actually seize control and operate the government machinery.

Facing them are "the others," a spectrum of high-level bureaucrats and semipermanent figures through whom executives must lead. This immensely larger number of bureaucratic officials is not so much fragmented as compartmentalized by agency and program. Most can be expected to have far more organizational and political experience than their political superiors. Unlike some foreign bureaucracies, these officials are not expected to have undivided loyalty to the minister of the day, but then neither are there well-established norms in Washington as to how ranking bureaucrats are to be held accountable for their important influence on public policy. On the contrary. Top bureaucrats gain more protections as they entrench themselves in particular bureaus and develop allegiances with outside power centers; their vulnerability increases insofar as they try to move with a broader government perspective and offer help to political executives.

The disparities between what is required for effective working relations and what is likely to occur in executive politics suggest structural weaknesses that cannot be cured simply by urging political executives to try harder or become more skilled in the statecraft of political administration. In fact, the more political appointees try to maneuver and to use people within the present strategic environment, the more likely they are to displace the basic civil service idea in government operations. The need for reform is inherent in the existing system. How, then, might the strategic environment be changed for the better? By creating institutions that could bridge the gap between a strictly political or bureaucratic solution.

The Shape of Reform

Considerable attention has already been given to the reasons why the self-interests of political leaders would be poorly served by adding even more political appointees. Far from improving control and performance, this would further bureaucratize the political layers and accentuate initial distrust and the mindless compulsion to change personnel with each new administration, as well as create more nonelected entrepreneurs trying to cut their own swath through Washington. Even if a President or a cabinet officer could achieve unambiguous control over his appointees, he would have done little to cope with the political-bureaucratic relationship discussed in this book. Like the court of the Medici, a system of ever more loyal and tougher political appointees would be a regime of absolutism tempered by suicide (as inexperienced appointees who had forgone the bureaucracy's services got into trouble) and by assassination (as alienated bureaucrats used their multiple sources of appeal and power).

Moreover, there are greater dangers in any reform that concentrates exclusively on responsiveness to political leadership. Without a sense of the civil service's independent responsibility to uphold legally constituted institutions and procedures, political control of the bureaucracy can easily go too far. Any single-minded commitment to executive energy is likely to evolve into arbitrary power. Recent revelations—not only about Watergate but about a long series of executive abuses of power in law enforcement, intelligence activities, tax administration, and domestic programs—have shown that, far from being abstract, these dangers are very real.[1] Americans may want government to cope with problems, but they are also right to continue their ancestral mistrust of executive power. As future public policy choices become more pressing, so too will the temptation for policymakers to rationalize ways of bypassing legitimate restraints on their power, including the restraint represented by a career civil service.

Should we then look for reforms to strengthen the civil service system in order to increase protections against arbitrary actions by political executives? Since the abuses of the Nixon administration, this has certainly been the general consensus among those trying to improve the system. Some of the signs can be observed in the recent growth of Civil Service Commission regulations noted in chapter 4. Other experts who once might have promoted the idea of an activist President-centered model of executive leadership now advocate detailed regulation of the number of presidential aides, prohibitions on what an attorney general may discuss

1. Evidence on the Internal Revenue Service, for example, is contained in *Political Intelligence in the Internal Revenue Service: The Special Service Staff, A Documentary Analysis*, Staff of the Subcommittee on Constitutional Rights of the Senate Committee on the Judiciary, 93 Cong. 2 Sess. (GPO 1974); and *Investigation of the Special Service Staff of the Internal Revenue Service*, Staff of the Joint Committee on Internal Revenue Taxation, 94 Cong. 1 Sess. (GPO, 1975). Recent evidence on improper FBI and CIA activities is cited in *Final Report of the Select Committee to Study Governmental Operations with Respect to Intelligence Activities*, S. Rept. 755, 94 Cong. 2 Sess. (GPO, 1976). Attempts to exert partisan influence in a number of other domestic agencies are described in *Presidential Campaign Activities of 1972*, Executive Session Hearings before the Senate Select Committee on Presidential Campaign Activities, bks. 18 and 19: *Watergate and Related Activities: Use of Incumbency–Responsiveness Program*, 93 Cong. 2 Sess. (GPO, 1974).

with the President, and many more checks on the political executives' discretion.[2] Still other reform proposals would make the Civil Service Commission a more self-contained bureaucracy operating with less dependence on the chief executive. Under this approach the three commissioners would be further removed from the reach of presidents, would report and seek funds directly from Congress, and would gain statutory authority to discipline individual employees anywhere in government.[3]

Such exclusive attention to constraining political executives and strengthening the present civil service structure has major drawbacks, however. An obvious disadvantage is that more detailed restrictions in the personnel process will merely add to the intricacies of the system described in chapter 4, intricacies that many supposed political leaders are already ill-prepared to cope with. Equally important, trying to limit executive discretion through a great many formal requirements and legal prohibitions is likely to be counterproductive. Frequently the problem is that political and bureaucratic officials fail to abide by the spirit, and at times the letter, of the law that already exists. More paper barriers against preferential personnel actions will simply be avoided by knowledgeable officials but will be extraordinarily troublesome to conscientious political executives who seek flexibility in adapting staffing arrangements to their needs.

Moreover, a further danger is that those setting the restrictions, either in Congress or the Civil Service Commission, can become so deeply involved in the details of managerial operations that they weaken their capacity to serve as independent critics of executive action and obscure the public executives' full measure of accountability for what is being done—not least to the spirit of the civil service laws. If, as some reformers propose, the Civil Service Commission is to acquire power for enforcing its sanctions directly on individual employees, the responsibility of top political executives seems bound to be diluted. Attention would be shifted to the commission's leadership role and away from the President's duty to faithfully execute the civil service law and to hold his chief appointees accountable for what they or their subordinates were doing to the career personnel system. In short, more detailed and legalistic pro-

2. See National Academy of Public Administration, *Watergate: Its Implications for Responsible Government* (Washington: NAPA, March 1974), pp. 38, 60.

3. See the report of Bernard Rosen, a retired executive director of the Civil Service Commission, *The Merit System in the United States Civil Service,* Committee Print 94-10, House Committee on Post Office and Civil Service, 94 Cong. 1 sess. (GPO, 1975).

scriptions concerning the personnel process would probably create more straitjackets on executive leadership. What is needed are more trip wires that send out early warning signals whenever managerial discretion oversteps its bounds and threatens the basic merit principles of the career civil service.

Beyond any of these drawbacks there are deeper problems in relying on the present structure of the federal personnel system. In theory the civil service idea should constitute a "third force" that is different from the self-interests of either political partisans or bureaucratic organization men. This idea is not an unsullied expression of *the* public interest. Instead, the civil service is supposed to express an institutional self-interest in politically neutral and professionally competent performance for the executive function as a whole. The civil servant's value lies in his or her capacity to respond effectively to a succession of different political leaders and to offer a service that is more positive and independent than mere passive obedience. In practice, however, the civil service concept in the United States has gradually come to be identified as synonymous with a body of procedural rules: the formal classification of specific job duties, competitive examinations open to all job seekers, numerical scoring of the applicants' merits, impersonal rankings, protections for an individual's hold on a given job, and all the rest of the civil service apparatus. For the bulk of government jobs, these procedures may or may not work adequately, but they are fundamentally unsuited to nonroutinized, high-level work.

Throughout this book I have emphasized that life at the top of the bureaucracy is highly personalized, both among bureaucrats and in their dealings with the political layers. It is not a world of anonymous procedures. Rather than relying on formal job classifications, administrators make highly personal judgments about who fits in what job. Instead of examinations and a job market open to all comers, there are personal networks and ladders where individual reputation is all-important. Executive politics has little to do with impersonal scores and rankings and everything to do with confidence and trust in different individuals.

Of course the Civil Service Commission recognizes the problems and creates exceptions and refinements to its rules (and ever more pages in the *Federal Personnel Manual*). And that is precisely the point. The present personnel system can deal with the realities of executive management only by exception. Personnel technicians curse the darkness that leads government managers to misuse the exceptions. Always, it seems, some people are treating others in a personally preferential manner. The technicians' feeling is likely to be that there is something wrong with the people. My argument is that there is something wrong with the rules and their premises. Reforms that simply create refinements in the present civil service system will still be at odds with the human reality of executive politics. Such reforms would intensify the vicious cycle that already exists in Washington. As the formal requirements run up against the personal calculations of trust, confidence, and mutual advantage among high-level personnel, both bureaucrats and political appointees attempt to circumvent these requirements. Sometimes the purpose of this kind of accommodation—job tailoring, name requests, special treatment, and so on—is laudable and sometimes not. In any case circumvention only devalues the basic idea of the civil service.

To try to break this vicious cycle by grafting more formal rules and regulations onto the present personnel system is unlikely to help. It may in fact hurt the ultimate integrity of the civil service. In the past no one became more adept than experienced bureaucrats at manipulating procedures in order to gain the flexibility they felt they could legitimately claim. It was the well-established tolerance for these informal personnel arrangements that facilitated the efforts of Nixon aides to politicize the bureaucracy. The unanswerable question was "If manipulation of the civil service would work for them, why not for us?" Rather than party spoils, centralized management control by the President's men over the bureaucracy became the rallying cry, but it was no less political for that.

A Middle Way

Does all this mean there should be no rules or no reform at all? Quite the contrary. Reforms are obviously needed, but any new rules also need to be compatible with, rather than antipathetic to, the personal realities of executive politics. It is tempting to choose up sides between the two perspectives, but reform will be of little help if it is based on either the current political structure or the civil service system. Instead of trying to sharpen the formal distinction between political and bureaucratic personnel, what is needed is a way to institutionalize the blurring that inevitably occurs. To do so could both help political leadership and strengthen the basic idea of a federal civil service.

To choose the middle way in reform would mean accepting the fact that at the higher reaches of the bureaucracy, personal acceptability and sympathetic working relations are vital. Officials rising to the top of the bureaucracy would have to accept more risks and less security in their hold on any particular job. At the same time, political agency heads could not expect to treat these top positions in the bureaucracy as if they were at the absolute disposal of each new administration. Selections would have to be made from among people with established records of competence. Unlike rank and file civil servants, the new type of officials would be movable across a variety of jobs; unlike political appointees they would expect to have career continuity in the civilian service of the national government. The new approach would aim to institutionalize what the myth of continual in-and-outers to Washington incorrectly assumes to exist: a pool of competent, experienced government executives able to serve a variety of political leaders.

This third force would give expression to the fact that the United States, unlike a number of foreign countries, cannot presume to create a closed senior civil service elite that acquires security from outside scrutiny by offering undivided loyalty to the government ministers of the day. Instead, such a reform would recognize that a good deal of bureaucratic maneuvering and divided loyalty is inherent in the uniquely American structure of divided institutions sharing powers. Reforms should institutionalize a means by which new administrations could reconstitute government leadership without undermining the continuity of its institutional life. Political appointees should have someone to talk to in addition to the personal loyalists they bring in with them and the more narrow program and staff specialists they inherit in the bureaucracy. Ambitious civil servants should have something more in government service to aspire to than an appointee's retinue or a bureaucrat's promotion ladder. Ordinary citizens should feel more confident that when political or bureaucratic enthusiasms threaten the integrity of government operations, there are officials with an independent career status who could exercise their right to say "No."

Of course, such a change would not be quite as novel as the preceding comments suggest. Gradually and indeliberately, executive politics in Washington have already begun evolving in this direction. Recall, for example, the large number of "political" appointees who have few credentials in a party political sense and strong backgrounds in a technical or professional sense. Lower down, one-third to one-half of the noncareer supergrades are de facto careerists. Likewise, throughout this discussion of the bureaucracy, the third force has been emerging at the margins—

bureaucrats with the institutionalists' disposition, those who feel an obligation to offer positive help or move, those who try to overcome the appointees' initial distrust, and those who count on their general standing in the Washington networks rather than on specific patrons for protection.

Yet without some institutionalized form, all these tendencies are hostages, not to fortune, but to the suspicions of each new political executive and his natural compulsion to change personnel. Even with goodwill on the part of political appointees and higher civil servants alike, an absence of institutionalized processes means that any major personnel change is subject to a kind of inadvertent politicizing through the reactions of outsiders. Lacking a collection of high-level officials secure in their career status, if not in particular jobs, top political agency heads are unable to change subordinate executives without identifying the vacated job as fair game for all the familiar political pressures from congressmen, White House aides, and lobbyists.

No reforms are likely to change the basic need for statecraft in political administration. Neither is there much likelihood of improvement by urging people in government to behave differently. What reforms can do is to try to change the strategic setting so as to create somewhat different incentives and calculations for using people. Without some new effort to create a third force in executive politics, there is little prospect of coping with the recurring and growing Washington dilemma. Trying to depoliticize the higher civil service will create more procedural formalities safeguarding individual claims to top bureaucratic jobs and encouraging circumvention. Trying to debureaucratize the political layers will facilitate new intrusions into the higher civil service.

A Third Force: The Federal Service

Both horns of the dilemma can be avoided by establishing a group of high-level officials who are more changeable and mobile than bureaucrats but more institutional and enduring than political appointees. This group of officials, whom I call Federal Executive Officers, would not acquire a rank, as officials do now, by virtue of a particular job classification. Instead, individuals would be appointed to a new Federal Service on the basis of their nonpartisan qualifications for high-level government work and would carry a rank and salary dependent on their individual record of performance (as in the U.S. military and foreign service).

Under the proposed system, a new civil service agency in the Executive Office of the President would establish public standards and evaluation procedures for making all appointments to the Federal Service of the executive branch. In order to create a system that is open and protected from arbitrary acts of favoritism, all applicants for the Federal Service would be judged by evaluation boards composed of distinguished career executives and representatives of the general public. Assessment centers would be used to compare the applicants' qualifications in a variety of work situations over a number of days. At the completion of each year's evaluation sessions, the results would be open to public scrutiny and the civil service agency would appoint the most competent applicants of that year's class as Federal Executive Officers.

In filling particular career executive positions, a political agency head would be free to choose from among any members of the Federal Service. He would be able to move Federal Executive Officers among various jobs but could not revoke their status as career officers and would have to choose a replacement from the pool of federal executives. Likewise, members of the Federal Service would be able to seek reassignments to any job falling vacant in this executive system.

To extend across the interface of political and bureaucratic levels, the jobs in question should include all those below the level of the major political appointees (assistant secretaries or the equivalent) and above the bulk of middle-management positions in the present civil service. In practice this would mean that the positions open to members of the Federal Service would encompass roughly the present range of GS 17, GS 18, and executive schedule V positions, or about 1,800 jobs in all. Once admitted to the Federal Service, an official would be eligible to have his qualifications considered for any of these 1,800 career executive positions. Under this new arrangement the present much larger group of GS 16 government jobs (almost 4,000 in 1976) would constitute a major recruitment group from the civil service into the Federal Service. At the same time, however, applicants from outside government could have their qualifications considered for appointment to the service.[4] Thus the

4. A transition period for instituting such a system would obviously be needed. All the officials currently holding these 1,800 positions should not be replaced en masse, but if there is to be fresh blood and opportunities for outside applicants, these officials also should not be automatically transferred into the Federal Service. A reasonable approach would be to start gradually by instituting the system in only one grade level (e.g., GS 17) at first and only in agencies that already have a similar internal executive program of their own.

present system of mixing some temporary political appointments into the ranks of career officials would be abolished; all Federal Executive Officers would be appointed on the basis of their commitment to a career in government service. Those whose competence eroded over the years or who could not be placed in a new position should be made eligible for early retirement benefits, or if qualified, could move to a less demanding position at the GS 16 level or below.

With such a Federal Service, the strategic environment would differ significantly from the present one. Currently almost half of the 1,800 jobs proposed for Federal Executive Officers are noncareer appointments; that is, they are not subject to competitive civil service examinations. The term "noncareer," however, covers a multitude of confusions with respect to whether or not it signifies that a job is a "political" appointment. Participants continually argue about how political the 160 or so schedule A lawyers at this level are supposed to be, why some personnel with policy-making responsibilities are among the 600 noncareer executive assignments while hundreds of other career executives are not, and how far the White House should involve itself in the 200 presidential appointees at this level or if it should leave discretion to the responsible agency heads. In these and many other respects, any political interest is likely to be part of a disorganized, unreliable process for recruiting, evaluating, and selecting key government executives. Under the Federal Service reform, political pressures would remain, but instead of preoccupation with "What kind of job is it?" more attention would be directed to how people are actually performing. Those unacceptable could be removed from a particular position, but no outside replacements could be arbitrarily brought into the Federal Service. For higher political appointees, incentives would shift away from trying to bring "my guy" into a job toward choosing from among a variety of people with the continuity to help political leaders.

For the present 900 or so civil service jobs that would be incorporated into the 1,800 positions under the new plan, there would also be important changes. As shown in chapter 4, the current arrangements for managing career supergrades involve a kind of snakes and ladders process of preparing specific job classifications and qualification requirements, of formally searching within the organization and in outside agencies, of following an additional even more complex process for any recruitment outside the government work force, of assembling lists that lack personal evaluations, and of obtaining approval for each procedure and individual appointment from the Civil Service Commission. Under the system I propose, the present complicated process for dealing with top career executives would be replaced with central selection into the Federal Service, and department managers would be given far more flexibility in using people within this pool.

Like similar plans published in 1972, this proposal would help improve managerial flexibility; unlike the Nixon administration formula, it would put career officials in higher-level government work, eliminate the dangerous mixture with so-called political appointments, and yield far more career continuity than can be provided by a short-term contract of service.[5] And unlike the plan for a senior civil service in the 1950s, the new Federal Service would be relatively accessible to applicants outside the bureaucracy, open to public scrutiny, and part of a reorganized presidential capability in personnel management.

For ambitious career civil servants, the proposed Federal Service would provide more challenging opportunities for advancement and would make governmentwide mobility and close working relations with political executives less threatening. For top political executives it would make the movement of subordinate personnel less difficult and less likely to attract outside political pressures. For the executive system as a whole the proposed Federal Service would help reduce much of the unjustified suspicion that new political figures now direct toward job-tenured bureaucrats. It would also mark a major switch away from the traditional approach of creating a few high-level positions for careerists (e.g., assistant secretaries for administration) and then trying to protect these particular salients from surrounding political pressures, all the while reassuring the political managers in charge that they can move top careerists if they really want to.

Above all, such a change in the approach to public executives would be more realistic than the incessant attempts to clarify and defend the blurred lines between political and bureaucratic jobs at the top of the bureaucracy. The Federal Service would be more realistic, and thus more stable, because it would not depend on the dubious idea of finding a line separating policymaking from administration. As I have stressed, political sensitivity and important policymaking responsibilities are inherent in the positive services of high-level civil servants. Likewise, top political "policymakers" may issue decisions, but without strategic attention to admin-

5. For a discussion of the 1972 proposals, pro and con, see *The Federal Executive Service*, Hearings before the Subcommittee on Manpower and Civil Service of the House Committee on Post Office and Civil Service, 92 Cong. 2 sess. (GPO, 1972).

istrative detail there is likely to be little real policymaking, at least not in the sense of changing the way people in government behave. A Federal Service of career public executives would preserve the basically valuable idea of civil service in the personalized world of executive politics, where policy, administration, and political sensitivity are all inextricably linked.

Civil Service Leadership

Despite a host of modern management techniques, there seems to be no alternative superior to the time-honored idea of, first, putting a political figure at the head of a government organization and holding him accountable, and second, providing a competent career system both to serve that political leader and to safeguard the continuity of government institutions. It is in the latter regard that the new Federal Service could facilitate intermediation between strictly political and bureaucratic interests. Still, how should central responsibility for the Federal Service and the civil service be organized and how could protections against politicizing be assured?

At present the question of policymaking for civilian career personnel remains in its traditional state of limbo. The Civil Service Commission tries to combine its independence as protector of the merit system with its more independent managerial status as the President's central personnel agency, a role it now also has to share with the President's Office of Management and Budget. Historically, the ambiguous arrangement has been subject to continual tinkering, usually with unfortunate consequences. Off and on, first presidential assistants and then Civil Service Commission chairmen have had responsibilities for both political and civil service personnel. Special White House assistants used in this way have often been removed from involvement in civil service policies and have been prone to mixing in political patronage cases. Civil Service Commission chairmen used as personal presidential advisers have been vulnerable to the appearance, if not the fact, of abandoning protection of the civil service. Meanwhile the commission has continued to oversee not only career civil service policy but also schedule C and many other noncareer appointments. In theory these positions are merely exempt from competitive examination and continue to be subject to civil service rules, such as merit qualifications for office, Hatch Act prohibitions against political activity, and so on. In practice these rules are seldom enforced, especially when there is real political interest in the appointment and when the commission is worried about gaining access to the White House and presidential support for its policies.

None of this suggests a promising structure in which to entrust the establishment of a new approach such as the Federal Service. The current inclination to criticize presidential power should not obscure the basic strength of the case made during the past forty years of truncated reform. The presidency is the one and only focus available for bringing a strong, overall perspective to executive branch personnel policies. This focus is particularly important if there is to be anyone accountable for the growing governmentwide problems surrounding such policies as bargaining with public employee unions, controlling the immense payroll costs and pension commitments of government workers, and developing competent managers who can run public programs effectively. That does not mean that the President is legally managing director of the federal government or that politically he could be. It does mean that the presidency is the place where people should be able to look for a coherent sense of the administration's purpose and responsibility; this is particularly important if the Federal Service is to be something more than a collection of top rungs on existing bureau career ladders. If congressionally enacted laws regarding the Federal Service and civil service were being violated or bent, then the President and through him his top executives should be able to be held accountable. At present the President has no lack of responsibilities, in fact more than he can handle. What is needed is the creation of organizational means by which a feasible range of presidential responsibilities can actually be exercised on some enduring institutional basis.

These organizational deficiencies would be substantially reduced by creating a statutory civil service agency under the President, an office that would take over responsibilities from the Civil Service Commission and the Office of Management and Budget for establishing governmentwide policies for civilian career personnel. Politically, Congress and opposition party members would not and should not accept such an organization if it were simply another adjunct to the President's personal staff in the White House Office. If it is to be both an adviser to presidents and an institutional arm of the presidency, such an organization should be a statutory part of the Executive Office of the President, with a rank equivalent to the present OMB, one director and a deputy appointed by the President and confirmed by the Senate, and a career staff. A change of this kind would for the first time give concrete meaning to the chief executive's overall responsibilities, not only for budgeting and grand policy, but also for conducting the personnel policies that produce millions of government employees and billions of dollars in public expenditures.

With certain exceptions, the presidency's civil service agency should *not* have day-to-day operating responsibility for individual personnel actions. Within central guidelines, department responsibility for individual personnel actions, job classifications, examinations, and so on should rest with department managers and their own personnel offices. One exception is that the civil service agency should become operationally involved by inspecting and spot-checking periodically to see that its general policies are being observed. Where they are not, the new agency should have the power to enforce policy by suspending or overturning department personnel actions. Another exception is that the civil service agency should, of course, have operating responsibility for the evaluation and appointment of applicants to the Federal Service. It should also conduct periodic training and counseling sessions on a governmentwide basis to encourage broader career mobility and development in government officials.

The major area where the central civil service agency should become involved in day-to-day personnel operations is with regard to career employees in the Executive Office of the President. In addition to setting broad policy for the civil service as a whole and administering admission to the Federal Service, the new organization should act as personnel agency for the various units in the Executive Office of the President. This is most vital because of the limited opportunities at present for careerists to learn to work and advance in an interdepartmental environment, much less any system that would make the presidency part of civil service career patterns. As public policies become more interdependent and as the missions of different agencies increasingly overlap, the need grows for career personnel in domestic policy who can deal with each other from a wider perspective than as paladins for bureau X or program Y. Yet under present arrangements, such interdepartmental careerists are unlikely to be developed on any reliable basis. With little organizational coherence, the Executive Office of the President is hardly more than a terminological convenience for preparing the appropriation accounts.

The new central civil service agency would be in a favorable position to encourage a more general presidential perspective in bureaucratic careers. It could provide a personnel capability to facilitate the movement of career staff throughout the Executive Office units (primarily the OMB, Council of Economic Advisers, and National Security Council) and it could foster exchanges of personnel between the Executive Office and the departments as a regular part of career development planning. The new agency could also regularize the present hit-and-miss process for using civil servants on interagency task forces, special study groups, and other flexible staffing arrangements to help scrutinize and rethink government policies. But the placement of Federal Executive Officers and lower civil servants in the Executive Office of the President should be totally separate from any identification with persons working for a given president in the White House Office.

Instituting Better Safeguards

The preceding suggestions contain two obvious dangers. One is that a career personnel agency in the presidency and a more distinct, central role for civil servants in the Executive Office complex could increase bureaucratic power out of all proportion to the political executives' ability to cope with it. For the time being, however, this drawback seems rather remote; any careerist trying to survive in the politically charged atmosphere of the presidency will have a strong self-interest in operating with considerable discretion and in urging colleagues to do the same.

The experience of recent administrations suggests that a second danger is far more likely: if they were so inclined, presidents and their personal aides could find it much easier to invade and politicize a career civil service system that is more closely attached to the presidency. Trying to build a more comprehensive, high-level civil service may simply further jeopardize the basically nonpartisan norms of such a fragile institution in Washington.

The dangers of politicizing are real under the proposed system, but they are under existing arrangements too. Even if responsibilities for the career civil service remained as they are where they are, the past trends and questionable practices that reached their highest point yet during the Nixon administration are not reassuring. The present system depends on the vigilance of one minority member among the three Civil Service commissioners, on the interest of congressmen in two civil service subcommittes, on employees' unions, and on individual officials complaining to Civil Service Commission investigators. Under the Nixon administration all these protections for the higher civil service system evidently were not enough, at least not until late in the administration when the White House was already vulnerable for other reasons.

A number of new legal prohibitions have been proposed to buttress the protections of the civil service. It is difficult, for example, to see why almost unbridled scope is allowed to anyone who wishes to make political referrals for career jobs, while sanctimonious regulations prohibit appointing officers from considering the political content of the referrals they receive. More stringent penalties could well be created in statutory law for both the improper giving and using of political referrals or clearances for career jobs.[6] By and large, however, more written rules and prohibitions will be of little help, since powerful government figures cannot be counted on to follow the rules that already exist. In an ideal world every public official would have the inner strength to "blow the whistle" against executive wrongdoing. In practice safety will be more certain if less heroism is required and if an official can more confidently report to superiors that, however much he might want to help, determined outsiders are watching who are bound to create trouble for everyone concerned if questionable demands are carried forward. As the Founders suggested, there is more security to be had by sharing powers among different sets of people so that personal self-interests correspond with the duty to protect against improper encroachments of power.

To some extent the proposed high-level Federal Service might help by creating a more distinctive self-awareness among leading careerists as a group. That, however, is a long-term proposition. Some margin of safety can also be provided by making the director and the deputy director of the President's civil service agency subject to Senate confirmation; by requiring that the agency be staffed only by civil service employees; and by prohibiting it from receiving political referrals, acquiescing to any political clearances, or advising on any political appointments by the President. Yet under these or any other arrangements a need would remain for safeguards that are independent from the executive branch officials whose conduct is being monitored. A Civil Service Commission that is semi-independent of the President but also supposed to be his central personnel agency cannot be counted on to perform that function.

Watching, investigating, and reporting on the operation of civil service laws should be a responsibility outside the reach of presidents and their personal aides and appointees. The President's civil service agency would obviously want to use managerial inspections to see to it that presidential aims and standards are being implemented. But policing the civil service

6. Current prohibitions are in 5 U.S. Code 3303. A number of other new legal prohibitions were proposed in H.R. 12080, 94 Cong. 2 sess., 1976.

merit system ought to be separate from its management. For this reason congressional oversight of career personnel policies needs to be improved. Protections should not depend mainly on particular congressmen and their staffs, since such individualistic protections from Congress are one of the chief means of politicizing the civil service. Rather, the changes needed are those that would strengthen the institutional resources of Congress as a whole. Oversight of the civil service law should be institutionalized by making the General Accounting Office of Congress responsible for auditing and reporting annually on the operation of the career civil service system in accord with the congressionally mandated civil service law. In addition to this General Accounting Office "personnel audit," Congress could make a coherent impact on personnel policy by revising its own committee activities. Establishing a single committee focus in each house for questions of government personnel policy (on the model of the new congressional budget committees) would go far in helping Congress become aware of the implications of its various actions, not only on the career civil service system, but also on the size and allocation of total government employment.

The problem of coping with grievances by individual government employees would remain. Given the natural inclination in Washington to exchange favors for protection, it seems unwise to count either on congressmen or the presidential and departmental personnel offices. In the former case too many extraneous strings would be attached to a particular redress of grievance; in the latter case the employee might justly feel that "management" was sitting in judgment on its own rules and actions. The present Civil Service Commission, with a clearer standing as an independent regulatory commission, seems best suited to handling grievances. Commissioners should serve for a fixed term of years, be confirmed by the Senate, and be removable by the President for no other cause than neglect of duty or malfeasance in office. Hearing and deciding individual appeals arising from personnel actions or labor-management agreements should be a separate safeguard institutionalized in the commission. Where appropriate, the commission should have power to order individual reinstatements but not to issue general rules and regulations for the management of federal personnel systems.

My concern here has been to protect the values of the civil service idea from political abuse and bureaucratic cronyism. Other larger values must also be secured, particularly in those situations when powerful political and bureaucratic executives get along only too well and at the expense of democratic norms. An improved structure of remedies may well be needed to provide timely protection against lawlessness within the executive branch itself—triggering mechanisms that would prevent abuses from going too far in the first place and that would provide better channels for administrative redress even when improprieties stop short of criminal activity.[7] Arguments concerning a permanent special prosecutor or government ombudsman, however, have little to do with my central topic. It is enough to note that these issues, like that of the civil service, remain as unwanted but unavoidable items on the future U.S. political agenda.

Improving the Political Personnel System

Reforms to create a new kind of federal executive officer, a central personnel agency, and better civil service safeguards would significantly improve the strategic setting for executive politics. Higher civil servants would find it more advantageous to their careers to serve a succession of political appointees in good faith and to stand up against improper political demands. Top political appointees would find their legitimate desires for change facilitated by using career officials and threatened by expedient attempts to cut corners and avoid responsibility.

A Federal Service to replace the mixture of civil service and political positions in the GS 17, GS 18, and executive schedule V range would not improve the rest of the chaotic system for political personnel. Here, as suggested earlier, the primary responsibility for more effective organization would rest with each president. Of course no president or anyone else could force political appointees to combine into one uniform team or to stay on the job long enough to be effective. But the musical chairs and disunity at the top of government agencies could be significantly reduced by more systematic White House efforts to make careful selections in the first place, to subsequently identify those who perform well, and to show the strength to remove those who are not effective for the administration. Thus while any president should be free to organize his personal political staff as he sees fit, every president would be well advised to provide a White House Office for Political Personnel with exclusive jurisdiction over all staff work on presidential appointments.

7. For a recent analysis, see American Bar Association, *Preventing Improper Influence on Federal Law Enforcement Agencies: A Report of the American Bar Association Special Committee to Study Law Enforcement Agencies* (Washington, D.C.: ABA, 1976).

Such an office should help the President to specify his requirements for a particular political vacancy. After receiving such specifications it should recruit actively and evaluate objectively all applications for presidential appointments. The Office for Political Personnel should be explicitly prohibited from having any hand in career appointments. Once a political appointment has been made, the office should prepare periodic follow-up reports to the President, using data from all available sources to assess the performance of presidential appointees as it pertains to furthering the administration's aims and to managing effectively in the bureaucracy. The staff in the President's personnel office should be selected for their competence as skilled recruiters and political analysts. They should be able to impartially lay out the political, substantive, and managerial merits of alternative personnel actions, and they ought to be discouraged from using their staff work as a stepping-stone to prestigious presidential appointments for themselves. There should be clear operating procedures to separate treatment of the political executive positions that are so vital to an administration's competent performance from the semihonorary and ceremonial posts that can be used for repaying political favors.

Even then, current arrangements require more high-caliber political appointees than may be available and certainly more than can be carefully selected and held accountable for their stewardship. The number of ranking political executives requiring the attention of the White House personnel office should be reduced and confined to the levels of cabinet secretary, undersecretary, and assistant secretary, or the equivalent operating heads of major program administrations. Cutting back on the bureaucracy of political appointees at the middle management and lower levels would focus more attention on the qualities and leadership responsibilities of the highest political executives in the agencies. It would provide both the President and Congress with a more practical opportunity to assess the selection and performance of political executives, and it would help reduce intra-agency conflict between the top and middle political layers. Concentrating on the top executive positions would clarify both the political signals sent to bureaucrats and the lines of political support between the White House and executive agencies.

Undoubtedly top political executives will always feel a need for a number of their own personal advisers, assistants, confidential secretaries, and so on. These positions, however, now carry civil service grades, depend on formal rules and regulations about job classifications, and are generally mixed up with the organization and procedures of the career civil service. The best way out of this tangled system is not to create more detailed rules about what can and cannot be done with these subordinate political positions vis-à-vis career appointments. Instead, the Gordian knot should be cut by creating a small pool of ungraded positions outside the formal hierarchy of classified government jobs. These positions could be allocated at the discretion of the presidentially appointed department heads, who would be able to hire whomever they wanted and (within a given range) to pay any salary they chose—as long as they stayed within their appropriated budget for this purpose. Such appointees could be used only as personal political assistants and policy advisers to the executive. They would have no specific classified rank within the government hierarchy of jobs. And, once in office, they could not be "blanketed-in" to the civil service.

The advantages of such a pool of political positions would be two-fold and complementary. It would strengthen the leadership resources of cabinet officers by giving them more flexibility in choosing their personal advisers and more resources with which to reward or punish subordinate political executives who would want their own part of the pool. Equally important, it would clarify the distinction between government career officials in the civil service or Federal Service on the one hand and temporary personal assistants and advisers on the other.

Other reforms, of course, could help strengthen the capacity for effective executive leadership. These changes might range all the way from more disciplined party organizations as a means of incubating executive teams to major reorganizations that would rearrange agencies. But within the confines of my subject—that is, matters of statecraft and personnel in executive politics—selectively centralizing, cutting, and pooling partisan appointments seem to be the most important changes that could be made among political executives.

Costs and Prospects

Particular features of the preceding recommendations are much less important than the question of whether, taken as a whole, they represent a generally sensible direction for change. Views on that will differ, if only because any such reforms would entail costs to a number of powerful interests in Washington.

Higher civil servants would have a more uncertain claim on given jobs; it is not clear, however, why any particular public position should be regarded as an individual's property. Political appointees and presidents would have less freedom to manipulate the career personnel system and would be more accountable for what was happening to it; but at least these constraints would be in the nature of trip wires rather than of straitjackets on managerial discretion in moving officials. Some power of the subgovernments operating across executive bureaus, congressional committees, and interest groups would be reduced or at least made more visible insofar as they sought to stake out claims on particular career or political jobs. But at present these shadowy networks offer neither energy in executive leadership nor safety from abuses of power. Institutional separation between the legislative and executive branches would be increased in the sense that political and career executives would have more reason to trust each other, while individual congressmen might be more cut off from special bureaucratic favors derived from protecting individual bureaucrats. That, too, could have advantages if Congress were thus encouraged to increase its own institutional capabilities (as opposed to increasing congressmen's personal staffs) for holding executive branch officials accountable for what they are doing.

These are high costs to expect of the established political forces in Washington. Yet the costs of avoiding major changes in the structure of political leadership and bureaucratic power are likely to be much greater. To leave arrangements largely as they are would imply complacency backed by the very dubious hope that successions of new political executives can learn enough quickly enough to be able to manage their own policymaking responsibilities (individually and together) and to maintain the integrity of the career civil service. The prospects are not encouraging. Policy challenges are growing, and if executive disorderliness, layering, and fragmentation are any guide, government capabilities are declining. As political leadership becomes more bureaucratized and the bureaucracy more politicized, any effort to compensate for one condition is apt to exacerbate the other. Although it is still too early to reach a verdict on the post-Nixon years, such problems appear to have intensified with each succeeding administration since World War II. Thus accepting the momentum of present arrangements will impose its own costs. The price of business as usual in Washington will be paid by future political leaders interested in instituting timely changes (either of a conservative or liberal nature), by the government civil service as a career for first-rate minds, and thus ultimately by American democracy itself.

If experience with past reforms is any guide, the prospects for improvement depend on a number of difficult conditions.

First, anything like the proposals suggested above would require a president who is not only willing to give strong priority to personnel matters (that would be exceptional enough) but who also has a keen appreciation for the value of the civil service idea in managing the executive branch.

Second, since any president taking such a lead will be accused of sinister motives in any event, the push for reform would have to be timed so that at a minimum it did not become entangled with other major controversies between the President and Congress. At best it should be timed to coincide with one of the rare eras of good feeling between the two branches.

Third, there would have to be forces in Congress willing to fight for improvement in executive performance and for increases in the legislature's own institutional capacities to deal with personnel policy. Without such congressional leadership the persisting alliances between specialized committees and government bureaus will dominate any effort at reform.

Fourth, if bureaucratic cooperation is to be gained for the reforms, some type of "hold harmless" provision would undoubtedly be necessary so that the personnel changes applied mainly to those newly hired rather than to all existing personnel and so that established bureaucratic figures entering the system could stipulate conditions under which they would join (e.g., no major geographic moves, a chance to concentrate in a particular area, and so on). A careful, step-by-step approach would be required to prevent the Federal Service reform from being immediately destroyed by everyone with a stake in the present bureau ladders—which is to say, every senior bureaucrat and every subordinate who is only one promotion away from where he wants to be. Probably only a small number of lower positions should be identified at first with the Federal Service, in part so that the strongest probable opponents (bureau chiefs) would not be met head on and in part so that those who would otherwise wait in the seniority line could have time to learn about the greater prospects for advancement under the new system.

All these conditions depend in turn on a larger requirement: a broad base of public support and pressure to convince both the President and Congress that there is indeed a climate for reform. Without that, no other appeals to self-interest in either branch are likely to be successful. If even

Watergate was unable to create that kind of public momentum, the immediate prospects do not look promising.

Reformers who are not content to await the next major scandal can expect to settle for many half-loaves: a limit on political referrals here, a new personal grievance procedure there. Yet even that course carries dangers. Under present arrangements it would be unwise to adopt any one particular line of reform without at the same time pursuing others. To make the bureaucracy more responsive to political executives without also improving civil service safeguards would simply increase the arbitrary influence of free-wheeling political entrepreneurs. Uncontrolled powers would also grow if the protections afforded civil servants were increased without requiring a corresponding increase in the employees' responsibility to offer impartial service to political executives. Given the difficulty of pursuing the needed balance of changes, it may seem best to leave bad enough alone.

But the difficulty of serious reform is only a symptom of its importance. To take it as a sign of hopelessness would leave an unsatisfactory situation even more intolerable, at least from the perspective of this book. As things stand, the energy that could be supplied by constructive working relations between appointees and higher civil servants is extracted only with great difficulty in the executive branch. The safety that should derive from respect for the distinctive duties of political representatives and career officials is often lost amid more narrow personal and agency loyalties. New executives seeking legitimate changes through their role as political spokesmen face unreasonable odds; so, too, do government officials who seek civil service careers that are both challenging and unbeholden to particular interests or patrons. A vast number of rules and regulations define the formal restrictions on using people in government; but what often exists in practice is a kind of covert flexibility for those clever or ruthless enough to shape the operation of regulations to their own purposes. It has become too difficult in Washington to gain political control of the bureaucracy through the right means—openly exercising political leadership—and too easy by the wrong means—quietly manipulating procedures behind the scenes. There are too many political appointees and too few accountable politicians in Washington, too many bureaucrats and not enough civil servants.

Index

Aberbach, Joel D., 160n, 183n
Adverse action, civil service procedures for, 39
Affirmative action programs, 115n
Agricultural Extension Service, 149, 200
Agricultural Soil and Conservation Service, 200
Agricultural Stabilization Service, 44
Anderson, Jack, 176
Animal and Plant Inspection Service, 45
Assistant secretaries: for administration, 76–78, 79, 252; bureaucratizing of, 66–67; tenure of, 103–05, 118
Atomic Energy Commission, 40n, 44

Barton, Allen H., 183n
Baruch, Ismar, 29n, 71n
Bernstein, Marver H., 1n
Blanketing-in, 41–42
Buchanan, Bruce, 191n
Budget: appeals limited under Nixon, 164; congressional review of, 17–18; as constraint on political executives, 174; cycles, 199; staff officials dealing with, 115, 149, 150
Bureau chiefs, 128–29, 150, 210n
Bureaucracy: activity of, during Nixon resignation, 8–9; contrasted with civil service, 19–21; control of, 1, 3–5, 34, 213–14, 240, 244; culture in 47–48, 116; growth of, 15, 20; need for, 5–6; politicizing of, 14, 49–54, 68–76, 82–83, 123–37, 170, 218–20, 236, 247, 256, 262; public suspicion of, 44; re-

sistance to political leadership, 176–77, 204–05, 210, 224–32; responsiveness of, 4–5, 20, 115, 142, 147, 177, 236–37, 264; theory of representative, 115; variations in, 153, 181, 183. *See also* Bureaucratic power; Bureaucrats
Bureaucratic power: contrasted with political leadership, 19, 21; growth in, 22, 64, 83, 256; meaning of, 1, 7, 171–73, 181; sources of, 4–5, 14–15, 173–80; vulnerability of political executives to, 112
Bureaucratic veto, 172
Bureaucrats: careers of, 30, 62–64, 116–19, 129, 145, 213, 241–42; caution of, 144, 186, 189; conflict among, 144, 185; conflict with Nixon appointees, 97–98, 183; dispositions of, 142–48, 199, 208; firing of, 140, 217–18; lack of common identity, 115–16, 133, 154; lack of presidential perspective, 129, 255–56; methods for reassuring political executives, 186–87; networks among, 111–12, 128–30, 132–33, 144, 146–47, 180; numbers of, 38; political activism among, 70; in political appointments, 23, 46–49, 131–32, 248; and self-protection, 63–64, 141, 180–81; in staff positions, 49, 149–50; services of, 5–6, 171–80, 235; as source of control over each other, 180–81, 215–16, 240; suspicions against, 3, 44, 113, 182–87; tenure of, 101, 118; ties to patrons, 14–15, 136, 141, 144–45,

265

243; types of, 142, 148–53, 173, 181, 183, 194, 204–05, 243; vulnerability to political identification, 22, 149–50, 180, 184–86, 218–20, 241, 249
Bureau of the Budget, 27, 57, 78, 80, 108
Bureau of Executive Manpower, 30, 37n, 39n, 103n, 104n, 117
Bureau of Prisons, 47
Bureau of Reclamation, 56–58
Bureau of Standards, 47
Business Organization of the United States, 57

Cabinet secretaries, 1, 14; appeals to president, 161, 164–65; attitudes toward bureaucracy, 187; conflict with president, 95, 98, 109–10, 160, 222–23; as departmental advocates, 196; number of, 36, 84, 85; right to select subordinates, 39, 95–98, 215; strengthening position of, 261; tenure of, 103–05
Career executive assignments, 30n
Carter, Jimmy, 92, 94
Cater, Douglass, 225n
Census Bureau, 56, 62, 149, 159
Central Intelligence Agency, 40n, 244
Central Personnel Agency, 24
Chayes, Abram, 18n
Cincinnatus, 102
Civil servants, 21–22. See also Bureaucrats
Civil service: as aid to political leadership, 23, 49, 171, 173–80, 232–33, 234, 240, 246; concept of, 19–21, 69, 220, 240; deficiencies of, summarized, 240–42; examinations, 20, 120, 121, 126–27, 246; extensions of, 68–69; fragmentation of, 44, 115–19, 133, 154, 241–42; grade escalation in, 62; job classifications, 120, 246; job security in, 20, 137, 140–42, 217–18; management by political executives, 133, 135–36, 138–39, 180, 183, 185–86, 213–20, 241–42; origins of, 22–23, 68, 113; as a precarious idea, 21–24, 32–33, 64, 70, 76, 243; presidential organization for, 33, 132, 145, 242, 253–56; procedures, 3, 39, 120–28, 133–34, 140–41, 246–47, 251; promotions, 131; reform of, 24–28, 29–31, 41, 44, 244, 247–53; vacancies in, 117–18. See also Civil service protections
Civil Service Act of 1883, 20n, 23, 24
Civil Service Board, 24
Civil Service Commission: chairman of, 25, 26–27, 124, 242; definition of ex-
ecutive population, 37; disciplinary powers of, 139–40, 245; under Eisenhower, 25–26, 29; executive development program, 30, 119, 130–32, 242; under Johnson, 26–27, 30; under Kennedy, 26; minority member's role, 23, 137; and name requests, 125n; under Nixon, 23–24, 28–29, 31, 50, 54, 77–78, 139–40; origins of, 23; personnel procedures of, 19, 28, 30, 33, 40, 120–22, 245–48, 251; and political clearances, 51–54; and political referrals, 123–24; presidential leadership role of, 26, 33, 113, 129, 242, 253; protective functions of, 28, 53–54, 133, 136–40, 244–45, 257; under Roosevelt, 24; supergrade quotas of, 31–32, 121
Civil service protections: dangers of, 83, 264; decline in, 28–29, 33, 68–83, 256; ineffectiveness of, 53–54, 218–20; need to increase, 240, 241, 256–59; reform of, 244–45, 247–53, 257–58; sources for providing, 133–42, 151, 241; tradition of, 23–24, 32–33, 63–64, 69, 127–28
Classification Act of 1949, 29, 135
Clearance: for civil service jobs, 49, 50–53, 70–76, 184; of political appointments, 71, 75, 96–97
Clifford, Clark M., 102
Coast Guard, 149
Coffey, Matthew B., 48n
Cohen, Richard E., 18n
Cohen, Wilbur, 145
Collegial presidency, 109
Commission on the Organization of the Executive Branch of the Government. See Hoover Commission
Commodity and Future's Trading Commission Act of 1974, 45n
Commodity Exchange Authority, 44–45
Common Cause, 87n
Communication: among bureaucrats, 111–12, 129, 146–47, 179–80; between bureaucrats and political executives, 175–76, 195–96, 205–07; effects of breakdown in, 232–33; among political executives, 104, 107, 163; unauthorized, 226–27. See also Leaks
Comptroller General, 17n, 40n
Conditional cooperation: defined, 193–94; effects of breakdown in, 232–34; outside influences on, 222; value of, 220, 221
Confidence, 246, 247; defined, 158–59; loss of, 163, 164, 227; political execu-

tives' difficulty in establishing, 170–71; scale of, 168–70

Congress, 2, 4, 87, 99, 109; administrative intervention by, 17–18, as control on bureaucracy, 6, 22; delegation of authority to department heads, 12; growth of bureaucracy in, 59–60, 229, 240; institutional versus personal staff, 257–58, 262; as job outlet for bureaucrats, 131; as means of politicizing bureaucracy, 51, 123–24, 249; political executives' relations with, 8–9, 11, 166–68, 228–30; as protector of the civil service, 133, 134–35, 257–58; resistance to presidential proposals for reforming personnel policy, 25–26, 31, 29, 135, 263; role in making federal personnel policy, 31–32, 33, 37–38, 40, 45, 46, 134–35, 245, 258, 263; and selection of political executives, 44–45, 92, 95, 99, 184–85; tenure of members, 118; ties with bureaucracy and interest groups, 13, 46, 111–12, 147, 150, 157, 159, 166–68, 171, 173, 183–84, 224, 225, 262

Cost of Living Council, 44

Council of Economic Advisers, 255

Courts, 6, 18

Cronin, Thomas E., 13n

Davidson, Robert, 77n

Defense Manpower Commission, 140n

Democratic National Committee, 71, 93

Democratic party: conflict with Republicans, 111; intrusions into civil service, 50, 51; patronage desires of, 71, 72–73; resistance to Eisenhower reforms, 25, 27; suspicions of bureaucracy, 182; use of bureaucrats in political appointments, 48

Departmentalism: as focus for political leadership, 12–14, 109, 160, 222–23; need to coordinate, 16; as source of bureaucratic identity, 129, 151, 255–56

Department of Agriculture, 40, 60, 77, 200, 203

Department of Commerce, 30, 41n, 43, 46, 77

Department of Defense, 8, 10, 44, 140n

Department of Health, Education, and Welfare, 9, 10, 145; assistant secretary for administration in, 77; lawsuits against, 18; opposition to Nixon appointees, 111, 183, 192; politicizing of, 50, 54

Department of Housing and Urban Development, 8–9, 39, 41, 116; assistant secretary for administration in, 77; internal organization of, 40, 42; politicizing of, 135, 219

Department of the Interior, 32n, 39, 132; internal organization of, 56, 58; political appointees in, 66; staff units started in, 60

Department of Justice, 9, 39, 77, 148

Department of Labor, 9, 10, 41n, 77

Department of State, 40n, 66, 132

Department of Transportation, 9, 10, 41n, 77, 130

Department of the Treasury, 8, 10, 50, 116, 132; assistant secretary for administration in, 77; internal organization of, 66; staff units started in, 60

Derthick, Martha, 183n

Destler, I. M., 2n

Doig, Jameson W., 100n, 102n, 103n, 106n

Domestic and International Business Administration, 46

Due process, in executive politics, 164–66, 208–09

Dye, Thomas R., 100n

Ehrlichman, John D., 164n

Eisenhower, Dwight D., 13, 101n; and assistant secretaries for administration, 77; attempts to reform civil service, 29, 135; political appointments under, 71–72, 74, 89, 95; staff organization for personnel policy, 25–27

Elections: limited influence of, 4, 14; mixed mandates from, 10–11; as source of political leadership, 86, 87, 109–10

Employment, federal government: civil service coverage of, 68–69; growth in, 15, 17, 55–59; 62, 63; numerical classification of, 36–40; social representativeness of, 114–15; uncontrollability of total size, 32

Environmental Protection Agency, 9, 41n

Estes, Billie Sol, 203

Executive Assignment System, 30

Executive development, 30–31, 130–31

Executive Inventory, of Civil Service Commission, 122, 127

Executive Office of the President: creation of, 25; as manager of personnel policy, 113; and reform of civil service, 250, 254–55

Executive politics: fragmentation of, 64; 133, 242–43; networks in, 111–12, 129, 132–33, 147, 207; personalized

quality of, 2–3, 55, 121–27, 246–47; reputations tested in, 132–33, 144–45, 184–85, 188–89
Executives, federal government: definition of, 37; increased number of, 62, 63; civil service procedures for, 39–40. *See also* Bureaucrats, Political executives
Executive schedule, of government positions, 36, 38, 85

Fabricant, Solomon, 15n
Federal Bureau of Investigation, 45, 200, 244
Federal Energy Administration, 9
Federal Executive Development Program, 30–31
Federal Executive Officers, proposal for, 249–53, 256
Federal Executive Service, 31, 252n
Federal Personnel Manual, 30n, 120, 246
Federal Reserve Board, 8
Federal Service, proposal for, 249–53, 254, 257, 259, 261, 263
Fenno, Richard F., Jr., 99n
Fesler, James W., 114n
Finch, Robert H., 145
Flemming, Arthur S., 137
Ford, Gerald R., 9–10, 55n
Foreign service officers, 118, 249
Foulke, William D., 23n
Frank, Thomas M., 107n
Freedom of Information Act of 1966, 18
Frisbie, Parker, 66n

Gardner, John W., 145
Garfield, James A., 68
Gawthorp, Louis C., 154
General Accounting Office, 59, 168, 203, 258
General schedule, of civil service jobs, 36
General Services Administration, 129, 174
Generalists, in government, 64, 207
Geological Survey, 130
Germany, 60, 61
Goheen, Howard W., 140
Goldberg, Arthur, 184
Gradualism, as bureaucratic disposition, 143–44, 178, 199
Graham, George A., 20n, 29n
Graham, William K., 191n
Great Society, programs of, 150
Griffenhagen-Kroger, Inc., 16n
Guiteau, Charles, 68
Guttman, Daniel, 17n, 89n, 119n

Halperin, Morton J., 172n
Hamilton, Alexander, 21n, 86n
Harriman, Averell, 102
Harris, Joseph P., 32n
Hatch Act, 253
Havemann, Joel, 94n
Heclo, Hugh, 16n, 78n
Henry, Laurin L., 48n, 49n, 67n, 89n
Herzberg, Frederick, 191n
Hill, John Philip, 60n
Hoover, J. Edgar, 45, 145
Hoover Commission, 25, 29, 60, 76
Horowitz, Donald L., 18n
Huddleston, Robert H., 140n

Implementation, 5, 179–80, 200, 233
In-and-outers, 100, 102–03, 118–19, 248
Institutionalists, as bureaucratic type, 151–52, 208, 249
Interest groups: as allies with Congress and bureaucracy, 13, 47, 111–12, 147, 166–68, 171, 173, 183–84, 200, 224–25, 228, 236; as control on bureaucracy, 6; as job outlet for bureaucrats, 131; and permeability of executive branch, 17; and selection of bureaucrats, 123, 185, 249; and selection of political executives, 44, 89, 92, 94, 95, 99; as source of political executives' power, 68, 87, 166–67
Internal Revenue Service, 30n, 45, 130, 244n
Iron triangles. *See* Interest groups, as allies with Congress and bureaucracy

Jay, John, 21n, 86n
Job tailoring, in civil service, 125
Johnson, Lyndon B., 13, 60; assistant secretaries for administration under, 77; and politicization of the bureaucracy, 73–74; reform of civil service under, 30; selection process for political executives, 90–91, 93; staff organization for personnel policy, 26; use of civil servants by, 48, 145
Joint Administrative Task Force, 108n
Joint Commission on Reclassification of Salaries, 56n

Kaufman, Herbert, 15n, 61, 129n, 172n
Kennedy, John F., 13; assistant secretaries for administration under, 77; and politicization of the bureaucracy, 72–73; selection process for political executives, 90, 93, 95; staff organization for personnel policy, 26

Key, V. O., Jr., 224n
Kissinger, Henry A., 164n
Kranz, Harry, 115n

Leaks: by bureaucrats, 171, 175, 208–09; methods of countering, 228–29; types of, 226; value of, 231–32
Legislative vetoes, 172
Leupp, F. E., 152n
Liason Officer for Personnel Management, 25
Lincoln, Abraham, 94
Lyden, Fremont James, 191n

Machiavelli, 214
McAllister, William, 68n
McGregor, Douglas, 191n
MacGregor, Eugene B., Jr., 118n
Mackenzie, Calvin, 90n
McKinsey and Company, 62n
Macmahon, Arthur W., 34n, 50n, 66n
Macy, John W., Jr., 90n, 117, 118n, 119n, 134n
Madison, James, 21n, 86n
Malbin, Michael J., 59n
Management, 1, 57, 220; identification of higher civil service with, 18, 133; missions for, 201–02; participatory, 209–10; and personnel policy reform, 245; as staff specialty, 62, 149, 150; theories of, 34, 191–92, 209–10, 233
Management by objectives, 188, 201, 220
Mann, Dean E., 100n, 102n, 103n, 106n
Marvin, Keith E., 151n
Mathews, F. David, 145
Mayers, Lewis, 57n
Medina, William A., 30n, 116n
Meier, Jon Kenneth, 114n
Meltsner, Arnold J., 150n
Meriam, Lewis, 63n, 137n
Merit Staffing Review Team, 28n, 123n
Millett, John D., 34n, 66n
Minority groups: in the bureaucracy, 114–15; and selection of political executives, 93–94, use of, 168
Mitchell, James P., 184
Mosher, Frederick C., 62n, 128n, 209n

Name requests, in civil service hiring, 125–26
Nathan, Richard P., 13n, 75n
National Academy of Public Administration, 245n
National Aeronautics and Space Administration, 44, 159, 201, 202

National Civil Service League, 113
National Institutes of Health, 149
National Park Service, 130
National Security Council, 255
NEA. See Noncareer executive assignments
Networks, 55, 111–12, 246; among bureaucrats, 128–30, 132–33, 144, 146–47, 176, 180; among political executives, 107–08, 183–84; political execututives' need to build, 158–59, 166–69, 191, 207
Neustadt, Richard, 92
New Federalism, 150
Nixon, Richard M., 17n, 150, 188; abuses of civil service under, 23, 28–29, 74–76, 135–36, 139–40, 244, 256; assistant secretaries for administration under, 77–78; attempts to reform civil service under, 31, 252; centralized political management under, 13–14, 74–75, 97–98; eliminates budget appeals, 164–65; and Office of Management and Budget, 80–81; political appointees' characteristics under, 101n, 103, 106–07; resignation of, 8, 12n; selection process for political executives, 93–94, 97–98; suspicions of bureaucracy, 24, 27, 183, 192; and Undersecretaries' Group, 108–09
Norton, Clark F., 17n
Noncareer executive assignments: defined, 30n, 38–39; civil servants in, 48, 248; and civil service immobility, 119–20; procedures for, 39, 251; tenure of, 101–04

Office of Management and Budget 129, 164n, 221; creation of, 78; and executive development, 130, 242; and personnel ceilings, 32n; political clearances in, 52–53; politicizing of, 78–81; and presidential responsibility for personnel policy, 27, 30, 242, 253–55
Office of Special Projects, 54
OMB. See Office of Management and Budget

Patronage: and civil service reform, 20, 125; declines in, 66–68, 69, 82, 93–94, 133; as means of controlling bureaucracy, 214; procedures for managing, 26–27, 70–76, 135, 238. See also Political appointments
Patterson, Bradley H., Jr., 12n
Patton, Arch, 105n

Personal Qualifications Statement (SF-171), 126
Pickering, John W., 100n
Plum Book, 92
Polenberg, Richard, 27n
Policy: bureaucratic view of, 177, 178, 208; changing nature of, 14–19, 236; contrasted with administration, 20, 134, 252–53; difficulty of changing quickly, 16–17, 110, 221, 237; effects of executive politics on, 232–34; political complexity of, 156; political executives' objectives for, 99, 155, 160, 198–204; and political power, 197
Policy analysts in bureaucracy, 150–51, 216
Political appointments, 1, 44–45, 65, 154; ambiguity of vis-à-vis career positions, 34–41, 55, 76, 82, 131, 154, 213, 251, 252; bureaucrats in, 46–49, 131–32, 248; clearance procedures for, 96–97; as control on bureaucracy, 4–5, 6–7, 85–86, 213–14, 243–44; need for reform of, 252, 259–61; number of, 36–41, 65–66, 85; types of, 84–85, 159–60; vacancies in, 46–47. See also Patronage
Political commissars, 50, 96
Political executives, 1–2, 11, 21, 155; ambiguous position of, 86–88, 112, 195–98, 237–39; appointment of subordinates by, 95–98, 213–20; characteristics of, 160–61, 192–93, 242; congressional relations of, 8–9, 11, 166–68, 228–30; divided loyalties, 95, 98, 109–10, 160, 222–23; growing challenges to, 18–19; inexperience of, 100–03; lack of teamwork among, 11, 106–97, 110, 237–39; learning by, 156–58; as managers of civil service, 53, 133, 135–36, 138–39, 180, 183, 185–86, 213–20, 241–42; methods of dealing with sabotage, 227–31; need for trust from bureaucracy, 181, 187–90; number of, 84–85; policy objectives of, 160, 198–204; resignations of, 107–08; salaries of, 7n; selection of, 88–99, 110, 238; and self-help, 156, 158–170, 235; socioeconomic background of, 100; suspicion of bureaucracy, 44, 182–87, 216–17, 249, 252; tenure of, 103–05, 238–39; as threat to civil service, 135–36, 233–34, 243; use of strategic resources in bureaucracy, 180, 191, 195–217
Political leadership; bureaucratization of,

14, 35, 46–49, 65–68, 82–83, 101, 170, 214, 236, 262; civil service as aid to, 23, 49, 171, 173–80, 232–33, 234, 240, 246; effects of interest groups on, 68, 87, 166–67; effects of political selection process on, 99, 110; meaning of, 7, 21, 195–98, 202–03; need for, 4, 6–7, 10, 14–19; from president versus departmental executives, 8–14, 109, 222–23; relation of to participatory management, 209–10; requirements for, 111–12, 155, 237–39; weakness of in executive branch, 19, 46–47, 88, 104–05, 110–11, 233–34, 248–49
Political parties, 4, 51, 86, 261; and civil service reform, 22, 32, 69; declining role of, 66–68, 70–75, 82, 92–95; failure of to produce executive teams, 11, 14, 87–88, 106, 110–11; irrelevance of to program politics, 148, 173. See also Democratic party, Republican party
Post office, 44
Prescott, Arthur Taylor, 86n
President, 2, 3; appeals to by cabinet officers, 164–65; appointments by, 67–68, 88–98, 110, 119, 238; centralized control under, 8, 10–14, 16, 34, 64, 68, 239, 247, 259–60; conflict with departmental executives, 95–98, 109, 160, 222–23; creation of office, 85–86; as head of civil service, 22–28, 33, 40, 45, 46, 135, 242, 250, 254, 263; incentives to politicize bureaucracy, 68, 247; as protector of civil service, 138–39; proposals to restrict power of, 244–45; relations with bureaucrats, 4, 129, 155, 233, 255–56; as source of political executives' support, 11, 14, 86–88, 161, 238; tenure of, 118
President's Commission on Personnel Interchange, 119n
President's Committee on Administrative Management, 25n
Press: leaks to, 171, 228, 231; relations with bureaucrats, 147, 166, 175–77
Prewitt, Kenneth, 68n
Private sector: bureaucrats' movement into, 118–19; contrast of public executives' leadership with, 101, 166, 201–02, 227, 232; grade creep in, 62
Professionalism: bureaucrats' identification with, 116, 125, 128; contrasted with craft knowledge, 3; as force for bureaucratic change, 143; growth of, in federal employment, 61, 62; as

means of bureaucratic self-protection, 63; among political appointees, 67–68; as source of bureaucratic power, 14, 159, 174–75, 178, 233, 234
Program bureaucrats, as a type, 148–49
Public Law 313 positions, 9

Reformers, 150–51, 208
Regional directors, 40–41
Reorganization: of civil service, 24–28, 29–31, 249–56, 257–58; departmental, 77, 261; limited impact of, 5, 13, 220
Republican National Committee, 72
Republican Party: conflict with Democrats, 111; patronage, 50, 51, 72, 74; political appointments of, 48, 93; in power during 1920s, 57; suspicions of bureaucracy, 182, 183
Richardson, Elliot L., 145, 160
Roberts, Karlene H., 191n
Rockefeller, Nelson, 102, 160
Rockman, Bert A., 183n
Roosevelt, Franklin D; civil service reform and, 24–25, 135; government growth under, 57; use of patronage, 70–71
Roosevelt, Theodore, 20n, 56, 152
Rose, Richard, 188n
Rosen, Bernard, 245n
Rosenberg, Charles F., 68n
Rourke, Francis E., 1n, 15n
Rouse, Andrew M., 151n
Rusk, Dean, 222

Sabotage: by bureaucrats, 171–72, 205, 223–32; examples of, 226–27; meaning of, 176–77, 224–25
Sadler, Philip, 209n
Schedule A, 30n, 37, 251
Schedule B, 30n, 37
Schedule C, 30n, 37, 39, 119, 253
Schwartz, Bernard, 206n
Scism, Thomas E., 117n
Seidman, Harold, 13n, 47n
Self, Peter, 61n
Senior corps proposal, 29–30
Shafritz, Jay M., 120n
Shultz, George P., 184
Simon, Herbert A., 61n, 209n
Small Business Administration, 41n, 135
Smith, Harold, 57
Smithburg, Donald W., 61n
Social Security Administration, 149, 159
Soil Conservation Service, 130
Staff: concept of, 61; growth in, 60–61;

as bureaucratic type, 149–50, 208; as source of networks, 129
Stanley, David T., 100n, 102n, 103n, 106n, 119n
Statecraft: absence of, 192, 212–13, 232–234; different for cabinet officers and President, 222–23; examples of, 153, 162–64, 167–68, 169–70, 192–93, 227–31; limitations on, 221, 243; meaning of, 3, 7, 112, 155, 181, 233, 235; need for, 220, 249
Sullivan, Robert, 206n
Sunshine laws, 18
Supergrades: creation of, 29, 31, 71; duration of experience, 101, 102, 103–04; mobility of, 117–19, 131; numbers of, 37, 57, 59; proportion of noncareerist, 40, 48; personnel procedures for, 30n, 120–22, 127; socioeconomic characteristics, 114–15. See also Bureaucrats, Noncareer executive assignments
Szanton, Peter L., 16n

Tennessee Valley Authority, 40n
terHorst, Jerald F., 165
Thompson, Victor A., 61n
Truman, Harry S.; political appointments under, 25, 27, 48, 89, 93; scandals during term, 45; use of patronage, 71
Trust: as aspect of conditional cooperation, 183, 192, 237; defined, 158–59; among political executives, 107, 166; between political executives and bureaucrats, 170, 181, 187–90, 246, 247; between political executives and outside groups, 168; relation to communication, 209; relation to consultation, 212

Undersecretaries: teamwork among, 108–09, tenure of, 103–05
Undersecretaries' Group, 108–09
Unions, federal employee, 18, 26, 41, 133

Van Riper, Paul P., 20n, 119n

Waldo, Dwight, 110n
War Department, 60
Warwick, Donald P., 2n, 233n
Washington, George, 102
Watergate, 72, 76, 97, 264; efforts to reduce presidential powers following, 244–45; operations of bureaucracy during, 8–10
Weather Service, 47
Weinberger, Casper, 145

Weisband, Edward, 107n
Whistle blowing, 141, 257
White, Leonard D., 34n
White House staff, 1; as advisers on civil service policies, 24–27, 242, 253–255; executive weakness of, 12–14, 15, 86–87; negotiations on political appointments, 44, 65, 95–98; organization in political personnel 110, 259–60; polit

reaucracy, 51, 55n, 72–74, 82, 249; size of, 65–66
Willis, Charles, 26, 72, 74
Willner, Barry, 17n, 89, 119n
Wirtz, W. Willard, 184
Wood, Robert C., 1n

Young, Stuart, 50n

ORGANIZING THE PRESIDENCY
STEPHEN HESS

The present power base in the White House began to take form under Franklin Roosevelt, with the concurrence of Congress. Succeeding presidents, faced with problems of world leadership and domestic turmoil, have augmented this base, until it reached its ultimate point during the tenure of Richard Nixon.

But as the White House has increased in size and functions, so have tensions and mistrust grown between the President and his political appointees in the executive branch, between the President and Congress, and between the President and the bureaucracy. At the same time, Hess contends, the present structure of the White House has also lessened the President's ability to perform the legitimate duties of his office.

A White House staff member under two former presidents, Hess bases his conclusions on a perceptive appraisal of the modus operandi of six men who have occupied the modern presidency. Presidents, he believes, have assumed too many roles and have been woefully miscast in one—that of manager. He further points to the propensity of presidents to increasingly seek advice from those most congenial to them rather than from those responsible for carrying out policy.

These weaknesses, he suggests, could be overcome if the present arrangement were replaced by a more collegial presidency. He explores what this would mean and why it should be seriously considered, with strategies for redesigning future administrations to be responsive, efficient, and accountable.

Stephen Hess, a senior fellow in the Brookings Governmental Studies program, is the author of six other books on American politics, including *The Presidential Campaign* (Brookings, 1974).

". . . a new and magnificent study of the presidential process." *The New Republic.*

". . . destined to become necessary reading for all those interested in the institutionalized presidency and in administrative politics generally." *Perspective.*

228 pp. / 1976 / cloth and paper

DATE DUE

GAYLORD			PRINTED IN U.S.A.